School Figures

The Data behind the Debate

The Hoover Institution gratefully acknowledges the following individuals and foundations for their significant support of the

Initiative
on
American Public Education

KORET FOUNDATION
TAD AND DIANNE TAUBE
LYNDE AND HARRY BRADLEY FOUNDATION
BOYD AND JILL SMITH
JACK AND MARY LOIS WHEATLEY
FRANKLIN AND CATHERINE JOHNSON
JERRY AND PATTI HUME
BERNARD LEE SCHWARTZ FOUNDATION
ELIZABETH AND STEPHEN BECHTEL, JR. FOUNDATION

The Hoover Institution gratefully acknowledges

FRANKLIN AND CATHERINE JOHNSON
for their generous support
of this book project.

School Figures
The Data behind the Debate

Hanna Skandera and Richard Sousa

HOOVER INSTITUTION PRESS
Stanford University
Stanford, California

www.hoover.org

Hoover Institution Press Publication No. 494

First printing, 2003
10 09 08 07 06 05 04 03   9 8 7 6 5 4 3 2 1

Manufactured in the United States of America

Library of Congress Cataloging-in-Publication Data
Skandera, Hanna, 1973–
School figures : the data behind the debate / by Hanna Skandera and Richard Sousa.
       p. cm.
Includes bibliographical references and index.
ISBN 0-8179-2822-7 (alk. paper)
 1. Educational indicators—United States. 2. Education—United States. I. Sousa, Richard, 1949– . II. Title.
LB2846.S54 2003
370'.2'1—dc22
                              2003020781

To our first and best teachers, our parents

Harry and Carol Skandera

and

Mary and Ed Sousa

Contents

Propositions

Chapter 1: Schools

Chapter 2: Teachers

Chapter 3: Achievement

Chapter 4: Expenditures

Figures and Tables: By Chapter

Chapter 1: Schools

Figures

Tables

Chapter 2: Teachers

Figures

Tables

Chapter 3: Achievement

Figures

Tables

Chapter 4: Expenditures

Chapter 5: School Reform

Figures

Tables

Chapter 6: Students and Their Families
Figure

Tables

Appendix: Basic Data
Tables

Acronyms

AFT	American Federation of Teachers
ALEC	American Legislative Exchange Council
CSR	California's Class Size Reduction (initiative)
EAHCA	Education for All Handicapped Children Act
EEOC	Equality of Educational Opportunity Commission
ESEA	Elementary and Secondary Education Act
GAO	General Accounting Office
IDEA	Individuals with Disabilities Education Act
MPS	Milwaukee Public Schools
NAEP	National Assessment of Educational Progress
NCES	National Center for Education Statistics
NCS	National Computer Systems
NEA	National Education Association
NELS	National Educational Longitudinal Survey
NHES	National Household Education Survey
NLSY	National Longitudinal Survey of Youth
OECD	Organisation for Economic Co-operation and Development
PTA	Parent Teacher Association
SAT	Scholastic Aptitude Test (old scale)
SAT I	Scholastic Assessment Test I
TFA	Teach for America
TIMSS	Third International Math and Science Study
TIMSS-Repeat	Third International Math and Science Study—Repeat

Manuscript Notes

All citations are placed at the end of the respective paragraph or body of text to which they refer. All references to tables and figures are also placed at the end of the respective paragraph or body of text to which they refer to ensure ease of readability.

All web page addresses were current at the time of manuscript completion; however, due to the changing nature of the World Wide Web, some references may become obsolete over time.

The abbreviation "na" is used throughout *School Figures* to signify that data was "not available."

Due to the vast amount of numbers used throughout *School Figures,* with rare exception, numbers are rounded to the nearest single decimal or, when deemed appropriate, whole number. In addition, due to rounding, numbers may not add to totals.

Distinction between the usage of "race" and "ethnicity" throughout *School Figures* was determined by usage in the original source material.

Distinction between the usage of "black" or "African-American" throughout *School Figures* was determined by usage in the original source material.

About the Authors

Hanna Skandera is a research fellow at the Hoover Institution.

Richard Sousa is a senior associate director and research fellow at the Hoover Institution.

Introduction

In recent years, the American public has become increasingly concerned about the academic performance of its children and the structure and organization of the nation's elementary and secondary schools. According to a 2000 Gallup Poll, the majority, 61 percent, of those surveyed are somewhat dissatisfied or completely dissatisfied with the quality of education that students receive in kindergarten through twelfth grade. The public wants quality education for the children in the United States but is not getting it. Despite the terrible tragedy of September 11 and the country's subsequent focus on terrorism, domestic security, and international relations, President Bush has restated his mantra "No child left behind" and reaffirmed the administration's resolve to return its interest to education—the main focus of his domestic policy agenda during the 2000 presidential campaign.

Many remedies to the perceived problems have been offered. Some emphasize fixing the system—better teachers, smaller classrooms, changes in curriculum. Others offer "outside the box" solutions that wander far from the current pedagogical path—school vouchers, charter schools, home schooling. Whatever the solution—and there are merits to most options offered—to discuss the problems intelligently, one must argue from reliable data and with recognized source material. Consistent and accurate data and well-defined and critical analysis are imperative if we are to separate the true problems from myth and then proffer solutions to solve the problems.

Reasonable people can disagree; however, we feel participants in discussions about students and their educational performance and environment cannot enter into a sound debate without first stipulating to the facts. In this volume, we hope to help establish the baseline for discussion and debate by providing relevant data in words, graphs, and tables.

It seems, too often, what masquerades as debate is really argument and polemics. Debates about academic performance, resources, teacher quality, and school choice sometime appear more like a *Monty Python* skit than a discussion among learned education professionals. We invite and encourage debate, but debate based on well-documented facts.

Harry Truman said, "We must have strong minds, ready to accept the facts as they are." One of the functions the Hoover Institution provides is to act as an educator—a provider of facts from which public policy debate can be launched. We were motivated to write this book by our desire to contribute to achieving this institutional goal in an area we feel is of vital importance if the United States is to continue as a world leader in freedom and commerce. We believe this volume will contribute to educating, raising the level of the public policy debate, and increasing awareness regarding issues of vital importance to Americans.

We do this not with our original research. Rather, our aim is to find data, to review previously published analysis, and to report on survey results. We organize these data and, then, present them in a user-friendly format.

To be all-inclusive would require a volume much greater than ours. We did not undertake that task, and we do not purport that our volume is that—we do not tackle every topic in the field. Moreover, there are numerous resources available to provide much more data than we do. Our goal is to identify selected, salient facts that will provide fodder for discussion, cause people to think, and equip them to refute what has become accepted wisdom when it may be fictitious or misleading.

Investing in human capital through education can only lead to a more economically prosperous nation, to a country better prepared to listen to and understand the policies our government leaders propose, and to innovation that will secure a better way of life—economically, socially, and politically. What follows are six chapters, each addressing a specific area of the educational experience. Our first chapter is about schools—after all, they are a fundamental aspect of the educational experience. If our goal is to better educate today's youth (measuring improvement by whatever metric one may choose), we must first know what is happening in our schools.

In some sense our presentation parallels *A Primer on America's Schools* (Hoover Press, 2001). That volume, authored by the Koret Task Force on K–12 Education, provides more in-depth analysis and history. Chapters 2–5 are on teachers, achievement, expenditures, and school reform. Finally, we close with a chapter on students and their families. Clearly students are what the educational experience is all about. Moreover, student's families provide the foundation for a successful education.

We finish with an appendix that includes the most basic of demographic and educational data. This section provides the facts we think every reader should have some knowledge of—for example, the U.S. population and its makeup (by age, sex, race, ethnicity, family size), the number and composition of schools in the United States, and family income levels.

We believe our presentation is unique. Within each chapter, we present a number of propositions. Some are obvious, some controversial, and some just plain informative. Based on each proposition, we lay out facts. In some cases, the facts fully support the proposition; in other cases, our factual finding may startle the reader—the accepted norm may not be factual and, hence, should not be accepted. Furthermore, what was true in 1960 may no longer be true in the new millennium.

Our Hoover colleagues, who serve as editors for the journal *Education Next*, state that the research reported in their journal takes them where the facts lead. In this volume, we hope to provide the readers with facts that will better equip them on a journey to make their own assessments.

This project could not have been undertaken without the guidance and support of a number of people. At the earliest stages, Hoover fellows Williamson Evers, Terry Moe, and Peter Montgomery helped define the issues, and Michael Kirst of the Stanford School of Education provided us with leads to numerous data sources that proved most valuable. Mark Boucher, Matthew Nobe, Nicole Saltzman, Andrew Schnell, and Hope Skandera provided valuable research assistance by collecting, collating, and checking vast amounts of data that are the basis for this volume. Members of Hoover's Koret Task Force on K–12 Education (John Chubb, Williamson Evers, Checker Finn, Rick Hanushek, Paul Hill, E.D. Hirsch, Caroline Hoxby, Terry Moe, Paul Peterson, Diane Ravitch, and Herb Walberg) were most generous with their time and comments; special thanks go to Herb and Rick, who went above and beyond to help us avoid pitfalls. Finally, our deepest debt goes to Hoover Institution Director John Raisian, who gave us the opportunity and encouraged us every step of the way throughout this project.

"Honesty is the first chapter of the book of wisdom."
—Thomas Jefferson

Chapter 1:
Schools

Propositions

▸ THE LANDSCAPE OF ELEMENTARY AND SECONDARY SCHOOL ENROLLMENT IN PUBLIC AND PRIVATE SCHOOLS IS CHANGING.

▸ PUBLIC EDUCATION IS BECOMING INCREASINGLY CONSOLIDATED, WHICH MEANS LESS PARENTAL INVOLVEMENT.

▸ SMALLER SCHOOLS CAN MAKE A DIFFERENCE.

▸ HIGH RATES OF STUDENT MOBILITY ARE ONE REASON FOR THE PERSISTENT GAP BETWEEN DISADVANTAGED AND NONDISADVANTAGED STUDENTS.

▸ STUDENTS IN THE UNITED STATES SPEND MORE HOURS PER YEAR IN THE CLASSROOM THAN THEIR PEERS IN OTHER DEVELOPED COUNTRIES.

▸ SCHOOL ENVIRONMENT MATTERS.

▸ SCHOOL VIOLENCE IS ON THE DECLINE.

Highlights

▶ In 2000, approximately 86 percent of students were enrolled in public schools, nearly 11 percent were in private schools, and 3 percent attended school at home.[1]

▶ Confidence in public schools has declined since the 1970s. In 1973, 58 percent of the public had a "great deal/quite a lot of confidence" in public schools; in 1999, only 36 percent did.[2]

▶ In 2000, there were fewer than 95,000 public elementary and secondary schools; in 1930, there were more than 260,000.[3]

▶ In the 1999–2000 school year, the average public elementary school had 477 students; the average public secondary school, excluding alternative schools, had 785 students.[4]

▶ In the 1999–2000 school year, 236 school districts (1.6 percent of districts nationwide) had 25,000 students or more enrolled in their district; these districts account for 32.1 percent of enrollment nationwide.[5]

▶ In the 1999–2000 school year, there were more than 35,000 private schools, nearly three times as many as there were in 1930.[6]

▶ In 2000, there were more than 2,300 charter schools, enrolling nearly 580,000 students.[7]

▶ In 2000, an estimated 61,525 vouchers were used in private schools, accounting for more than 1 percent of private school enrollment.[8]

▶ Crime rates in elementary and secondary schools have decreased in recent years. Between 1993 and 1999, the percentage of students in grades 9 through 12 who reported being victims of crime at school decreased from 10 percent to 8 percent.[9]

In 2000, the average public school had a total of 110 computers, 77 percent of instructional rooms had access to the Internet, and 98 percent of schools had access to the Internet.[10]

Overview

Since the mid-19th century, public schools have been the linchpin of the American education system. The vast majority of American children have always been educated in public schools, and they still are. In 2000, more than 86 percent of children were enrolled in the nation's public schools. Public schools have been effective and have contributed significantly to insuring our continued, productive democracy. Most of our country's political, intellectual, business, cultural, and military leaders have come through the ranks of the public schools. Public schools are the primary source of America's human capital, and, according to many economists, our human capital accounts for the greatest share of capital in our economy. Education has become the primary engine for economic growth.

Enrollment trends over the last few decades, however, have changed, reflecting a subtle shift in sentiment toward public education. The bottom line is that parents are voting with their feet—fleeing the cities for better educational opportunities in the suburbs, enrolling their children in private and religious schools, or simply choosing to teach their children themselves.

Not only have new enrollment patterns emerged, but due to growth in the educational system overall, a move to consolidate within the school system has been underway throughout the 20th century. While there were nearly 120,000 school districts in the 1930s, there are now fewer than 15,000 nationwide. The average number of students in a school district has increased dramatically, as the total number of students has increased while the number of districts has declined. The public school system is a behemoth and, in the opinion of some, a faceless bureaucracy. The distance between parents and school administration has grown. Have parents just thrown up their hands, or are the administrators ensconced in ivory towers? Worse yet, are administrators overly burdened by bureaucracy and government regulations that distract them from their basic mission of teaching?

The romanticized bucolic one-room schools are now a relic—a true rarity in 21st-century America; by the latest count, only 423 survive from the nearly 150,000 in the early part of the 20th century. Today's schools are much larger and more impersonal. Some say these reasons are why the schools are not doing as good a job as they once did. Schools today are no doubt different than they were 50 years ago. Has this changed schooling in America?

The classrooms—where the teaching and learning take place—have, over the years, remained relatively stable in size. Access to technology, however, has changed—now more than 75 percent of instructional rooms have computers in them. Teaching methodology and theories have evolved and changed, but the structure of the classroom has not changed much.

This chapter reports on the schools—how many there are, their composition, and how they have changed. Although only a fraction of students are enrolled in private and parochial schools, we don't ignore them—they are important components in the education equation.

PROPOSITION: THE LANDSCAPE OF ELEMENTARY AND SECONDARY SCHOOL ENROLLMENT IN PUBLIC AND PRIVATE SCHOOLS IS CHANGING.

Many have questioned the effectiveness of the current public school system. Recent enrollment and achievement trends suggest that some kind of educational reform is desired, if not required. Enrollment in public elementary and secondary schools grew rapidly during the 1950s and '60s and peaked in 1971, as a result of the "baby boom," the dramatic increase in births following World War II. From 1971 to 1984, total elementary and secondary school enrollment steadily decreased, reflecting a decline in the school-age population over that period. In 1985, however, enrollment in elementary and secondary schools started increasing, and record enrollment levels were established every year by the late 1990s. By 2000, public school enrollment totaled more than 47 million. Private school enrollment grew more slowly than public school enrollment over this period, from nearly 5.6 million in 1985 to nearly 6.0 million in 2000. (See table 1.1 and figure 1.1.)[11]

Table 1.1: **Elementary and Secondary School Enrollment 1950–2000**

Year	Total	Public schools	Private schools	Home education
1950	28,492,000	25,111,000	3,380,000	na
1970	51,257,000	45,894,000	5,363,000	na
1990	46,752,000	41,217,000	5,234,000	301,000
2000	54,804,000	47,160,000	5,944,000	1,700,000

Sources: Thomas D. Snyder, ed., *Digest of Education Statistics, 2001* (Washington, DC: U.S. Department of Education, National Center for Education Statistics, 2002), table 3, p. 12; Home School Legal Defense Association, *Homeschooling Research* (Purcellville, VA: Home School Legal Defense Association, National Center for Home Education), available online at http://www.hslda.org.

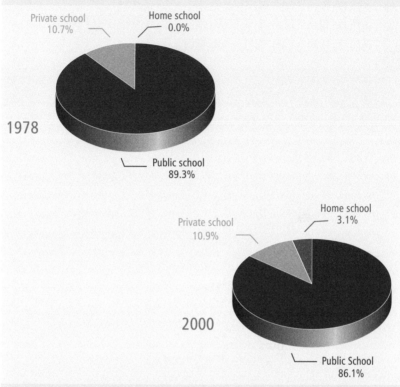

Sources: Thomas D. Snyder, ed., *Digest of Education Statistics, 2001* (Washington, DC: U.S. Department of Education, National Center for Education Statistics, 2002), table 3, p. 12; Home School Legal Defense Association, *Homeschooling Research* (Purcellville, VA: Home School Legal Defense Association, National Center for Home Education), available online at http://www.hslda.org.

Furthermore, the faces that comprise enrollment numbers have changed. In 1976, minorities comprised 24 percent of elementary and secondary school enrollment; in 1999, minorities comprised 38 percent. The most notable distinction among minorities is the growing Hispanic population. The percentage of Hispanic students nearly tripled between 1976 and 1999. (See table 1.2 and figure 1.2.)[12]

Table 1.2: **Elementary and Secondary Public School Enrollment**

Percentage Minority Students by Race, 1976 & 1999

Race	1976	1999
Black	15.5%	17.2%
Hispanic	6.4	15.6
Asian or Pacific Islander	1.2	4.0
American Indian/Alaskan Native	0.8	1.2
Total	23.9%	38.0%

Source: Thomas D. Snyder, ed., *Digest of Education Statistics, 2001* (Washington, DC: U.S. Department of Education, National Center for Education Statistics, 2002), table 42, p. 58.

Figure 1.2: **Elementary and Secondary Public School Enrollment**

By Race/Ethnicity, 1976 & 1999

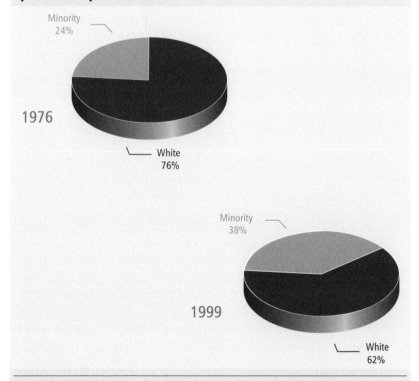

Minority
24%

1976

White
76%

Minority
38%

1999

White
62%

Source: Thomas D. Snyder, ed., *Digest of Education Statistics, 2001* (Washington, DC: U.S. Department of Education, National Center for Education Statistics, 2002), table 42, p. 58.

Enrollment in public and private schools has changed not only in numbers but in composition, as well. Over the last decade, three educational alternatives—home schooling, voucher programs, and charter schools—have emerged, altering the makeup of both public and private schools. (See table 1.3 and figure 1.3.)[13]

- In 1978, 89 percent of elementary and secondary students were enrolled in public schools, 11 percent in private schools, and 0.03 percent in home schools.
- In 2000, 86 percent were enrolled in public schools, 11 percent in private schools, and 3 percent in home schools.[14]

Home education surfaced as the largest portion of alternative enrollment.

- In 1990, 0.6 percent of total elementary and secondary school students were home educated.
- In 2000, home-educated students were 3.1 percent of total enrollment, more than five and one-half times as many as in 1990.[15]

Furthermore, within the last 10 years, voucher and charter school enrollments have grown considerably and do not appear to be slowing down.[16]

- In 1992, the first charter school emerged, with an enrollment of 35 students. In 2000, there were more than 2,300 charter schools, enrolling more than 575,000 students, nearly 1 percent of total elementary and secondary enrollment.
- In 1990, there were 341 public and private vouchers provided, a trivial percentage. In 2000, there were 61,525 vouchers used in private schools. Although very small in the overall scheme, voucher students total more than 1 percent of private school enrollment.[17]

Table 1.3: **Elementary and Secondary School Enrollment** By Type of School, 1900–2000

Total Enrollment

| Year | Total | Public Schools | | Private Schools | | |
		Traditional	Charter	Traditional	Vouchers	Home Education
1900	16,855,000	15,503,000	na	1,352,000	na	na
1910	19,372,000	17,814,000	na	1,558,000	na	na
1920	23,277,000	21,578,000	na	1,699,000	na	na
1930	28,329,000	25,678,000	na	2,651,000	na	na
1940	28,045,000	25,434,000	na	2,611,000	na	na
1950	28,491,000	25,111,000	na	3,380,000	na	na
1960	40,857,000	35,182,000	na	5,675,000	na	na
1970	51,257,000	45,894,000	na	5,363,000	na	na
1980	46,208,000	40,877,000	na	5,331,000	na	na
1985	45,162,000	39,422,000	na	5,557,000	na	183,000
1990	46,752,000	41,217,000	na	5,234,000	341	301,000
1992	48,848,000	42,823,000	na	5,322,000	4,798	703,000
1994	50,834,000	44,111,000	na	5,498,000	18,136	1,225,000
1996	52,600,000	45,611,000	105,100	5,764,000	25,853	1,225,000
1998 [a]	54,375,000	46,857,000	433,797	6,018,000	58,127	1,500,000
2000 [a, b]	54,804,000	47,160,000	522,199	5,944,000	61,525	1,700,000

Percentage of Total Enrollment

| Year | Public Schools | | Private Schools | | |
	Traditional	Charter	Traditional	Vouchers	Home Education
1900	91.98%	na	0.08%	na	na
1910	91.96	na	8.04	na	na
1920	92.70	na	7.30	na	na
1930	90.64	na	9.36	na	na
1940	90.69	na	9.31	na	na
1950	88.14	na	11.86	na	na
1960	86.11	na	13.89	na	na
1970	89.54	na	10.46	na	na
1980	88.46	na	11.54	na	na
1985	87.29	na	12.30	na	0.41%
1990	88.16	na	11.20	na	0.64
1992	87.67	na	10.90	0.01%	1.44
1994	86.77	na	10.82	0.04	2.41
1996	86.71	0.20%	10.96	0.05	2.33
1998 [a]	86.17	0.80	11.07	0.11	2.76
2000 [a, b]	86.05	0.95	10.85	0.11	3.10

Sources: Thomas D. Snyder, ed., *Digest of Education Statistics, 2001* (Washington, DC: U.S. Department of Education, National Center for Education Statistics, 2002), table 3, p. 12; Center for Education Reform, *Charter School Highlights and Statistics* (Washington, DC: Center for Education Reform, 2000), available online at http://www.edreform.com; Marquette University, Institute for the Transformation of Learning, Office of Research, *School Choice Enrollment Growth* (Milwaukee, WI: Marquette University, 2000), available online at http://www.schoolchoiceinfo.org; Children First America, *The Road to Success: Private Vouchers Helping American Children* (Bentonville, AR: Children First America, 1999); Home School Legal Defense Association, *Homeschooling Research* (Purcellville, VA: Home School Legal Defense Association, National Center for Home Education), available online at http://www.hslda.org.

Notes: a. For 1998 and 2000, traditional public and private school data are projected.
b. Charter school enrollment includes projections of new schools opening in fall 2000, which may vary as much as 10%.

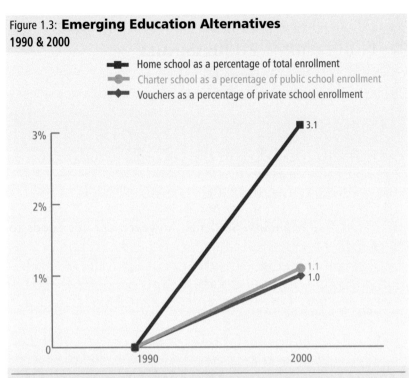

Figure 1.3: **Emerging Education Alternatives**
1990 & 2000

- ■— Home school as a percentage of total enrollment
- ●— Charter school as a percentage of public school enrollment
- ◆— Vouchers as a percentage of private school enrollment

Sources: Thomas D. Snyder, ed., *Digest of Education Statistics, 2001* (Washington, DC: U.S. Department of Education, National Center for Education Statistics, 2002), table 3, p. 12; Center for Education Reform, *Charter School Highlights and Statistics* (Washington, DC: Center for Education Reform, 2000), available online at http://www.edreform.com; Marquette University, Institute for the Transformation of Learning, Office of Research, *School Choice Enrollment Growth* (Milwaukee, WI: Marquette University, 2000), available online at http://www.schoolchoiceinfo.org; Children First America, *The Road to Success: Private Vouchers Helping American Children* (Bentonville, AR: Children First America, 1999); Home School Legal Defense Association, *Homeschooling Research* (Purcellville, VA: Home School Legal Defense Association, National Center for Home Education), available online at http://www.hslda.org.

While the general public appears to be mixed in its opinion regarding alternative educational routes, teachers unions and most education professionals have been quite adamant in their views. They find fault with any alternative that challenges the traditionally defined public school system. Enrollment numbers, however, are telling. The composition of enrollment, and therefore education, is different from how it was just 10 years ago. The changing enrollment patterns persist and may dictate respective adjustments.

PROPOSITION: PUBLIC EDUCATION IS BECOMING INCREASINGLY CONSOLIDATED, WHICH MEANS LESS PARENTAL INVOLVEMENT.

Over the past several decades, the public education system has become much more consolidated. If students were strictly economic goods, then the economies of scale associated with consolidation might make sense: more produced, lower cost, and, it is hoped, better quality. Students, however, are not goods to be uniformly manufactured, and the goal of education is not simply to push students through an assembly line process and check them off a list. Students are the future of America, and to this end, how they are educated is as important as, and will have more lasting impact than, a manufactured good.

The trend toward consolidation in the public school system has manifested itself in many ways. Since the early part of the 20th century, the number of public school districts and the number of schools has decreased dramatically. In the 1939–40 school year, there were 117,108 school districts; in the 1999–2000 school year, there were fewer than 15,000. At the same time, the number of public elementary and secondary schools decreased from roughly 260,000 to less than 95,000. Although annual enrollment has fluctuated, mirroring demographic trends, overall public school enrollment nearly doubled in this period, while the number of schools was cut by more than half. The results: The average public school size and the average school district size have gradually increased. In the 1930s, for example, the average enrollment in a public school was approximately 100 students. In the 1999–2000 school year, the average enrollment was more than 500 students. (See table 1.4 and figures 1.4 and 1.5.)[18]

Table 1.4: **Public School Districts and Public and Private Elementary and Secondary Schools**
1929–30—1999–2000

School year	Public school districts[a, b]	Public schools[c]			Private schools[c, d, e]	
		Schools with elementary grades		Schools with secondary grades	Schools with elementary grades	Schools with secondary grades
		Total	One teacher			
1929-30	na	238,306	149,282	23,930	9,275	3,258
1939-40	117,108	na	113,600	na	11,306	3,568
1949-50	83,718	128,225	59,652	24,542	10,375	3,331
1959-60	40,520	91,853	20,213	25,784	13,574	4,061
1970-71	17,995	65,800	1,815	25,352	14,372	3,770
1980-81	15,912	61,069	921	24,362	16,792	5,678
1989-90	15,367	60,699	630	23,461	na	na
1990-91	15,358	61,340	617	23,460	22,223	8,989
1991-92	15,173	61,739	569	23,248	23,523	9,282
1992-93	15,025	62,225	430	23,220	na	na
1993-94	14,881	62,726	442	23,379	23,543	10,555
1994-95	14,772	63,572	458	23,668	na	na
1995-96	14,766	63,961	474	23,793	25,153	10,942
1996-97	14,841	64,785	487	24,287	na	na
1997-98	14,805	65,859	476	24,802	24,915	10,779
1998-99	14,891	67,183	463	25,797	na	na
1999-2000	14,928	68,173	423	26,407	24,685	10,693

Source: Thomas D. Snyder, ed., *Digest of Education Statistics, 2001* (Washington, DC: U.S. Department of Education, National Center for Education Statistics, 2002), table 89, p. 98.
Notes: a. Includes operating and nonoperating districts.
b. Because of expanded survey coverage, all public school district data between 1989 and 2000 are not directly comparable with figures for earlier years.
c. Schools with both elementary and secondary programs are included both under elementary schools and under secondary schools.
d. Data for most years are partly estimated.
e. All private school data between 1989 and 1994 are from sample surveys and should not be compared directly with data for earlier years.

Figure 1.4: **Number of Public School Districts and Enrollment**
Public School Districts and Enrollment, 1939–40—1999–2000

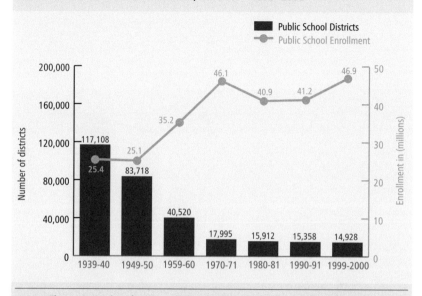

Source: Thomas D. Snyder, ed., *Digest of Education Statistics, 2001* (Washington, DC: U.S. Department of Education, National Center for Education Statistics, 2002), tables 3, 89, pp. 12, 98.

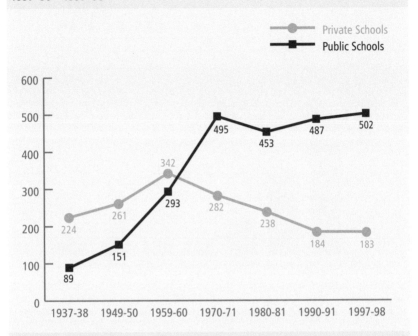

Source: Thomas D. Snyder, *120 Years of American Education: A Statistical Portrait* (Washington, DC: U.S. Department of Education, National Center for Education Statistics, 1993).

In just the last 10 years, the percentage of students concentrated in districts with 25,000 students or more has increased dramatically. In the 1988–89 school year, 177 school districts (1.2 percent of districts nationwide) had 25,000 students or more enrolled in their district; these 177 districts accounted for 21.4 percent of total enrollment nationwide. Contrast this with the 1999–2000 school year, when 236 school districts (1.6 percent of districts nationwide) had 25,000 students or more enrolled in their district; this represents 32.1 percent of total enrollment nationwide. (See table 1.5 and figure 1.6.)[19]

Table 1.5: **Public School Districts and Enrollment**
By Size of District, 1988–89 & 1999–2000

Enrollment of district	1988–89			1999–2000		
	Number of districts	Percent of districts	Percent of students	Number of districts	Percent of districts	Percent of students
Total	15,376	100.0%	100.0%	14,928	100.0%	100.0%
25,000 or more	177	1.2	21.4	238	1.6	32.1
10,000–24,999	473	3.1	20.6	579	3.9	18.7
5,000– 9,999	924	6.0	17.2	1,036	6.9	15.4
2,500– 4,999	1,907	12.4	17.8	2,068	13.9	15.6
1,000– 2,499	3,529	23.0	15.4	3,457	23.2	12.1
600– 999	1,813	11.8	3.6	1,814	12.2	3.1
300– 599	2,266	14.7	2.5	2,081	13.9	2.0
1– 299	3,984	25.9	1.5	3,298	22.1	1.0
Size not reported[a]	303	2.0	na	357	2.4	na

Source: Thomas D. Snyder, ed., *Digest of Education Statistics, 2001* (Washington, DC: U.S. Department of Education, National Center for Education Statistics, 2002), table 90, p. 98.
Note: a. Includes school districts reporting enrollment of 0.

Arguments for consolidation are based on increased efficiency and economies of scale; however, one consequence has been increased distance—further removing parents from those who administer their children's education. Increasingly, parents, teachers, and students are becoming faces in a crowd. Surveys from the state of Connecticut provide clear examples of the relationship between school consolidation and parental involvement. Between 1988 and 1992, as schools were consolidated (or otherwise grew as a result of reorganization), parental interaction greatly decreased.[20] Over this period, parents were

- 12 percent less likely to respond to questionnaires from the school
- 10 percent less likely to participate in parent-teacher organizations
- 10 percent less likely to attend a school open house
- 7 percent less likely to say that their school "communicate[d] well" with them
- 5 percent less likely to check their children's homework[21]

Figure 1.6: **Public School District Enrollment**
By Size of School District, 1999–2000

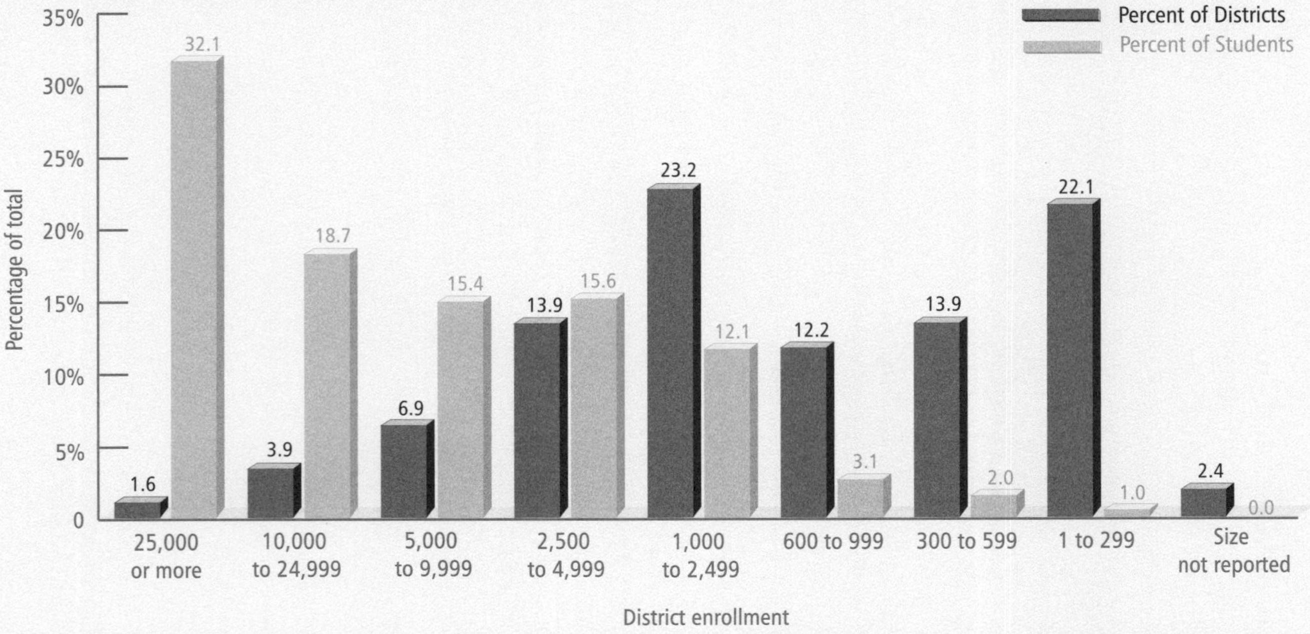

Legend:
- Percent of Districts
- Percent of Students

Percentage of total (vertical axis): 0, 5%, 10%, 15%, 20%, 25%, 30%, 35%

District enrollment (horizontal axis):

District enrollment	Percent of Districts	Percent of Students
25,000 or more	1.6	32.1
10,000 to 24,999	3.9	18.7
5,000 to 9,999	6.9	15.4
2,500 to 4,999	13.9	15.6
1,000 to 2,499	23.2	12.1
600 to 999	12.2	3.1
300 to 599	13.9	2.0
1 to 299	22.1	1.0
Size not reported	2.4	0.0

Source: Thomas D. Snyder, ed., *Digest of Education Statistics, 2001* (Washington, DC: U.S. Department of Education, National Center for Education Statistics, 2002), table 90, p. 98.

Clearly, there may be confounding factors, and the study measures the response of different sets of parents, but statistical tests indicate these differences are significant.

If parents—the third leg of the education tripod, which includes students, teachers, and parents—are distancing themselves from the process, a breakdown is inevitable.

The move toward a more consolidated public school system and fewer but larger schools is in stark contrast to private school trends. The number of private elementary and secondary schools has steadily increased: In 1930, there were roughly 12,500 private schools; in 2000, more than 35,000, nearly three times as many. During the same time period, the number of public schools decreased steadily. Over the past 70 years, the ratio of public to private schools has fallen from 20 public schools for every private school to 3 public schools for every private school. (See figures 1.7 and 1.8.)[22]

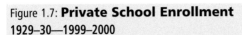

Figure 1.7: **Private School Enrollment**
1929–30—1999–2000

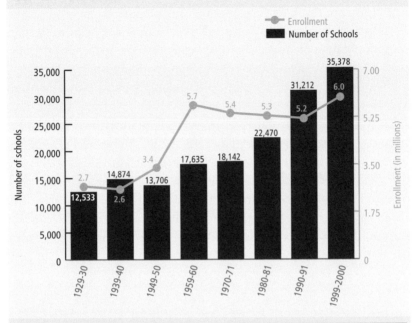

Sources: Thomas D. Snyder, ed., *Digest of Education Statistics, 2001* (Washington, DC: U.S. Department of Education, National Center for Education Statistics, 2002), table 89, p. 98; Thomas D. Snyder, *120 Years of American Education: A Statistical Portrait* (Washington, DC: U.S. Department of Education, National Center for Education Statistics, 1993).

Evidence points to the family as the most important determinant of a student's achievement.[23] As the public education system has become more consolidated, the administration and bureaucracy have grown, distancing parents from educational decisions and input. Theoretically, consolidation may be economically viable, but at a high cost to America's future—America's children.

Figure 1.8: **Public School Enrollment**
1929–30—1999–2000

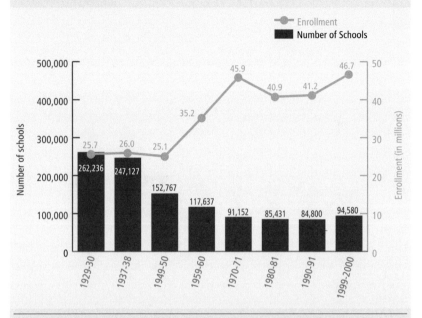

Sources: Thomas D. Snyder, ed., *Digest of Education Statistics, 2001* (Washington, DC: U.S. Department of Education, National Center for Education Statistics, 2002), table 89, p. 98; Thomas D. Snyder, *120 Years of American Education: A Statistical Portrait* (Washington, DC: U.S. Department of Education, National Center for Education Statistics, 1993).
Note: Data are not available for the 1939–40 school year.

▶ PROPOSITION: SMALLER SCHOOLS CAN MAKE A DIFFERENCE.

With America's renewed interest in the quality of education following the launch of the Soviets' *Sputnik* in 1957, new ideas for educational improvement proliferated; however, few were effective.[24] One little-noticed "improvement" was a more "scientific" approach to education. One piece of evidence was the consolidation of school systems. In the minds of "experts," consolidation meant economies of scale: more efficiency and more effectiveness. The literature at the time reinforced this mind-set. Franklin Keller's 1955 book, *The Comprehensive High School*, recommended consolidation. James Conant's 1959 book, *The American High School*, stated that the small high school was the number one problem in education and that its elimination should be a top priority.[25] Entitlement programs and desegregation compliance in the 1960s further contributed to the consolidation movement.[26]

Research today, however, contradicts the education experts of a few decades earlier. Many experts presumed, for example, that large schools, high schools in particular, offered a more diverse curriculum and more opportunities at a lower cost; there is mounting evidence that neither of these assertions is true. In fact, comprehensive research shows that small schools[27] are superior to large schools on most measures and equal to them on the rest.[28] A comprehensive review of 103 studies revealed the following several points regarding small schools.[29]

Academic achievement of students in small schools is at least equal to, and often superior to, that of large schools. A recent study documenting Chicago's small-school "reform" implementation, which included approximately 150 schools, showed improved standardized test scores or average test scores holding steady despite more students taking the test.

There is no research indicating that large schools are superior to small schools in their achievement effects. (See table 1.6.)[30]

Table 1.6: **Academic Performance of Students by School Size**
Chicago Public Schools, 1997 & 1999

Schools		Percentage of students at or above national norms	
Type	Number	Reading, 1997	Math, 1999
Small schools	40–45	48.1%	62.4%
Not small	360–390	29.1	44.3

Source: Patricia Wasley, Michelle Fine, Matt Gladden, Nicole E. Holland, Sherry P. King, Esther Mosak, and Linda C. Powell, *Small Schools: Great Strides: A Study of New Small Schools in Chicago* (New York: Bank Street College of Education, 2000), available online at http://www.bankstreet.edu/news/releases/smschool.html.

Marked improvement in achievement among ethnic minority students and students of low socioeconomic status (SES) is evident. A July 1997 study reported that "disadvantaged students in small schools significantly outperformed those in large ones on standardized basic skills tests." A study by the Consortium on Chicago School Research found that "for both reading and math, small schools produce greater achievement gains than larger schools, holding demographic and teacher characteristics constant." A study in 2000 showed that small schools helped close the achievement gaps between less affluent students and their wealthier counterparts.[31]

Student attitudes toward school in general and toward particular school subjects are more positive. Consistently, research favors small schools when it comes to student attitudes. Furthermore, research indicates that the attitudes of low-SES and minority students are especially sensitive to school size and benefit greatly from attending smaller schools.[32]

Cost-effectiveness is possible. When per-pupil costs are calculated on the number of students who actually graduate from school, rather than on the number attending (in school), the so-called savings of big schools largely disappears. If a small school attempts to maintain the large-school infrastructure, it will probably not be cost effective.[33]

Behavior problems are fewer. Research shows that in every instance, small schools have lower incidence rates of negative social behavior than larger schools. Research linking small schools and behavior has investigated everything from truancy and classroom disruption to vandalism, aggressive behavior, theft, substance abuse, and gang participation.[34] For example, according to the U.S. Department of Education, more than half of small-school principals report either minor or no discipline problems, compared to only 14 percent of big-school principals. Schools of 1,000 or more students experience 9 times more violent crime, 3 times more vandalism, and 11 times more weapons incidents as schools with fewer than 300 students.[35]

Participation in extracurricular activities is at a higher rate and more varied. The degree of satisfaction from participation is much higher among students. This holds true regardless of setting and is most applicable to minority and low-SES students. Furthermore, research has identified an important relationship between extracurricular participation and other desirable outcomes, such as positive attitudes and social behavior.[36]

Attendance patterns are better. Not only do students have better attendance records, but when secondary students switch from larger to smaller schools, their attendance generally improves. For example, in the previously referenced study documenting Chicago's small-school "reform" implementation, the average number of days missed in core courses per semester (controlling for eighth-grade achievement and demographics) was 13.56 for non-small schools but ranged from 8.09 to 10.45 days missed in small schools.[37]

Dropout and graduation rates are much better. Nine out of 10 reports reviewed confirmed lower dropout rates for small schools.[38]

Students are more likely to go to college. In Nebraska, 73 percent of students in districts with fewer than 70 high school students enrolled in postsecondary institutions, compared to 64 percent of those in districts of 600 to 999 high school students. These findings hold even when other variables, such as student attributes or staff characteristics, are taken into account.[39]

Interpersonal relationships are better. Between students and between students and teachers, relationships were perceived as better.[40]

No reliable relationship exists between school size and curriculum quality.[41] According to some researchers, the allegedly richer curriculum that larger schools offer tends to be made up of additional introductory courses outside core areas, not higher-level courses.[42]

In a recent Public Agenda poll of high school parents and teachers, 66 percent of the parents and 79 percent of the teachers favored smaller high schools.[43]

Proposals for small schools have emerged all over the United States. In New York, Chicago, and Philadelphia, more than 300 downsized public schools have opened over the past 15 years.[44] The popularity of smaller schools as an educational improvement appears to be on the rise; however, consolidation and its effects are still apparent. Approximately 70 percent of American high school students attend schools enrolling more than 1,000 or more students, and nearly 50 percent attend schools enrolling more than 1,500. In the 1937–38 school year, the average size of a secondary public school was approximately 200; in the 1997–98 school year, the average size was 779.[45] High schools with enrollments of 2,000 and 3,000 students are not uncommon around the nation; New York City has schools with enrollments of more than 5,000.[46] It is of note that the average size of public high schools varies extensively, depending on the state. For example, Florida's secondary public school average is 1,662; South Dakota's is 173.[47]

In the short run, there may be dollar savings resulting from consolidation. Based on the evidence, however, there are noteworthy and long-standing cost savings when schools are smaller: higher achievement, less violence, fewer discipline problems, and higher attendance and graduation rates. After examining both curriculum quality and cost-effectiveness, researcher Kathleen Cotton stated, "The perceived limitations in the program that small high schools can deliver and their presumed high cost regularly have been cited as justifications for our steady march toward giantism. The research convincingly stamps both of these views as misconceptions."[48] Smaller schools produce positive results. America should take notice of the impact smaller schools are making.

PROPOSITION: HIGH RATES OF STUDENT MOBILITY ARE ONE REASON FOR THE PERSISTENT GAP BETWEEN DISADVANTAGED AND NONDISADVANTAGED STUDENTS.

The achievement gap between advantaged and disadvantaged children is a constant concern. Although many attribute the gap to inequalities in resources and poor learning environments at home and at school, data from the U.S. General Accounting Office (GAO) indicate that low achievement scores are more often related to high rates of student mobility, that is, of students changing schools frequently. One explanation for this relationship, according to E.D. Hirsch and others, is the curricular inconsistency in the American educational system.[49]

A common measure of mobility is the percentage of students who have transferred in or out of a school in the past school year. Mobility rates typically range between 45 and 80 percent in inner-city schools and between 25 and 40 percent in suburban schools. Children from low-income families or children who attend inner-city schools are more likely than others to change schools frequently, where "changed schools frequently" is defined as third-graders who have changed schools three or more times since the first grade.[50] According to the 1994 GAO study,

- About 17 percent of all third-graders—more than 500,000—have changed schools frequently.
- More than 24 percent of third-graders have attended two schools since the first grade.
- Of third-graders from low-income families (incomes below $10,000), 30 percent have changed schools frequently, compared with approximately 10 percent from

families with incomes between $25,000 and $50,000 and 8 percent of children in families with incomes of $50,000 or more. (See figure 1.9.)

- About 25 percent of third-graders in inner-city schools have changed schools frequently, compared with about 15 percent of third-graders in rural or suburban schools.[51]

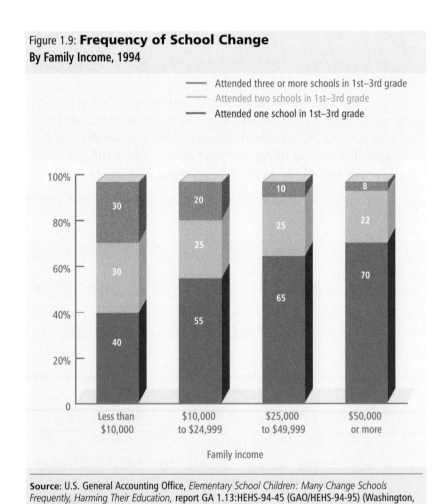

Figure 1.9: **Frequency of School Change**
By Family Income, 1994

Source: U.S. General Accounting Office, *Elementary School Children: Many Change Schools Frequently, Harming Their Education,* report GA 1.13:HEHS-94-45 (GAO/HEHS-94-95) (Washington, DC: U.S. General Accounting Office, 1994).

Studies have shown that high mobility rates and poor academic performance are related, and mobility rates are higher in the inner-city. Of the many factors that contribute to high rates of mobility in inner-city areas, three stand out: family income, population density, and home ownership.

The home environments of children from low-income families are not as stable as those from families with higher incomes. In lower-income families, the rates of illegitimacy, divorce, and single-parent households are higher, and there is a greater dependence on the extended family to provide care and housing for children. This means that low-income children are shuttled from house to house more often than those from high-income families.

With lower population densities, suburban school districts often cover larger geographic areas than do inner-city districts. Whereas a move within the inner-city almost assuredly requires a change of school, a move of equal distance in a suburban district is much less likely to require a school transfer.[52]

Home ownership affects school mobility because renters are more common in urban areas, and they tend to move much more frequently than do homeowners. In 1999, 35 percent of renters had moved within the last year, compared with only 8 percent of homeowners.[53]

Some of the characteristics of students with high mobility rates include these:

- About 40 percent of migrant children change schools frequently.

- White and Asian-American third-grade students change schools at a rate of approximately 12 percent; Hispanic students, 25 percent; black students, 26 percent; and Native American students, 35 percent. (See figure 1.10.)

- Among children with limited English proficiency, about 34 percent change schools frequently.[54]

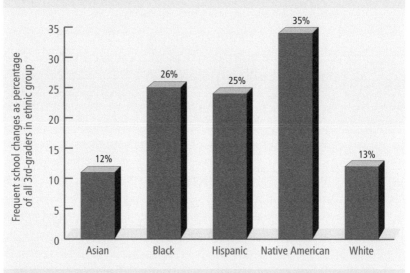

Figure 1.10: **Likelihood of Frequent School Change** By Race and Ethnicity, 1994

Source: U.S. General Accounting Office, *Elementary School Children: Many Change Schools Frequently, Harming Their Education,* report GA 1.13:HEHS-94-45 (GAO/HEHS-94-95) (Washington, DC: U.S. General Accounting Office, 1994).
Note: "Frequent" is defined as third-graders who had changed schools three or more times since the 1st grade.

Do high mobility rates matter? Of the nation's third-graders, 41 percent of those who have changed schools frequently are low achievers (below grade level) in reading, compared with 26 percent of third-graders who have never changed schools. Results are similar for math. Thirty-three percent of children who have changed schools frequently perform below grade level, compared with 17 percent of those who have never changed schools. (See figure 1.11.)[55] In addition,

- Overall, third-graders who have changed schools frequently are two and a half times as likely to repeat a grade as third-graders who have never changed schools (20 versus 8 percent).

- For all income groups, children who have changed schools frequently are more likely to repeat a grade than children who have never changed schools.
- Children who changed schools four or more times by the eighth grade were at least four times more likely to drop out than those who remained in the same school; this is true even after taking into account the socioeconomic status of a child's family.[56]

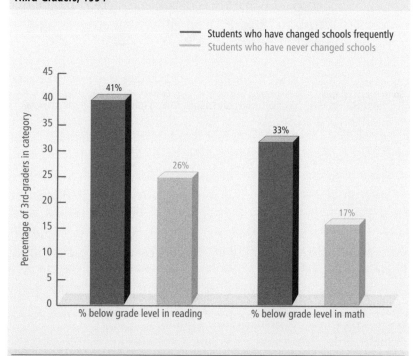

Figure 1.11: **Student Mobility Rates and Achievement**
Third-Graders, 1994

Students who have changed schools frequently
Students who have never changed schools

Percentage of 3rd-graders in category

41%
26%
33%
17%

% below grade level in reading   % below grade level in math

Source: U.S. General Accounting Office, *Elementary School Children: Many Change Schools Frequently, Harming Their Education,* report GA 1.13:HEHS-94-45 (GAO/HEHS-94-95) (Washington, DC: U.S. General Accounting Office, 1994).
Note: "Frequent" is defined as third-graders who had changed schools three or more times since the 1st grade.

In grouping children who have changed schools frequently into four income categories, the GAO study found that within each category, children who have changed schools most frequently are more likely to be below grade level in reading and math than those who have never changed schools.

Why do student mobility rates have such a strong effect on performance? Some theorize that the lack of coherency in curricula across the United States, within states, and often between schools in the same district is a major cause. After much research, Herbert Walberg concluded, "Common learning goals, curriculum, and assessment within states (or within an entire nation) ... alleviate the grave learning disabilities faced by children, especially poorly achieving children who move from one district to another with different curricula, assessment, and goals."[57]

High mobility rates may be inevitable for some subsets of the population. School choice could contribute to a partial solution by breaking the link between a child's home address and school address, thus allowing students to remain at the same school despite changing residences. Hirsch and other experts argue, however, that what is needed is a strong and coordinated core curriculum to provide a solid, consistent foundation in the basics.[58] Although a national curriculum may be questionable because of its potential for superceding local control, a well-defined, basic core curriculum would be beneficial. Without a coordinated sequence, too much time is spent repeating certain fundamentals of a student's education and completely ignoring others. Higher mobility may be inevitable for lower-income and immigrant children, but the combination of choice, local control, clear standards, and a coordinated sequence of study should provide a foundation for closing the achievement gap.

PROPOSITION: STUDENTS IN THE UNITED STATES SPEND MORE HOURS PER YEAR IN THE CLASSROOM THAN THEIR PEERS IN OTHER DEVELOPED COUNTRIES.

Although it is difficult to determine which educational inputs have the greatest impact on student achievement, the amount of time spent learning, whether in school or at home, matters. Lengthening the school day, prolonging the school year, and decreasing class size are a few of the most frequently promoted recommendations for improving student achievement. Although the length of the school day and school year do not determine the quality of education received, they are important inputs to the education production function, and they do signify students' exposure to educational opportunities in the classroom. Time spent out of the classroom on educational endeavors, such as doing homework or other education-enhancing activities, clearly has an impact on achievement, as well.

Among industrialized nations, there are distinct differences in the amount of time spent in instruction because of either school day or school year length. The number of annual classroom hours for 14-year-olds varies greatly between countries, with the United States falling just above the 1994 and 1998 averages of 952 and 944 hours a year, respectively. In 1998, a handful of nations averaged more than 1,000 hours of instruction a year, while England and Sweden reported lows of 720 and 741 hours a year, respectively. (See table 1.7 and figure 1.12.)[59]

Table 1.7: **Hours of Instruction Time per Year**
Selected Countries, 1998

Country	Age 12	Age 13	Age 14	Three-year total
Australia	1,022	1,027	1,027	3,076
Austria	987	987	1,048	3,022
Belgium (Flemish)	na	1,067	1,067	na
Belgium (French)	1,048	1,048	1,048	3,145
Czech Republic	782	811	869	2,461
Denmark	840	900	930	2,670
England	720	720	720	2,160
Finland	686	855	855	2,396
France	833	975	975	2,783
Germany	860	921	921	2,702
Greece	1,064	1,064	1,064	3,192
Hungary	780	902	902	2,584
Ireland	957	957	957	2,872
Italy	1,105	1,105	1,105	3,315
Japan	875	875	875	2,625
Rep. of Korea	867	867	867	2,601
Mexico	1,167	1,167	1,167	3,500
Netherlands	1,067	1,067	1,067	3,200
New Zealand	985	988	988	2,961
Norway	770	855	855	2,480
Portugal	878	878	878	2,635
Scotland	975	975	975	2,925
Spain	851	957	957	2,765
Sweden	741	741	741	2,222
Turkey	720	720	696	2,136
United States	na	na	980	na
26-country mean	899	937	944	2,768

Source: Organisation for Economic Co-operation and Development, Education Database (Paris: Organisation for Economic Co-operation and Development, 2003), updated from year to year, available online at http://www.oecd.org/els/edu/EAG98/list.htm.
Note: The data present the number of hours students are exposed to instructional activities in school. The figures do not include hours spent studying, completing homework, or participating in extracurricular tutoring or additional instruction.

Test scores from the Third International Math and Science Study (TIMSS) and the TIMSS-Repeat provide context and insight when comparing the amount of time spent on instruction in the classroom. Many nations where students spend fewer hours in instruction score higher in math and science than the United States, notably Japan and the Republic of Korea, both of which have significantly higher test scores com-

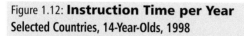

Figure 1.12: **Instruction Time per Year**
Selected Countries, 14-Year-Olds, 1998

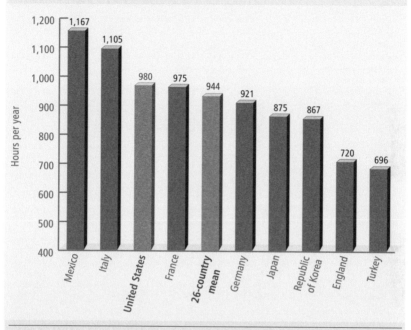

Source: Organisation for Economic Co-operation and Development, Education Database (Paris: Organisation for Economic Co-operation and Development, 2003), updated from year to year, available online at http://www.oecd.org/els/edu/EAG98/list.htm.

pared to eighth-grade students in the United States. Moreover, England and Sweden, whose instruction hours are particularly low, score higher than the United States, as well. Although Sweden's total instruction hours are low, the amount of time it devotes to math and science instruction as a percentage of its total time of instruction is quite high. (See tables 1.8 and 1.9 and figures 1.13, 1.14, and 1.15.)[60]

Table 1.8: **Instruction Time per Subject**
As a Percentage of Total Intended Instruction Time for Students,
Selected Countries, 12- to 14-Year-Olds, 1998

Country	Reading and writing mother tongue	Math	Science	Social studies	Modern foreign languages	Technology	Arts	P.E.	Religion	Vocational skills	Other	Total compulsory part	Flexible part
Australia	13%	13%	10%	10%	6%	8%	8%	7%	na	na	3%	77%	23%
Austria	12	15	14	12	10	6	12	11	6%	na	na	100	na
Belgium (Fl.)	13	13	3	6	14	6	3	6	6	na	na	70	30
Belgium (Fr.)	15	14	7	11	12	2	2	8	6	na	7	82	18
Czech Republic	14	14	13	18	11	na	9	7	na	4%	5	94	6
Denmark	20	13	12	11	10	na	9	7	3	na	3	90	10
England	12	12	14	11	11	12	10	8	4	1	5	100	na
Finland	18	11	10	10	9	na	6	8	4	na	22	100	na
France	17	14	12	13	11	7	8	11	na	na	na	93	7
Germany	14	13	11	11	21	na	9	9	na	na	8	95	5
Greece	12	11	10	10	15	5	6	8	6	1	16	100	na
Hungary	13	13	13	10	10	na	6	6	na	3	3	78	22
Ireland	23	12	9	19	na	na	na	5	7	na	2	77	23
Italy	23	10	10	14	11	9	13	7	3	na	na	100	na
Japan	14	12	11	12	13	8	11	10	na	na	8	100	na
Rep. of Korea	14	12	12	11	12	5	10	9	na	4	6	93	7
Mexico	14	14	19	18	9	9	6	6	na	na	3	100	na
Netherlands	10	10	8	11	14	5	7	9	na	na	3	78	22
New Zealand	18	16	14	14	4	8	4	11	na	5	na	93	7
Norway	16	13	9	11	16	na	8	10	7	na	10	100	na
Portugal	13	13	15	17	10	na	10	10	3	na	10	100	na
Scotland	10	10	10	10	10	10	10	5	5	na	na	80	20
Spain	19	12	11	11	8	5	14	9	na	na	2	90	10
Sweden	22	14	12	13	12	na	7	7	na	4	na	93	7
Turkey	17	13	10	7	13	na	3	3	7	10	17	99	na
United States	17	16	14	12	7	3	7	12	1	5	7	100	na
26-country mean	15	13	11	12	11	5	8	8	3	2	5	92	8

Source: Organisation for Economic Co-operation and Development, Education Database (Paris: Organisation for Economic Co-operation and Development 2003), updated from year to year, available online at http://www.oecd.org/els/edu/EAG98/list.htm.
Note: The data present the number of hours students are exposed to instructional activities in school. The figures do not include hours spent studying, completing homework, or participating in extracurricular tutoring or additional instruction.

School Figures: The Data behind the Debate

Table 1.9: **Intended Instruction Time per Year in Mathematics and Science**
Selected Countries, 14-Year-Olds, 1998

Country	Hours
Australia	232
Austria	370
Belgium (Fl.)	167
Belgium (Fr.)	247
Czech Republic	261
Denmark	240
England	217
Finland	177
France	257
Germany	229
Greece	274
Hungary	250
Ireland	200
Italy	221
Japan	223
Rep. of Korea	204
Mexico	367
Netherlands	200
New Zealand	320
Norway	171
Portugal	198
Scotland	195
Spain	198
Sweden	189
Turkey	168
United States	**295**
26-country mean	**233**

Source: Organisation for Economic Co-operation and Development, Education Database (Paris: Organisation for Economic Co-operation and Development, 2003), updated from year to year, available online at http://www.oecd.org/els/edu/EAG98/list.htm.
Note: The data present the number of hours students are exposed to instructional activities in school. The figures do not include hours spent studying, completing homework, or participating in extracurricular tutoring or additional instruction.

Figure 1.13: **Instruction Time per Subject**
Selected Countries, 12- to 14-Year-Olds, 1998

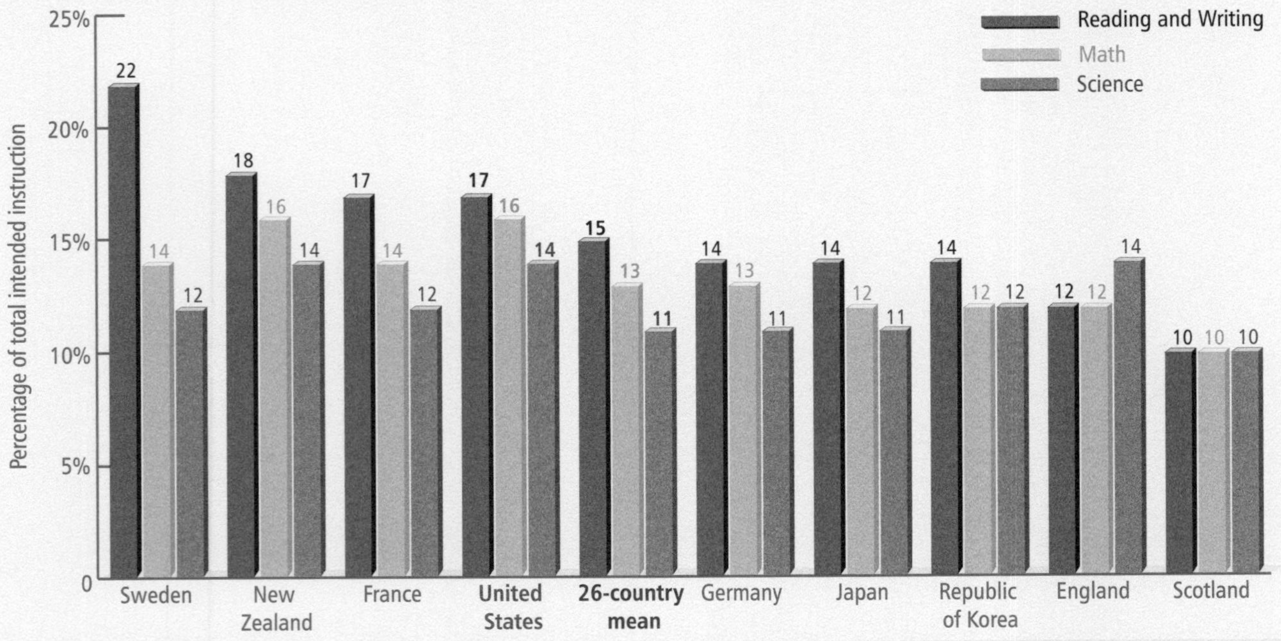

Reading and Writing
Math
Science

Percentage of total intended instruction

Sweden: 22, 14, 12
New Zealand: 18, 16, 14
France: 17, 14, 12
United States: 17, 16, 14
26-country mean: 15, 13, 11
Germany: 14, 13, 11
Japan: 14, 12, 11
Republic of Korea: 14, 12, 12
England: 12, 12, 14
Scotland: 10, 10, 10

Source: Organisation for Economic Co-operation and Development, Education Database (Paris: Organisation for Economic Co-operation and Development, 2003), updated from year to year, available online at http://www.oecd.org/els/edu/EAG98/list.htm.

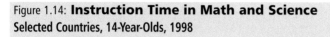
Figure 1.14: **Instruction Time in Math and Science**
Selected Countries, 14-Year-Olds, 1998

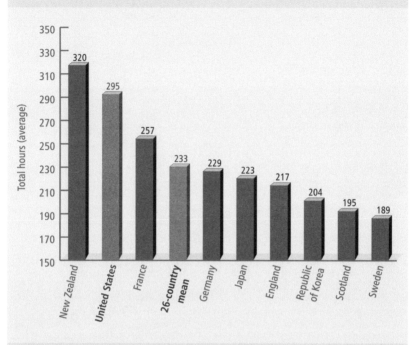

Source: Organisation for Economic Co-operation and Development, Education Database (Paris: Organisation for Economic Co-operation and Development, 2003), updated from year to year, available online at http://www.oecd.org/els/edu/EAG98/list.htm.

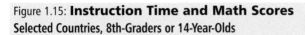

Figure 1.15: **Instruction Time and Math Scores**
Selected Countries, 8th-Graders or 14-Year-Olds

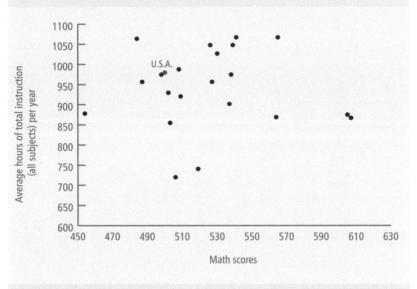

Sources: Organisation for Economic Co-operation and Development, Education Database (Paris: Organisation for Economic Co-operation and Development, 2003), updated from year to year, available online at http://www.oecd.org/els/edu/EAG98/list.htm; Harold W. Stevenson, "A TIMSS Primer: Lessons and Implications for U.S. Education," *Fordham Report* (Washington, DC: Thomas B. Fordham Foundation) 2, no. 7 (July 1998).

Data on the quantity of instruction hours dedicated to particular subjects provide information on how much time students spend learning different subjects, but they do not reveal anything about the use of the time. Classroom practices and curricula determine the way that educational information is presented. In addition, even if a nation dedicates a high percentage of instruction time toward given subjects, percentage is only half of the equation. If total instruction time for all subjects is low, students may still receive an insufficient amount of instruction in a particular subject.

While it is difficult to provide convincing evidence of the direct relationship between the number of hours received in instruction and test scores, there is one classroom activity that has a negative effect on test scores. According to a report published by the National Center for Education Statistics (NCES), students in countries who work more frequently in groups achieve at a lower level than those who worked less frequently in groups. For the United States, this is significant. In 1994, 49 percent of U.S. students worked problems in groups, a percentage of students similar to or higher than all other countries compared, except Spain. Interestingly, Spanish and American students scored at the same level as or below their peers in other nations. Although group work is certainly not the sole contributor to lower rankings, its impact should not go unmentioned.[61]

Furthermore, according to Geoffrey Borman, researchers have consistently documented "summer slide," or the depreciation of skills and habits and the deterioration of acquired knowledge during the summer months. This requires teachers to undertake extensive review when students return from a long summer vacation. This is important to note because while the U.S.'s number of instruction hours is well above the mean, its number of instruction days is not. Countries like Japan and Korea, two nations who clearly outperform the U.S., have fewer instruction hours per year but have a significantly higher number of school days each year. On average, the traditional U.S. public school year is 180 days; Japan and Korea's school years last between 220 and 225 days. In addition, most students from Asian countries do more homework and attend more private tutorials, in comparison to students in the United States. Comparing instructional time and test scores clearly illustrates that classroom time is important, but it is not everything.[62]

▶ PROPOSITION: SCHOOL ENVIRONMENT MATTERS.

Clearly, elementary and secondary education is designed to provide children with the academic knowledge and skills they need to function successfully in society and to prepare them to pursue further education, enter the workforce, and be responsible, active citizens. Research indicates that the quality of the school environment, including the overall culture and atmosphere of the school, affects student learning.[63]

Teacher quality, curriculum effectiveness, and resource quantity are often given the most consideration in discussions regarding enhancing achievement. One easily overlooked and hard-to-quantify component is school environment—specifically, peer-to-peer interaction. While at school, students spend the majority of their time with, and interact primarily with, fellow students; what their peers do, in and out of the classroom, matters. Evidence indicates that regardless of race, ethnicity, and socioeconomic status, a positive disciplinary environment is directly linked to high achievement in high school.[64]

In an ideal educational environment, students would be completely focused on enhancing their studies. At the extreme, drug and alcohol use and teen pregnancy keep students from attending school; and, at a minimum, students tend to be more easily distracted and less able to focus on their studies. Moreover, according to recent studies, approximately one-half of all classroom time is taken up with activities other than instruction, and discipline problems are responsible for a significant portion of this lost time.[65]

What are students doing today? According to Phi Delta Kappa's "Annual . . . Gallup Poll of the Public's Attitudes toward the Public Schools," which surveyed a sample of adults 18 years and older, many disciplinary problems facing public schools—drug use, alcohol, teenage pregnancy, and cigarette smoking—have actually declined over time, but concern regarding the general "lack of discipline" remains. While the percentage of those concerned regarding discipline has declined over time, it is consistently ranked as a top concern; in 2001, it tied for first. (See table 1.10.)[66]

Table 1.10: **Public's Perception of Public Schools**
Selected Problems, 1980–2001

Problems	1980	1990	2001
Lack of discipline	26%	19%	15%
Use of drugs	14	38	9
Drinking/alcoholism	2	4	na

Source: Lowell C. Rose and Alec M. Gallup, "The 33rd Annual Phi Delta Kappa/Gallup Poll of the Public's Attitudes toward the Public Schools," *Phi Delta Kappan 83*, no. 1 (September 2001), available online at http://www.pdkintl.org/kappan/kimages/kpoll83.pdf.
Note: Selected responses to question asking for the "biggest problems with which the public schools of your community must deal."

Drugs

Drug use by adolescents can have serious immediate as well as long-term health and social consequences. Drug use contributes to crime and decreased economic productivity, and requires a disproportionate share of health care services for those affected.[67]

After a short decline in reported drug use between 1980 and 1990, drug use marched upward again in the late 1990s, although not reaching the level reported in 1980.

- In 2001, 26 percent of twelfth-graders reported using illicit drugs in the previous 30 days, as did 23 percent of tenth-graders and 12 percent of eighth-graders.

- The percentage of students in each grade level reporting illicit drug use in the past 30 days increased substantially between 1992 and 1996, from 14 percent to 25 percent for twelfth-graders, from 11 to 23 percent for tenth-graders, and from 7 to 15 percent for eighth-graders. Since 1996, rates have remained relatively stable. (See table 1.11 and figure 1.16.)[68]

Table 1.11: **Illicit Drug Use by Students**
By Grade, Gender, and Race, 1980–2001

Characteristic	1980[a]	1990	1995	1996	1997	1998	1999	2000	2001
8th-graders									
Total	na	na	12.4%	14.6%	12.9%	12.1%	12.2%	11.9%	11.7%
Male	na	na	12.7	14.6	13.3	11.9	12.6	12.0	13.2
Female	na	na	11.9	14.1	12.3	11.9	11.7	11.3	9.9
White	na	na	18.9	13.2	13.7	12.4	11.3	11.2	11.2
Black	na	na	9.1	10.5	10.8	10.2	11.1	10.8	9.6
Hispanic[b]	na	na	16.7	16.5	15.9	15.9	17.0	15.2	15.0
10th-graders									
Total	na	na	20.2	23.2	23.0	21.5	22.1	22.5	22.7
Male	na	na	21.1	24.3	24.8	22.5	23.7	25.4	24.9
Female	na	na	19.0	21.9	21.0	20.5	20.4	19.5	20.5
White	na	na	19.7	22.4	23.8	23.1	22.6	23.0	23.4
Black	na	na	15.5	17.0	17.7	16.4	15.8	17.0	17.6
Hispanic[b]	na	na	20.6	22.5	24.2	24.2	23.8	23.7	23.3
12th-graders									
Total	37.2	17.2	23.8	24.6	26.2	25.6	25.9	24.9	25.7
Male	39.6	18.9	26.8	27.5	28.7	29.1	28.6	27.5	28.4
Female	34.3	15.2	20.4	21.2	23.2	21.6	22.7	22.1	22.6
White	38.8	20.5	23.8	24.8	26.4	27.5	27.0	25.9	26.5
Black	28.8	9.0	18.3	19.7	20.0	19.4	20.2	20.3	18.7
Hispanic[b]	33.1	13.9	21.4	22.6	23.9	24.1	24.4	27.4	25.3

Source: Federal Interagency Forum on Child and Family Statistics, Writing Subcommittee of the Reporting Committee, *America's Children: Key National Indicators of Well-Being, 2002* (Washington, DC: U.S. Government Printing Office, 2002), available online at http://www.childstats.gov/americaschildren/.
Notes: Students who reported using illicit drugs in the previous 30 days.
Estimates for race and Hispanic origin represent the mean of the specified year and the previous year.
Data have been combined to increase subgroup sample sizes, thus providing more stable estimates.
a. Beginning in 1982, the question about stimulant use (i.e., amphetamines) was revised to get respondents to exclude the inappropriate reporting of nonprescription stimulants. The prevalence rate dropped slightly as a result of this methodological change.
b. Persons of Hispanic origin may be of any race.

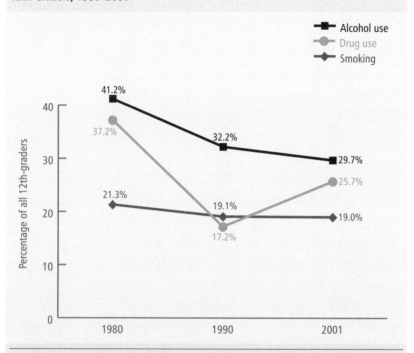

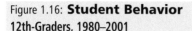

Source: Federal Interagency Forum on Child and Family Statistics, Writing Subcommittee of the Reporting Committee, *America's Children: Key National Indicators of Well-Being, 2002* (Washington, DC: U.S. Government Printing Office, 2002), available online at http://www.childstats.gov/americaschildren/.
Note: Smoking students are 12th-graders who reported smoking cigarettes daily in the previous 30 days. Alcohol use is defined as having 5 or more drinks in a row in the previous 2 weeks. Drug use is defined as using illicit drugs in the previous 30 days.

Comparing boys' and girls' use patterns, boys are more likely to use drugs. The race and ethnic differences are not as marked. Blacks use less drugs at all three measurement points, and white students show the greatest prevalence for use at younger ages. The difference between whites and Hispanics is not as clear. At younger ages, Hispanics are more likely to use drugs, but for twelfth-grade students, drug use is more common among white students than Hispanics.[69]

Alcohol

Alcohol use among adolescents is linked to a host of problems, including motor vehicle crashes and deaths, difficulties in school and the workplace, fighting, and breaking the law. In addition, heavy drinking by youths (having five or more drinks in a row at some point in the previous 2 weeks) is associated with higher levels of illicit drug use.[70]

- In 2001, 30 percent of twelfth-graders, 25 percent of tenth-graders, and 13 percent of eighth-graders reported heavy drinking.

- The reported percentage of regular drinking (having an alcoholic beverage on more than two occasions in the previous 30 days) has increased slightly among eighth-graders, from 9.1 percent in 1991 to 11.6 percent in 1996, and remained relatively constant among tenth-graders during the same time period. Among twelfth-graders, however, the percentage decreased noticeably over time, from 49.9 percent in 1980 to 30.6 percent in 1996, then remaining relatively constant throughout the late 1990s.

- Among twelfth-graders, rates of heavy drinking fell from a high of 41.2 percent in 1980 to 27.5 percent in 1993. Between 1993 and 1997, rates edged up modestly, from 27.5 percent in 1993 to 31.3 percent. But by 2001, they had leveled off to 29.7 percent. (See table 1.12 and figure 1.16.)[71]

Among tenth- and twelfth-graders, males are more likely to drink heavily than are females. In 2001, 36 percent of twelfth-grade males reported heavy drinking, compared to 24 percent of twelfth-grade females. Twenty-nine percent of tenth-grade males, compared to 21 percent of females, reported heavy drinking. Furthermore, heavy drinking is much more common

Table 1.12: **Alcohol Consumption by Students**
By Grade, Gender, and Race, 1980–2001

Characteristic	1980	1990	1995	1996	1997	1998	1999	2000	2001
8th-graders									
Subtotal	na	na	14.5%	15.6%	14.5%	13.7%	15.2%	14.1%	13.2%
Male	na	na	15.1	16.5	15.3	14.4	16.4	14.4	13.7
Female	na	na	13.9	14.5	13.5	12.7	13.9	13.6	12.4
White	na	na	13.9	15.1	15.1	14.1	14.3	14.9	13.8
Black	na	na	10.8	10.4	10.4	9.0	9.9	0.1	9.0
Hispanic[a]	na	na	22.0	21.0	20.7	20.4	20.9	19.1	17.6
10th-graders									
Subtotal	na	na	24.0	24.8	25.1	24.3	25.6	26.2	24.9
Male	na	na	26.3	27.2	28.6	26.7	29.7	29.8	28.6
Female	na	na	21.5	22.3	21.7	22.2	21.8	22.5	21.4
White	na	na	25.4	26.2	26.9	27.0	27.2	28.1	27.4
Black	na	na	13.3	12.2	12.7	12.8	12.7	12.9	12.6
Hispanic[a]	na	na	26.8	29.6	27.5	26.3	27.5	28.3	27.7
12th-graders									
Subtotal	41.2%	32.2%	29.8	30.2	31.3	31.5	30.8	30.0	29.7
Male	52.1	39.1	36.9	37.0	37.9	39.2	38.1	36.7	36.0
Female	30.5	24.4	23.0	23.5	24.4	24.0	23.6	23.5	23.7
White	44.3	36.6	32.3	33.4	35.1	36.4	35.7	34.6	34.5
Black	17.7	14.4	14.9	15.3	13.4	12.3	12.3	11.5	11.8
Hispanic[a]	33.1	25.6	26.6	27.1	27.6	28.1	29.3	31.0	28.4

Source: Federal Interagency Forum on Child and Family Statistics, Writing Subcommittee of the Reporting Committee, *America's Children: Key National Indicators of Well-Being, 2002* (Washington, DC: U.S. Government Printing Office, 2002), available online at http://www.childstats.gov/americaschildren/.
Notes: Students who reported having five or more alcoholic drinks in a row in the previous 2 weeks. Estimates for race and Hispanic origin represent the mean of the specified year and the previous year.
Data have been combined to increase subgroup sample sizes, thus providing more stable estimates.
a. Persons of Hispanic origin may be of any race.

among Hispanic and white secondary school students than among their black counterparts. For example, among twelfth-grade students, 12 percent of blacks reported heavy drinking, compared to 35 percent of whites and 28 percent of Hispanics.[72]

Sexual Experience and Pregnancy

Sexual experience and, particularly, age at first intercourse represent critical indicators of the risk of pregnancy and sexually transmitted diseases. Trends over the past several decades show that increasing proportions of teens are sexually experienced, defined as ever having had sexual intercourse. The birth rate for teenagers, however, peaked in 1995 and has consistently declined through 2000.[73]

- In the mid-1990s, 37 percent of ninth-grade students reported having had sexual intercourse. This percentage rose with each grade and reached 66 percent by the twelfth grade.

- The United States has the highest teenage pregnancy rate of all developed countries. About 1 million teenagers become pregnant each year, nearly 1 in 10 teenage girls ages 15–19.

- The estimated teen pregnancy rate in 1996 was 98.7 per 1,000 women age 15–19, down 15 percent from its high point of 116.5 in 1991. The 1996 rate was the lowest since 1976.

- The birth rate for teenagers in 1998 was 51.1 live births per 1,000 women age 15–19, 2 percent lower than the rate in 1997, and 18 percent lower than in 1991. (See table 1.13.)

- Specifically, birth rates have dropped sharply for black teenagers (age 15–19) since 1991, declining overall by 26 percent, from 115.5 per 1,000 live births to 85.3, lower than any year since 1960 when data first became available.

Table 1.13: **Birthrates for Unmarried Women**
By Age of Mother, 1980–2000

Age of mother	1980	1990	1995	1996	1997	1998	1999	2000
15–17	20.6	29.6	30.5	29.0	28.2	27.0	25.5	24.4
18–19	39.0	60.7	67.6	65.9	65.2	64.5	63.3	62.9
20–24	40.9	65.1	70.3	70.7	71.0	72.3	72.9	74.5
25–29	34.0	56.0	56.1	56.8	56.2	58.4	60.2	62.2
30–34	21.1	37.6	39.6	41.1	39.0	39.1	39.3	40.7
35–39	9.7	17.3	19.5	20.1	19.0	19.0	19.3	20.0
40–44	2.6	3.6	4.7	4.8	4.6	4.6	4.6	5.0
Total 15–44	29.4	43.8	45.1	44.8	28.2	44.3	44.4	45.2

Source: Federal Interagency Forum on Child and Family Statistics, Writing Subcommittee of the Reporting Committee, *America's Children: Key National Indicators of Well-Being, 2002* (Washington, DC: U.S. Government Printing Office, 2002), available online at http://www.childstats.gov/americaschildren/.
Note: Live births per 1,000 unmarried women.

Race and ethnicity differences are distinct. Black students are more likely than white and Hispanic students to have had their first sexual experience while still in high school. In 1995, 49 percent of both male and female white students reported having had sexual intercourse, 62 percent of male Hispanic students and 53 percent of Hispanic female students, and 81 percent of black male students and 67 percent of black female students.[74]

Cigarette Smoking

The Centers for Disease Control and Prevention estimates that one in five deaths is caused by tobacco use. Youthful smoking can have severe, lifelong consequences because a large portion of those who start smoking in adolescence will continue to smoke as adults. Furthermore, youth who smoke are also more likely to use illicit drugs and to drink more heavily than their peers who do not smoke. Rates of daily smoking peaked in 1996 for eighth- and tenth-graders (between 1991 and 2001) and in 1997 for twelfth-graders (between 1980 and 2001). Among eighth- and tenth-graders, daily smoking declined steadily between 1996 and 2001. It is no surprise that as children get older, so does the prevalence of smoking. In 2001, 5 percent of eighth-graders, 12 percent of tenth-graders, and 19 percent of twelfth-graders reported smoking cigarettes daily in the previous 30 days.[75]

Rates of smoking differ substantially between racial and ethnic groups. White students have the highest rates of smoking, followed by Hispanics and then blacks. In 2001, 24 percent of white twelfth-graders reported daily smoking, compared with 12 percent of Hispanics and 8 percent of blacks. There is little difference, however, in the prevalence of smoking between males and females, with the exception of blacks. In grades 9 through 12, black males are more likely than black females to smoke. (See table 1.14 and figure 1.16.)[76]

While data show overall improvement when it comes to high-risk behavior among students, there is consistent concern regarding the general disciplinary environment in the classroom.

Table 1.14: **Cigarette Smoking by Students**
By Grade, Gender, and Race, 1980–2001

Characteristic	1980	1990	1995	1996	1997	1998	1999	2000	2001
8th-graders									
Subtotal	na	na	9.3%	10.4%	9.0%	8.8%	8.1%	7.4%	5.5%
Male	na	na	9.2	10.5	9.0	8.1	7.4	7.0	5.9
Female	na	na	9.2	10.1	8.7	9.0	8.4	7.5	4.9
White	na	na	10.5	11.7	11.4	10.4	9.7	9.0	7.5
Black	na	na	2.8	3.2	3.7	3.8	3.8	3.2	2.8
Hispanic[a]	na	na	9.2	8.0	8.1	8.4	8.5	7.1	5.0
10th-graders									
Subtotal	na	na	16.3	18.3	18.0	15.8	15.9	14.0	12.2
Male	na	na	16.3	18.1	17.2	14.7	15.6	13.7	12.4
Female	na	na	16.1	18.6	18.5	16.8	15.9	14.1	11.9
White	na	na	17.6	20.0	21.4	20.3	19.1	17.7	15.5
Black	na	na	4.7	5.1	5.6	5.8	5.3	5.2	5.2
Hispanic[a]	na	na	9.9	11.6	10.8	9.4	9.1	8.8	7.4
12th-graders									
Subtotal	21.3%	19.1%	21.6	22.2	24.6	22.4	23.1	20.6	19.0
Male	18.5	18.6	21.7	22.2	24.8	22.7	23.6	20.9	18.4
Female	23.5	19.3	20.8	21.8	23.6	21.5	22.2	19.7	18.9
White	23.9	21.8	23.9	25.4	27.8	28.3	26.9	25.7	23.8
Black	17.4	5.8	6.1	7.0	7.2	7.4	7.7	8.0	7.5
Hispanic[a]	12.8	10.9	11.6	12.9	14.0	13.6	14.0	15.7	12.0

Source: Federal Interagency Forum on Child and Family Statistics, Writing Subcommittee of the Reporting Committee, *America's Children: Key National Indicators of Well-Being, 2002* (Washington, DC: U.S. Government Printing Office, 2002), available online at http://www.childstats.gov/americaschildren/.

Notes: Percentage of students who reported smoking cigarettes daily in the previous 30 years. Estimates for race and Hispanic origin represent the mean of the specified year and the previous year.

Data have been combined to increase subgroup sample sizes, thus providing more stable estimates.

a. Persons of Hispanic origin may be of any race.

Proposition: School violence is on the decline.

For some time, violence in our schools has been a concern. Highly publicized and extremely violent school shootings in the 1990s (Columbine, Jonesboro, and so on) further heightened fears. Schools should be houses of learning, not of fear; however, without a safe environment, teachers cannot teach and students cannot learn. The seventh goal of the National Education Goals states that by the year 2000, "all schools in America will be free of drugs and violence and the unauthorized presence of firearms and alcohol, and offer a disciplined environment that is conducive to learning."[77] In response to this goal, Congress passed the Safe and Drug-Free Schools and Communities Act of 1994, which provides for support of drug and violence prevention programs. Although school crime has not been extirpated, rates are decreasing.

Students

In 1999, students age twelve through eighteen were victims of about 2.5 million crimes at school. In the same year, these students were victims of about 186,000 serious violent crimes (defined as rape, sexual assault, robbery, and aggravated assault) at school. In the 1990s, however, counter to popular perception, the total nonfatal crime rate for young people generally declined.[78]

- Between 1995 and 1999, the percentage of students who reported being victims of crime at school decreased from

10 percent to 8 percent, dropping from 11 to 8 percent among seventh-graders, 11 to 8 percent among eighth-graders, and 12 to 9 percent among ninth-graders.

- Between 1993 and 1998, the number of nonfatal crimes against students ages 12 through 18 occurring at school or on the way to or from school decreased by 40.6 percent, from 155 crimes to 92 per 1,000 students.

- In 1993, white children were much more likely to be victims of crime. By 1998, black children were the most likely victims. (See table 1.15 and figure 1.17.)[79]

Table 1.15: **Nonfatal Crimes against Students 1993 & 1999**

Characteristic	Total crimes		Theft		Violent[a]		Serious violent[a]	
	1993	1999	1993	1999	1993	1999	1993	1999
Gender								
Male	171	98	101	62	70	37	14	8
Female	137	85	91	57	46	28	11	6
Age								
12–14	190	120	111	74	79	46	16	11
15–18	125	70	83	48	42	23	9	4
Ethnicity[b]								
White	170	98	106	64	63	34	11	6
Black	128	106	76	63	52	43	22	14
Hispanic	118	62	68	40	50	21	9	6
Other	99	77	70	52	29	26	6[c]	5[c]
Overall	155	92	96	59	59	33	12	7

Source: P. Kaufman, X. Chen, S.P. Choy, K. Peter, S.A. Ruddy, A.K. Miller, J.K. Fleury, K.A. Chandler, M.G. Planty, and M.R. Rand, *Indicators of School Crime and Safety: 2001*, reports NCES 2002-113, NCJ-190075 (Washington, DC: U.S. Departments of Education and Justice, 2001), available online at http://www.ojp.usdoj.gov/bjs/pub/pdf/iscs.pdf.
Notes: Rate per 1,000 students, at or on the way to school.
a. "Serious violent" crimes are also included under "violent" crimes.
b. "Hispanic" does not overlap into the three other groups.
c. Estimate based on fewer than 10 cases.

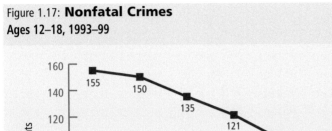

Figure 1.17: **Nonfatal Crimes**
Ages 12–18, 1993–99

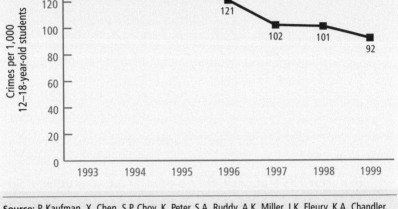

Source: P. Kaufman, X. Chen, S.P. Choy, K. Peter, S.A. Ruddy, A.K. Miller, J.K. Fleury, K.A. Chandler, M.G. Planty, and M.R. Rand, *Indicators of School Crime and Safety: 2001*, reports NCES 2002-113, NCJ-190075 (Washington, DC: U.S. Departments of Education and Justice, 2001), available online at http://www.ojp.usdoj.gov/bjs/pub/pdf/iscs.pdf.
Note: Crimes committed against students at or on the way to school.

Although concerns regarding school violence are well-founded, in 1999, school-age children were more than twice as likely to be victims of serious crime away from school as at school. The publicity surrounding the most deadly incidents at school, such as Columbine, belies the true conditions at most schools—violence and crime rates are down.[80]

School Environment

As crime has decreased, students' confidence in the security of the school environment has increased. Between 1995 and 1999, the percentage of students ages 12 through 18 who reported being fearful of being attacked or harmed at school decreased from 9 percent to 5 percent. During the same time period, the percentage of students fearing they would be attacked while traveling to and from school fell from 7 percent to 4 percent.[81]

- Between 1993 and 1999, the percentage of students in grades 9 through 12 who reported carrying a weapon on school property within the previous 30 days fell from 12 percent to 7 percent, a 42 percent reduction. (See figure 1.18.)

- Between 1995 and 1999, the percentage of students ages 12 through 18 who avoided one or more places at school for fear of their own safety decreased from 9 percent to 5 percent.

- Between 1995 and 1999, the percentage of students who reported that street gangs were present at their schools decreased by more than more than 40 percent, from 29 percent to 17 percent. (See figure 1.19.)[82]

Figure 1.18: **Students Carrying Weapons**
Grades 9–12, 1993–99

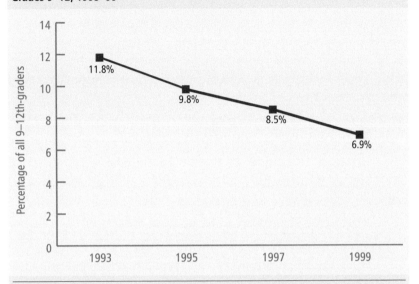

Source: P. Kaufman, X. Chen, S.P. Choy, K. Peter, S.A. Ruddy, A.K. Miller, J.K. Fleury, K.A. Chandler, M.G. Planty, and M.R. Rand, *Indicators of School Crime and Safety: 2001,* reports NCES 2002-113, NCJ-190075 (Washington, DC: U.S. Departments of Education and Justice, 2001), available online at http://www.ojp.usdoj.gov/bjs/pub/pdf/iscs.pdf.
Note: Students who reported carrying a weapon at least once within the previous 30 days.

The data all indicate that the students' perception of school has improved, as has their environment. What has led to this change? The national nonfatal crime rate per 100,000 of the population decreased by 15.8 percent between 1993 and 1998.[83] In addition, school programs have been established to help reduce crime and increase student awareness of drugs, gangs, and risky behavior and situations. For example, according to a 1995–96 National Center for Education Statistics (NCES) Survey on School Violence, 78 percent of public schools reported having some type of formal violence-prevention or violence-reduction program or effort. Furthermore, 50 percent of public schools with violence-prevention programs

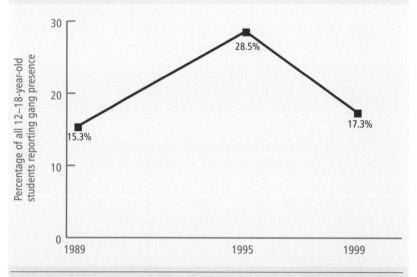

Figure 1.19: **Gang Presence**
Ages 12–18, 1989–99

Percentage of all 12–18-year-old students reporting gang presence

28.5%

15.3%

17.3%

1989   1995   1999

Source: P. Kaufman, X. Chen, S.P. Choy, K. Peter, S.A. Ruddy, A.K. Miller, J.K. Fleury, K.A. Chandler, M.G. Planty, and M.R. Rand, *Indicators of School Crime and Safety: 2001,* reports NCES 2002-113, NCJ-190075 (Washington, DC: U.S. Departments of Education and Justice, 2001), available online at http://www.ojp.usdoj.gov/bjs/pub/pdf/iscs.pdf.
Note: Students age 12–18 who reported that street gangs were present at school within the previous 6 months.

indicated that all or almost all of their students participated in these programs.[84]

There is no argument that a safe school is a better school. During the 1990s, crime awareness and prevention programs in schools proliferated, and there was an overall decline in crime in the United States. It remains to be seen which had a greater effect on the decline in violence in U.S. schools. This germinates a larger question: What is the tradeoff with the time spent on prevention programs? These programs may contribute to providing a better environment for education, but at the cost of time taken from core learning. Was the decline in school violence a reflection of changes in society, or did the increase in the number of crime awareness programs and get-tough, zero-tolerance policies in schools contribute to safer schools? The jury is out. No doubt interventionist activities in the schools take time away from teaching, but they may contribute to a more positive educational environment.

▶ Chapter Notes

1. Thomas D. Snyder, ed., *Digest of Education Statistics, 2001* (Washington, DC: U.S. Department of Education, National Center for Education Statistics, 2002), table 3, p. 12; Center for Education Reform, *Charter School Highlights and Statistics* (Washington, DC: Center for Education Reform, 2000), available online at http://www.edreform.com; Marquette University, Institute for the Transformation of Learning, Office of Research, *School Choice Enrollment Growth* (Milwaukee, WI: Marquette University, 2000), available online at http://www.schoolchoiceinfo.org; Children First America, *The Road to Success: Private Vouchers Helping American Children* (Bentonville, AR: Children First America, 1999); Home School Legal Defense Association, *Homeschooling Research* (Purcellville, VA: Home School Legal Defense Association, National Center for Home Education), available online at http://www.hslda.org.

2. Public Agenda Online, *Education: People's Chief Concerns* (New York, NY: Public Agenda Online), available online at http://www.publicagenda.org.

3. Snyder, *Digest of Education Statistics, 2001*, table 89, p. 98. Note: Schools with both elementary and secondary programs are included under elementary schools and also under secondary schools.

4. Ibid., table 96, p. 120.

5. Ibid., table 90, p. 98.

6. Snyder, *Digest of Education Statistics, 2001*, table 89, p. 98. Note: Schools with both elementary and secondary programs are included under elementary schools and also under secondary schools.

7. Snyder, *Digest of Education Statistics, 2001*, table 89, p. 98; Marquette University, Institute for the Transformation of Learning, Office of Research, *School Choice Enrollment Growth*; Children First America, *The Road to Success: Private Vouchers Helping American Children.*

8. Snyder, *Digest of Education Statistics, 2001*, table 89, p. 98; Marquette University, Institute for the Transformation of Learning, Office of Research, *School Choice Enrollment Growth*; Children First America, *The Road to Success: Private Vouchers Helping American Children.*

9. P. Kaufman, X. Chen, S.P. Choy, K. Peter, S.A. Ruddy, A.K. Miller, J.K. Fleury, K.A. Chandler, M.G. Planty, and M.R. Rand, *Indicators of School Crime and Safety: 2001*, reports NCES 2002-113, NCJ-190075

(Washington, DC: U.S. Departments of Education and Justice, 2001), available online at http://www.ojp.usdoj.gov/bjs/pub/pdf/iscs.pdf.

10. Snyder, *Digest of Education Statistics, 2001*, table 421, p. 493.

11. Snyder, *Digest of Education Statistics, 2001*, table 3, p. 12.

12. Snyder, *Digest of Education Statistics, 2001*, table 42, p.58.

13. Snyder, *Digest of Education Statistics, 2001*, table 3, p. 12; Center for Education Reform, *Charter School Highlights and Statistics*; Marquette University, Institute for the Transformation of Learning, Office of Research, *School Choice Enrollment Growth*; Children First America, *The Road to Success: Private Vouchers Helping American Children*; Home School Legal Defense Association, *Homeschooling Research*.

14. Ibid.

15. Ibid.

16. Snyder, *Digest of Education Statistics, 2001*, table 3, p. 12; Center for Education Reform, *Charter School Highlights and Statistics*; Marquette University, Institute for the Transformation of Learning, Office of Research, *School Choice Enrollment Growth*; Children First America, *The Road to Success: Private Vouchers Helping American Children*.

17. Ibid.

18. Snyder, *Digest of Education Statistics, 2001*, tables 89, 90, 96, pp. 98, 120.

19. Ibid., tables 89, 90, 96, pp. 98, 120.

20. Caroline M. Hoxby, "If Families Matter Most, Where Do Schools Come In?" in *A Primer on America's Schools*, ed. Terry M. Moe (Stanford, CA: Hoover Institution Press, 2001), pp. 89–123.

21. Ibid.

22. Snyder, *Digest of Education Statistics, 2001*, table 89, p. 98.

23. Hoxby, "If Families Matter Most, Where Do Schools Come In?"

24. Kathleen Cotton, *School Size, School Climate, and Student Performance*, School Improvement Research Series, Close-up #20 (Portland, OR: Northwest Regional Educational Laboratory, 1996), available online at http://www.nwrel.org/scpd/sirs/10/c020.html.

25. Interestingly, Conant's idea of a large school was approximately 300–400 students, which would be considered a small school today.

26. Cotton, *School Size, School Climate, and Student Performance*.

27. While there is no single definition of a "small school," some research has indicated that 300–400 students at the elementary level and 400–800 students at the secondary level is appropriate.

28. Cotton, *School Size, School Climate, and Student Performance*; Roger Ehrich, *The Impact of School Size*, available online at http://pixel.cs.vt.edu/edu/size.html; Mary Anne Raywid, *Current Literature on Small Schools*, ERIC Digest EDO-RC-98-8 (Charleston, WV: ERIC Clearinghouse on Rural Education and Small Schools, 1999), available online at http://www.ael.org/eric/digests/edorc988.htm; William Ayers, Gerald Bracey, and Greg Smith, *The Ultimate Education Reform? Make Schools Smaller* (Milwaukee, WI: University of Wisconsin-Milwaukee, School of Education, Center for Education Research, Analysis, and Innovation, 2000), available online at http://www.uwm.edu/Dept/CERAI/documents/archives/00/cerai-00-35.htm.

29. Cotton, *School Size, School Climate, and Student Performance*; Ehrich, *The Impact of School Size*; Raywid, *Current Literature on Small Schools*; Ayers, Bracey, and Smith, *The Ultimate Education Reform? Make Schools Smaller*; Patricia Wasley, Michelle Fine, Matt Gladden, Nicole E. Holland, Sherry P. King, Esther Mosak, and Linda C. Powell, *Small Schools: Great Strides: A Study of New Small Schools in Chicago* (New York: Bank Street College of Education, 2000), available online at http://www.bankstreet.edu/news/releases/smschool.html; Wisconsin Education Association Council, School Size, Great Schools Issue Paper (Madison, WI: Wisconsin Education Association Council), available online at http://www.weac.org/GreatSchools/Issuepapers/schoolsize.htm.

30. Cotton, *School Size, School Climate, and Student Performance*; Ehrich, *The Impact of School Size*; Raywid, *Current Literature on Small Schools*; Ayers, Bracey, and Smith, *The Ultimate Education Reform? Make Schools Smaller*; Wasley, Fine, Gladden, Holland, King, Mosak, and Powell, *Small Schools: Great Strides: A Study of New Small Schools in Chicago*; Wisconsin Education Association Council, *School Size*.

31. Cotton, *School Size, School Climate, and Student Performance*; Ehrich, *The Impact of School Size*; Raywid, Current Literature on Small Schools; Ayers, Bracey, and Smith, *The Ultimate Education Reform? Make Schools Smaller*; Wasley, Fine, Gladden, Holland, King, Mosak, and Powell, *Small Schools: Great Strides: A Study of New Small Schools in Chicago*; Wisconsin Education Association Council, *School Size*.

32. Cotton, *School Size, School Climate, and Student Performance*; Ehrich, *The Impact of School Size*; Raywid, *Current Literature on Small Schools*; Ayers, Bracey, and Smith, *The Ultimate Education Reform? Make Schools Smaller*; Wasley, Fine, Gladden, Holland, King, Mosak, and Powell, *Small Schools: Great Strides: A Study of New Small Schools in Chicago*; Wisconsin Education Association Council, *School Size*.

33. Cotton, *School Size, School Climate, and Student Performance*; Ehrich, *The Impact of School Size*; Raywid, *Current Literature on Small Schools*; Ayers, Bracey, and Smith, *The Ultimate Education Reform? Make Schools Smaller*; Wasley, Fine, Gladden, Holland, King, Mosak, and Powell, *Small Schools: Great Strides: A Study of New Small Schools in Chicago*; Wisconsin Education Association Council, *School Size*.

34. Cotton, *School Size, School Climate, and Student Performance*; Ehrich, *The Impact of School Size*; Raywid, *Current Literature on Small Schools*; Ayers, Bracey, and Smith, *The Ultimate Education Reform? Make Schools Smaller*; Wasley, Fine, Gladden, Holland, King, Mosak, and Powell, *Small Schools: Great Strides: A Study of New Small Schools in Chicago*; Wisconsin Education Association Council, School Size.

35. Stacy Mitchell, "The Answer Is Smaller Schools," *Michigan Education Report*, winter (15 February, 2002), available online at http://mackinac.org/pubs/mer/article.asp?ID=4074.

36. Cotton, *School Size, School Climate, and Student Performance*; Ehrich, *The Impact of School Size*; Raywid, *Current Literature on Small Schools*; Ayers, Bracey, and Smith, *The Ultimate Education Reform? Make Schools Smaller*; Wasley, Fine, Gladden, Holland, King, Mosak, and Powell, *Small Schools: Great Strides: A Study of New Small Schools in Chicago*; Wisconsin Education Association Council, *School Size*.

37. Ibid.

38. Ibid.

39. Mitchell, "The Answer Is Smaller Schools."

40. Ibid.

41. Ibid.

42. Cotton, *School Size, School Climate, and Student Performance*.

43. Tom Gregory, *Breaking Up Large High Schools: Five Common (and Understandable) Errors of Execution*, ERIC Digest EDO-RC-01-6 (Charleston, WV: Eric Clearinghouse on Rural Education and Small Schools, 2001), available online at http://www.ael.org/eric/digest/edorc01-6.htm.

44. Debra Viadero, "Research on Chicago High Schools Finds Benefits in Smaller Size," *Education Week* 19, no. 42 (12 July, 2000), p. 12, available online at http://www.edweek.org/ew/ewstory.cfm?slug=42small.h19; Allie Shah, "As New Schools Get Bigger, Report Argues Smaller Is Better" (*Minneapolis–St. Paul, Minnesota*) *Star Tribune* (10 September, 2001), available online at http://www.startribune.com/viewers/qview.php?slug=SKUL10&template=print_a.

45. Excluding special education schools, vocational schools, and alternative schools.

46. Wisconsin Education Association Council, *School Size.*

47. U.S. Department of Education, "Public Secondary Schools, by Grade Span and Average School Size, by State: 1997–98"(Washington, DC: U.S. Department of Education, National Center for Education Statistics), table 102, available online at http://www.nces.ed.gov.

48. Cotton, *School Size, School Climate, and Student Performance.*

49. E.D. Hirsch, Jr., "Curriculum and Competence," in *A Primer on America's Schools*, ed. Terry M. Moe (Stanford, CA: Hoover Institution Press, 2001), pp. 185–204; Deborah Cohen, "Moving Images," *Education Week* (3 August, 1994), available online at http://www.edweek.org/ew/ewstory.cfm?slug_40mobile.h13.

50. U.S. General Accounting Office, *Elementary School Children: Many Change Schools Frequently, Harming Their Education*, report GA 1.13:HEHS-94-45 (GAO/HEHS-94-95) (Washington, DC: U.S. General Accounting Office, 1994).

51. Ibid.

52. U.S. Census Bureau, American Housing Survey Branch, "Table 2-1. Introductory Characteristics—Occupied Units," in *American Housing Survey for the United States: 1999* (Washington, DC: U.S. Census Bureau, 2000), available online at http://www.census.gov/hhes/www/housing/ahs/ahs99/tab21.html.

53. Ibid.

54. U.S. General Accounting Office, *Elementary School Children: Many Change Schools Frequently, Harming Their Education.*

55. Ibid.

56. Ibid.

57. Hirsch, "Curriculum and Competence."

58. Ibid.

59. Organisation for Economic Co-operation and Development, Education Database (Paris: Organisation for Economic Co-operation and Development, 2003), updated from year to year, available online at http://www.oecd.org/els/edu/EAG98/list.htm. Note: The data present the number of hours students are exposed to instructional activities in school. The figures do not include hours spent studying, completing homework, or participating in extracurricular tutoring or additional instruction.

60. Ibid.

61. Marianne Perie, Joel D. Sherman, Gabriele Phillips, and Matthew Riggan, *Elementary and Secondary Education: An International Perspective*, report NCES 2000-033 (Washington, DC: U.S. Department of Education, National Center for Education Statistics, 2000), p. 70.

62. Ibid., pp. 19, 117, 118.

63. Federal Interagency Forum on Child and Family Statistics, Writing Subcommittee of the Reporting Committee, *America's Children: Key National Indicators of Well-Being, 2000* (Washington, DC: U.S. Government Printing Office, 2000), available online at http://www.childstats.gov.

64. Ibid.

65. Kathleen Cotton, *Schoolwide and Classroom Discipline*, School Improvement Research Series. Close-up #9 (Portland, OR: Northwest Regional Educational Laboratory, 1990), available online at http://www.nwrel.org/scpd/sirs/5/cu9.html.

66. Lowell C. Rose and Alec M. Gallup, "The 33rd Annual Phi Delta Kappa/Gallup Poll of the Public's Attitudes toward the Public Schools," *Phi Delta Kappan* 83, no. 1 (September 2001), available online at http://www.pdkintl.org/kappan/kimages/kpoll83.pdf.

67. Federal Interagency Forum on Child and Family Statistics, Writing Subcommittee of the Reporting Committee, *America's Children: Key National Indicators of Well-Being, 2002* (Washington, DC: U.S. Government Printing Office, 2002), available online at http://www.childstats.gov/americaschildren/; Child Trends, Inc., Donald J. Hernandez, and Kathryn Darke, *Trends in the Well-Being of America's Children & Youth: 1998* (Washington, DC: U.S. Department of Health and Human Services, Office of the Assistant Secretary for Planning and Evaluation, 1999), available online at http://aspe.hhs.gov/hsp/98trends/trends98.htm.

68. Federal Interagency Forum on Child and Family Statistics, Writing Subcommittee of the Reporting Committee, *America's Children: Key National Indicators of Well-Being, 2002*; Child Trends, Inc., Hernandez, and Darke, *Trends in the Well-Being of America's Children & Youth: 1998*.

69. Ibid.

70. Ibid.

71. Federal Interagency Forum on Child and Family Statistics, Writing Subcommittee of the Reporting Committee, *America's Children: Key National Indicators of Well-Being, 2002*; Child Trends, Inc., Hernandez,

and Darke, *Trends in the Well-Being of America's Children & Youth: 1998*.

72. Ibid.

73. Centers for Disease Control and Prevention, "Teen Pregnancy" (Atlanta, GA: Centers for Disease Control and Prevention, 2002), available online at http://www.cdc.gov.

74. Federal Interagency Forum on Child and Family Statistics, Writing Subcommittee of the Reporting Committee, *America's Children: Key National Indicators of Well-Being, 2002*; Child Trends, Inc., Hernandez, and Darke, *Trends in the Well-Being of America's Children & Youth: 1998*.

75. Ibid.

76. Ibid.

77. National Center for Education Statistics, *Violence and Discipline Problems in U.S. Public Schools: 1996–97: Executive Summary* (Washington, DC: U.S. Department of Education, National Center for Education Statistics, 1998), available online at http://nces.ed.gov/pubs98/violence/98030001.html.

78. Kaufman, Chen, Choy, Peter, Ruddy, Miller, Fleury, Chandler, Planty, and Rand, *Indicators of School Crime and Safety: 2001*.

79. Ibid.

80. Ibid.

81. Kaufman, Chen, Choy, Peter, Ruddy, Miller, Fleury, Chandler, Planty, and Rand, *Indicators of School Crime and Safety: 2001*.

82. Ibid.

83. U.S. Census Bureau, *Statistical Abstract of the United States: 2000* (Washington, DC: U.S. Census Bureau, 2001), available online at http://www.census.gov/prod/www/statistical-abstract-us.html.

84. National Center for Education Statistics, *Violence and Discipline Problems in U.S. Public Schools: 1996–97*.

Chapter 2:
Teachers

Propositions

▶ THERE IS NO REAL TEACHER SHORTAGE.

▶ ACROSS-THE-BOARD TEACHER SALARY INCREASES MAY NOT STAND ALONE AS AN EDUCATION REFORM SOLUTION.

▶ TEACHER CERTIFICATION DOES NOT NECESSARILY GUARANTEE TEACHER QUALITY, AND FOR SOME INTERESTED IN TEACHING, IT IS A DETERRENT.

▶ TEACHERS' EDUCATION LEVELS HAVE INCREASED; STUDENTS' ACHIEVEMENT HAS NOT.

▶ SOME ARE CONCERNED THAT CHILDREN IN PUBLIC SCHOOLS ARE RECEIVING LESS INDIVIDUALIZED ATTENTION; THE NUMBERS TELL A DIFFERENT STORY.

▶ SECONDARY PUBLIC SCHOOL TEACHERS ARE SPENDING MORE TIME PERFORMING THEIR TEACHING DUTIES, YET THEY ARE TEACHING FEWER STUDENTS.

▶ TEACHERS' UNIONS PROVIDE MORE THAN COLLECTIVE BARGAINING FOR TEACHERS.

▶ THE NATION'S LARGEST TEACHERS' UNIONS INVEST HEAVILY IN THE POLITICAL PROCESS, YET THEIR CONTRIBUTIONS DO NOT REFLECT THE POLITICAL VIEWS OF A LARGE SEGMENT OF THEIR MEMBERSHIP.

Highlights

▶ In 2000, there were approximately 3.3 million teachers in elementary and secondary schools, 2.9 million of them in public schools.[1]

▶ Of teachers in elementary and secondary public schools, approximately 75 percent are women, and approximately 9 percent are minorities.[2]

▶ In the mid-1990s, the average age of a public school teacher was 44. The average number of years of teaching experience was 15, up from 8 years in 1966.[3]

▶ In the mid-1990s, only 2 percent of public school teachers were in their first year of teaching, compared with 9 percent in 1966.[4]

▶ Nearly 55 percent of public elementary and secondary teachers today have a master's or specialist degree; only 23 percent did in 1966.[5]

▶ Today only 52 percent of public elementary and secondary instructional staff are teachers, compared with 70 percent in 1950.[6]

▶ In 2001, the public elementary and secondary student-to-teacher ratio was approximately 15:1; in 1950, it was 27:1.[7]

▶ In 1961, teachers' salaries were 51 percent of public K–12 education costs; in 2001, they were only 40 percent.[8]

▶ In 2001, the average teacher salary was $43,250.[9]

In 1966, 53 percent of teachers said they certainly would be willing to teach again; in 1996, only 32 percent said they would.[10]

In 2001, an estimated 75 to 80 percent of public school teachers were members of teachers' unions.[11]

Overview

In education, teaching is where the rubber meets the road. Teachers are clearly among the most important players in the field of learning.

However, today teaching and teachers are different than they were in the past. Teachers must address an increasingly diverse student body; the days of homogeneity in the classroom are dwindling. Teachers must master—and convey to their students—a greater body of knowledge, and they are confronted with higher expectations. In addition to teaching, a classroom teacher must act as role model, counselor, disciplinarian, friend, and, some say, babysitter. No one says the job is getting any easier.

While the teaching profession and the student body are changing, the teaching force does not seem to be changing as quickly. Proportionately, there are far more white teachers, for example, than white students, and the gap is widening. In 1971, 88 percent of teachers were white; in 1996, 91 percent of teachers were white. Moreover, in 1961, less than 69 percent of classroom teachers were women; by 1996, contrary to what one might think, that percentage had actually risen to nearly 75 percent. Of course, women's participation in the labor force has grown tremendously during this same time period, explaining some of the increase.

An alarming change is the aging of the teaching force; the average age of today's teacher is 44—fully 7 years older than the average age 30 years ago. More mature, more experienced teachers are an asset to any school district. But, will the next generation of teachers be as effective? And, will we be able to attract the best and the brightest?

Teachers now enter the profession with more education, and many continue their formal education throughout their careers. However, education and preparation are not always the same. As the body of knowledge grows, demand, particularly at the secondary level, is for more specialization in the profession. Yet large numbers of teachers do not have academic degrees in the fields in which they are teaching.

Despite, on the whole, more highly educated teachers, the achievement of students does not appear to be improving. This leads to the vexing problem of connecting pay to performance. Incentive pay structures and merit pay are virtually nonexistent in the profession. The unions, bureaucracy, lack of accountability, and inertia all work against innovative pay schemes—experience, academic degrees, and certification continue to define the pay structure.

In the latter half of the 20th century, the largest agents of change in relationship to teachers' pay and the profession overall had been the teachers' unions, primarily the National Education Association (NEA) and the American Federation of Teachers (AFT). For the most part, labor unions in most industries have become less organized over the past 50 years; American public education (both K–12 and postsecondary) is one of the rare exceptions.

In this chapter, we present data about teachers, their education, and the nature of their job.

PROPOSITION: THERE IS NO REAL TEACHER SHORTAGE.

Teachers are consistently at the center of education discussions—their quality, their pay, their commitment, their preparation, their impact on student performance, and most recently, their shortage. While shortage fears are well-founded, they are often misrepresented. On the whole, there is not a shortage of certified teachers. To be sure, in specific subject areas—math, science, foreign languages, and special education—there is a lack of certified teachers;[12] however, in the aggregate, there are plenty of teachers. Unfortunately, many choose not to teach.

More alarming is that the quality of certified teachers appears to be diminishing. It's no good to solve the teacher shortage problem if well-prepared and effective teachers are not part of the process. Research consistently confirms that a skilled and knowledgeable teacher can make an enormous difference in how well students learn.[13] The real problem—poorly performing students—is not solved simply if the number of teachers increases.

There is a clear discrepancy between the number of prepared teachers and teaching teachers.

- In the 1992–93 school year, American colleges produced 142,000 college graduates prepared to teach, but more than half did not even apply for teaching jobs in the year following graduation. An extreme example is the state of Pennsylvania, which produces approximately 20,000 newly certified teachers annually but hires only about 5,100 per year.[14]

- In 1998, an estimated 200,545 college graduates were prepared to teach. Between 1998 and 1999, approximately 156,000 first-time teachers were added to the total number of elementary and secondary teachers teaching, a far smaller number than those prepared to teach.[15]

- In the 1998–99 school year, 37 percent of newly hired public school teachers had previous teaching experience, and 63 percent were recent college graduates.[16]

- In addition to newly prepared teachers each year, the teacher "reserve pool" (those who are prepared to teach but are not teaching) in the U.S. is approximately 4 million strong.[17]

It is estimated that 20 percent of first-time teachers leave the field within the first 3 years and one-third leave the field within 5 years. In high-poverty schools, the situation is worse, with one-half leaving within 5 years. This would not necessarily be cause for concern if those who stayed were the most capable and most effective; however, there is mounting evidence that the teachers who leave are in fact the most promising. A recent study of college graduates found that novice teachers who scored in the top quartile on college-entrance exams were almost twice as likely to exit the field as those who scored lower.[18] Moreover, the people who choose teaching today aren't necessarily coming from the top half of the class. Sandra Feldman, president of the AFT, candidly stated, "You have in the schools right now, among ... the teachers who are going to be retiring, very smart people," she says. "We're not getting in now the same kinds of people."[19]

Why the discrepancies? While there are probably numerous reasons, three stand out: pay, working conditions, and bureaucracy. Many assume that poor pay is the primary reason for not retaining enough quality teachers. While it is clear that teachers' salaries lag in comparison to those for many other professional careers, this is not the sole source of potential shortages. There is no glaring teacher shortage facing private or charter schools, even though they pay no better and sometimes worse than public schools. For example, in the 1993–94 school year, the average base salary for public school teachers was $34,153; for a teacher in private school, it was only $21,968.[20]

Moreover, teaching may be the only professional field where you don't get a penny more for being good at what you do. Over the last few decades, teachers have acquired many new responsibilities and assume new tasks that they must perform; however, there has been no reward for their increased responsibilities, nor is there any incentive to excel as a teacher.

In 1961, 49.9 percent of teachers said they "certainly would teach again." In 1996, only 32.1 percent of teachers made this claim. For many, this dissatisfaction is directly linked to an increase in the discipline problems and poor overall school environment. Of the approximately 20 percent of teachers who leave the profession within the first 3 years, teachers dissatisfied with student discipline or school environment quit at twice the rate of those who are not.[21]

The current certification process is bureaucratic and often keeps qualified people from teaching. In response to public concerns regarding the lack of prepared teachers, states are currently in the process of piling on even more regulatory requirements. There is no established link between certification requirements and effective teaching, but there is evidence that bureaucracy is a barrier to entry.[22]

Teachers are important when it comes to a good education. According to a recent study, the strongest predictor of how well a state's students performed on national assessment tests was the percentage of well-qualified teachers.[23] There is clearly no quick solution to the challenge of ensuring high-quality teachers and having enough teachers who are willing to teach. Simply churning out more teachers is not the answer. How can we attract and keep high-performing teachers? A simplified system (less bureaucracy) where teachers are given enough support and autonomy to shape the culture of their classroom (working conditions) and a reward system that compensates teachers for results (pay) are possible starting points.

▶ Proposition: Across-the-Board Teacher Salary Increases May Not Stand Alone as an Education Reform Solution.

Over time, teachers' responsibilities have increased dramatically; teachers not only educate the children but often act as parents, counselors, social workers, and disciplinarians. Teachers' unions, and those steeped in the tradition of schools of education, feel higher salaries, across-the-board, would compensate for the increased responsibilities, bestow the proper respect on the teaching profession, and attract well-prepared teachers. According to NEA President Bob Chase, "Teaching is an emotionally, physically, and intellectually challenging career that today garners too little respect and low pay relative to comparable professionals." Others, however, are concerned about how to attract "better qualified" teachers and justify salary increases in the face of falling test scores. They recommend that teacher compensation be redirected from an input-driven system to an outcome-based system.[24]

Increasing teacher salaries has long been proposed as one solution to our current education woes. In 1983, the report *A Nation at Risk* highlighted low teacher pay as a major problem in American education. In the early 1980s, teachers earned only 2 to 3 percent more than the average worker. The forceful claim and persuasive message of teachers' unions are that teachers' salaries are not competitive within the job market, and, therefore, the profession has not attracted "the best and the brightest." According to the AFT, teachers' salaries have slipped, and the implementation of an innovative payroll package that might attract highly qualified personnel to teach has been stalled.

Some have made the case, however, that a blanket increase in salary or benefits or both, without a gauge to determine returns (achievement), defies market principles. If competitive teacher salaries are important, then an accountable and competitive environment should be part of the package. This might include modifying teacher compensation packages in the following ways:

- Superior teachers should earn more than average teachers.
- Poorly performing teachers should be expeditiously removed from the school system.
- Across-the-board pay hikes should be resisted, discontinued, or scaled down.[25]

Data from the AFT 2001 teacher salary survey show that despite annual increases, teachers' relative salaries, although still above the average worker's salary, have declined over the last 10 years.

- In 1990, the teacher's average salary was 20 percent higher than the earnings of the full-time worker's average salary in the U.S. economy. However, during the booming economy of the 1990s, relative to the average worker, teachers lost ground. In the 2000–2001 school year, the teacher advantage had fallen to less than 10 percent. (See table 2.1 and figure 2.1.)
- In 2001, a teacher earned less than 5 percent more than a government employee, clearly less than the approximately 15 percent advantage enjoyed in 1990.
- Although teachers' salaries have steadily increased over the past 40 years, the portion of education expenditures designated for those salaries has decreased. In 1961, 51 percent of K–12 public education expenditures were devoted to teacher salaries, compared to 39 percent in 2001. (See table 2.2 and figure 2.2.)[26]

Table 2.1: **Salary Comparisons**
Teachers, Average U.S. Workers, Government Workers, 1960–2001

Year	Average salary		
	Teacher	Worker	Government worker
1960	$29,618	$28,092	$27,272
1970	38,337	33,544	34,983
1980	32,965	32,283	32,100
1990	41,398	34,542	36,038
1991	42,234	34,786	36,950
1992	42,247	35,722	37,586
1993	42,423	35,775	37,605
1994	42,214	35,434	38,265
1995	42,295	35,658	38,436
1996	41,851	35,697	38,370
1997	42,031	36,575	38,815
1998	42,408	37,828	39,497
1999	42,495	38,505	40,579
2000	42,459	39,301	40,852
2001	43,250	40,132[a]	41,676[a]

Source: F. Howard Nelson, Rachel Drown, and Jewell C. Gould, *Survey & Analysis of Teacher Salary Trends 2001* (Washington, DC: Research & Information Services Department, American Federation of Teachers, AFL-CIO, 2002), available online at http://www.aft.org/research/salary01salarysurvey2001.pdf.
Notes: All figures in 2001 dollars.
a. Estimate.

Figure 2.1: **Teachers' and U.S. Workers' Salaries**
1960–2001

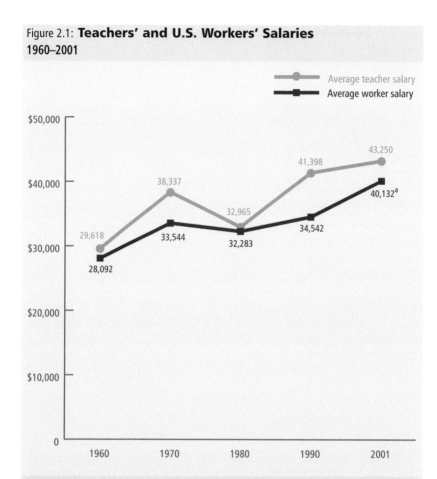

Average teacher salary
Average worker salary

Source: F. Howard Nelson, Rachel Drown, and Jewell C. Gould, *Survey & Analysis of Teacher Salary Trends 2001* (Washington, DC: Research & Information Services Department, American Federation of Teachers, AFL-CIO, 2002), available online at http://www.aft.org/research/salary01salarysurvey2001.pdf.
Notes: All figures in 2001 dollars.
a. Estimate.

Table 2.2: **Teacher Salaries**
1961–2001

Year	Average teacher salary	Total teacher salaries (in billions)	Total public K–12 costs (in billions)	Teacher salaries as a percentage of public K–12 costs	Gross domestic product (in billions)	Total public K–12 costs as a percentage of GDP
1961	$5,275	$7.4	$14.6	50.9%	$545	2.7%
1970	8,635	17.4	34.9	49.8	1,039	3.4
1980	16,100	35.1	87.0	40.4	2,795	3.1
1990	31,347	75.0	187.6	40.0	5,803	3.2
2001	43,250	132.1	334.5	39.5	10,208	3.3

Source: F. Howard Nelson, Rachel Drown, and Jewell C. Gould, *Survey & Analysis of Teacher Salary Trends 2001* (Washington, DC: Research & Information Services Department, American Federation of Teachers, AFL-CIO, 2002), available online at http://www.aft.org/research/salary01salarysurvey2001.pdf.
Note: All figures in 2001 dollars

Figure 2.2: **Public Teacher Salaries, K–12 Public Education Expenditures, and Gross Domestic Product**
1961–2001

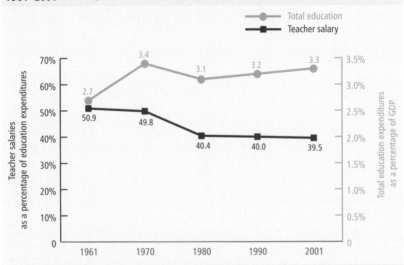

Source: F. Howard Nelson, Rachel Drown, and Jewell C. Gould, *Survey & Analysis of Teacher Salary Trends 2001* (Washington, DC: Research & Information Services Department, American Federation of Teachers, AFL-CIO, 2002), available online at http://www.aft.org/research /salary01salarysurvey2001.pdf.

School Figures: The Data behind the Debate

Although vast amounts of information are disseminated to the public regarding the low level of teacher salaries, some contend that teachers earn more per day than other professionals. The 2000–2001 public school teacher's average salary of $43,250, for example, was earned over a period of 185 days, in contrast to the 235 days worked by a typical wage earner. Moreover, teacher salary growth has still outpaced the price level over the last decade, increasing 31 percent, compared to 28 percent. (See table 2.3.)[27]

Table 2.3: **Salary Comparisons**
Teacher Salary, Consumer Price Index, Per Capita GDP, 1960–2001

Year	Average teacher salary	Consumer price index	Percentage change for teacher salary	Average teacher salary (2001 dollars)	Per capita GDP (2001 dollars)	Ratio of teacher salary to per capita GDP
1960	$4,995	29.8	2.7%	$29,618	$2,918	1.78
1970	8,635	39.8	2.9	38,337	5,069	1.70
1980	16,100	86.3	-4.4	32,965	12,276	1.31
1990	31,347	133.8	-0.3	41,398	23,215	1.35
1991	32,960	137.9	2.0	42,234	23,630	1.39
1992	33,927	141.9	0.0	42,247	24,618	1.38
1993	35,004	145.8	0.4	42,423	25,544	1.37
1994	35,764	149.7	-0.5	42,214	26,799	1.33
1995	36,766	153.6	0.2	42,295	27,784	1.32
1996	37,564	158.6	-1.1	41,851	28,993	1.30
1997	38,415	161.5	0.4	42,031	30,497	1.26
1998	39,360	164.0	0.9	42,408	31,822	1.24
1999	40,475	168.3	0.2	42,495	33,204	1.22
2000	41,810	174.0	-0.1	42,459	34,950	1.20
2001	43,250[a]	176.7	1.9	43,250	35,704[a]	1.21

Source: F. Howard Nelson, Rachel Drown, and Jewell C. Gould, *Survey & Analysis of Teacher Salary Trends 2001* (Washington, DC: Research & Information Services Department, American Federation of Teachers, AFL-CIO, 2002), available online at http://www.aft.org/research/salary01salarysurvey2001.pdf.
Note: a. Estimate.

The average teacher contract requires 7.3 hours of work a day, and teachers reported working an average of 2.5 additional hours a day (for a total of 9.8 hours of work a day).

Although many teachers work beyond the traditional school day, other professionals do also; thus, it is difficult to make direct comparisons based on daily or weekly hour totals. Furthermore, previously unpublished data from the NCES reveals that many teachers earn income in addition to their compensation as full-time teachers. In the 1993–94 school year, for example, more than one-third of teachers earned supplemental income.[28] Incorporating these factors into the analysis indicates that teachers' salaries per day of work are far greater than those of most U.S. workers.

Considering their abbreviated work year and the declining performance of their students on standardized tests and in international comparisons, some argue that teachers are overpaid. (See table 2.4.)[29] After conducting several years of detailed empirical analyses of teachers in both the public and the private sectors, the Upjohn Institute issued a report concluding that "dramatic increases in teacher salaries over the past twenty years have done nothing to improve the quality of American public school teachers." Furthermore, numerous reports on teacher compensation have concluded that attempts to recruit better teachers with global pay raises, irrespective of merit, make no discernible impact on new teacher recruitment.[30]

Table 2.4: **Teacher Duties**

Duty	Full-time teachers performing task	
	Number	Percentage
Classroom duties	2,340,443	100.0%
Extra duties	815,827	34.9
Summer school	401,516	17.2
Tutoring	118,601	5.1
Other education work	80,104	3.4
Other non-education work	237,177	10.1

Sources: John C. Bowman, *Teacher Compensation in Texas: Emerging Trends for Texas* (San Antonio: Texas Public Policy Foundation, July 2000), available online at http://www.tppf.org/education/report/report.html; Mike Antonucci, "Teacher Salaries and Benefits," in *One Yard Below* (Sacramento, CA: Education Intelligence Agency), available online at http://www.calnews.com/Archives/1YB_II_sal.htm.
Notes: Figures based on 1993–94 teacher survey.
Individual teachers may be performing more than one additional duty.

School Figures: The Data behind the Debate

Teachers' unions assert that blanket increases in teacher salaries are one key to an improved education system, yet others challenge this assertion. If the primary goal is to increase the supply of teachers (and in the short run this may be the case for those experiencing extreme teacher shortages), blanket increases in teacher salaries might be one solution. The evidence, however, seems clear: When salaries go up, schools run the risk of paying more for the teachers they already have or of increasing the quantity of teachers but not the quality.[31] Most Americans understand this concept. The majority of the general public believes that teachers are underpaid (62%), but most also say teachers' salaries should be very closely tied or somewhat closely tied to student achievement (60%).[32]

► Proposition: Teacher certification does not necessarily guarantee teacher quality, and for some interested in teaching, it is a deterrent.

While some policymakers and parents view "certified" teachers as synonymous with qualified teachers, being certified generally means little more than having completed state-approved training at a school of education. There is little evidence that certification leads to effective teaching, and many indications that it works against professionalism.[33] In 1997, over 63 percent of education professors admitted that their programs often failed to prepare teachers for the challenge of real-world teaching.[34]

The late Albert Shanker, president of the American Federation of Teachers, stated, "Many of the attributes that characterize a profession are not hallmarks of today's teaching profession." He continued, "To be considered a true profession, an occupation must have a distinct body of knowledge— acknowledged by practitioner and consumer alike—that undergirds the profession and forms the basis of delivering high-quality services to clients."[35]

Many certification advocates feel that certification would be more effective if programs were lengthened or if all certification programs were required to be accredited. However, there is no evidence to support these claims. Few differences have been found between graduates of accredited and nonaccredited programs. Furthermore, graduates of 5-year teacher training programs are not more effective than those of 4-year programs.[36]

One of the primary problems with traditional certification programs is their focus on inputs rather than results: Courses taken, requirements met, time spent, tests passed, credentials acquired, and activities engaged in are more important than actual evidence of classroom effectiveness. Research has consistently shown that there is little association between teachers' initial "qualifications" and their eventual effectiveness.[37] Moreover, critics charge that the current credentialing process, with its low standards and bureaucratic requirements, actually discourages the best and the brightest from becoming teachers.[38] Out of every 600 students entering 4-year teaching programs, only 180 complete them, only 72 become teachers, and only about 40 are still teaching several years later. (See figure 2.3.)[39]

Figure 2.3: **Teacher Attrition**

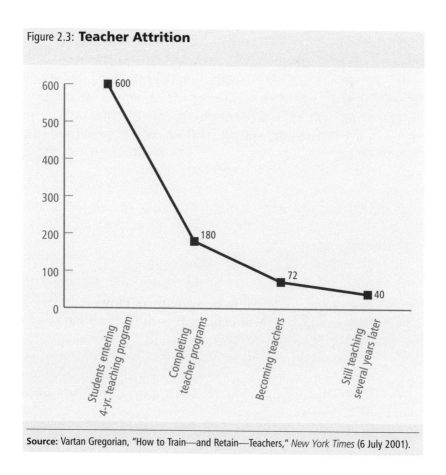

Source: Vartan Gregorian, "How to Train—and Retain—Teachers," *New York Times* (6 July 2001).

In most states, traditional certification programs enjoy monopoly control over classroom entry. Some states, however, are beginning to deregulate the process. Comparing teachers who were trained and licensed through traditional programs to teachers who bypassed these programs provides potent evidence. Alternative certification programs streamline the classroom entry process. Often the programs require a bachelor's degree, passing a competency test, and compressed intensive training, with specialized preparation that is usually completed on the job. Schools of education, however, require a narrow curriculum and student teaching. To date, studies show that students taught by teachers prepared via alternative certification programs have performed at least as well as students taught by teachers prepared by the conventional teacher certification process. Alternative routes of certification are gaining in momentum.[40] For example, Teach for America (TFA)—a program that recruits high-achieving students from prominent universities, offers them specialized training, funnels them through alternative certification routes, and then places them in some of the toughest U.S. public schools—has been quite successful. A recent evaluation of TFA teachers in the Houston Independent School District, the seventh largest district in the U.S., concluded that "on average, the impact of having a TFA teacher was always positive."[41]

Research shows that teachers who are prepared via alternative certification routes are more likely to have degrees with majors in subjects other than education, particularly in math and science. Both these fields have chronic shortages of teachers, and many teachers in these fields do not have academic degrees in these subjects. Furthermore, they are more apt to be men, members of minority groups, and older (characteristics that distinguish them from the typical teacher), and they have lower attrition rates. For example, after 6 years, 87 percent of the graduates of California's alternative certification programs are still teaching—83 percent in the schools where they began.[42] In contrast, of all new teachers in the United States, only two-thirds are still in the education field after 5 years, and only one-half in high-poverty schools.[43] Alternative certification teachers are also more likely to have work experience in occupations other than education, and they are more likely to teach where job demand is greatest—in inner cities and in outlying rural areas—and in high-demand subject areas.[44]

- The fiscal year 2001 budget for the U.S. Department of Education included $31 million specifically for the development of alternative teacher certification programs.[45]
- In 2001, 45 states and the District of Columbia reported having some type of alternative route for certifying teachers; in 1983, only 8 states reported alternative routes.[46]
- About 18 percent of new teacher hires in California come through alternative routes; in Texas, 16 percent; and in New Jersey, 22 percent.[47]

The degree of professionalism and esteem for teachers is further undermined by their standardized test results. The 1997 average SAT scores of high school seniors who intended to major in education were lower than the average scores of all test-takers. The average verbal score of all SAT candidates was 505, and the average math score was 511; those planning to major in education averaged 485 and 479, respectively. A closer evaluation of these data provide some encouragement. Test scores of students seeking teaching licenses in mathematics, for example, are comparable to math majors in general. Those seeking an elementary education license, the largest cohort of teacher licenses, however, have SAT and ACT scores that are substantially lower than the scores of those seeking licensure in specific content areas. (See table 2.5.)[48]

Table 2.5: SAT Scores
By Intended College Major, 2000–01

Intended major	Average SAT verbal score	Average SAT math score	Combined verbal and math score
Education	483	481	964
Business	489	511	1000
Social sciences and history	531	512	1043
Biological sciences	545	549	1094
Engineering	523	572	1095
Language and literature	606	549	1155
Physical sciences	568	588	1156
Mathematics	549	625	1174

Source: Thomas D. Snyder, ed., *Digest of Education Statistics, 2001* (Washington, DC: U.S. Department of Education, National Center for Education Statistics, 2002), table 136, p. 154.

There is no evidence supporting the notion that the current teacher credentialing process has been successful. The notable increase in alternative certification routes is evidence of the problem. A good process would produce tangible results, that is, better teachers who produce well-educated students. For too long, policymakers have tried to enhance the credentialing process by increasing requirements. These measures have acted as a deterrent to many who might otherwise teach. Today's training system has created a quality and quantity crisis.

PROPOSITION: TEACHERS' EDUCATION LEVELS HAVE INCREASED; STUDENTS' ACHIEVEMENT HAS NOT.

Debate surrounds the preparation and qualifications that characterize high-quality teachers. Compared to other fields, disputes and ambiguities regarding the knowledge base and competency level that should be required of teaching professionals are particularly striking. Many agree that teachers should possess strong basic knowledge of the subjects they teach, but does that knowledge translate into effective teaching? Over time, teachers' education levels have increased; however, the anticipated increase in students' achievement rankings has not followed.

The type of academic degree held is one measure used to determine teacher qualifications. Through the 1960s, the percentage of teachers with advanced degrees began to increase. The majority of public school teachers (56.2 percent in 1996) now have advanced degrees. Furthermore, heightened awareness regarding teacher education levels has been accompanied by an emphasis for teachers, particularly those in secondary schools, to have an academic major such as English, math, or history rather than a major in education.

Although dramatic change can be seen in the percentage of teachers with advanced degrees, in most fields, teachers do not hold their degrees in the fields in which they teach. (See table 2.6 and figure 2.4.)[49] Considering all primary subjects, in 1999, nearly 34 percent of public school teachers in grades 7 through 12 were teaching without a major or a minor in the academic field in which they were teaching. Contrasting the U.S. experience to other countries, 71 percent of 8th-grade math students from selected countries (those countries whose students participated in the TIMSS-Repeat) learned math from teachers who majored in mathematics in college, compared with only 41 percent of American 8th-grade math students. Moreover, it appears the more technical the subject, the less likely it is for the teacher to have advanced preparation in the subject.[50]

Table 2.6: **Teacher Educational Attainment 1961–96**

	Education level			
Year	Less than a bachelor's degree	Bachelor's degree	Master's or specialist degree	Doctor's degree
1961	14.6%	61.9%	23.1%	0.4%
1966	7.0	69.9	23.2	0.1
1971	2.9	69.6	27.1	0.4
1976	0.9	61.6	37.1	0.4
1981	0.4	50.1	49.3	0.3
1986	0.3	48.3	50.7	0.7
1991	0.6	46.3	52.6	0.5
1996	0.3	43.6	54.5	1.7

Source: Thomas D. Snyder, ed., *Digest of Education Statistics, 2001* (Washington, DC: U.S. Department of Education, National Center for Education Statistics, 2002), table 70, p. 81.
Notes: Data are based on sample surveys of public schoolteachers.
Data differ from figures appearing in other tables because of varying processing procedures and time period coverage.
Because of rounding, percentages may not add to 100.

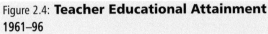

Figure 2.4: **Teacher Educational Attainment**
1961–96

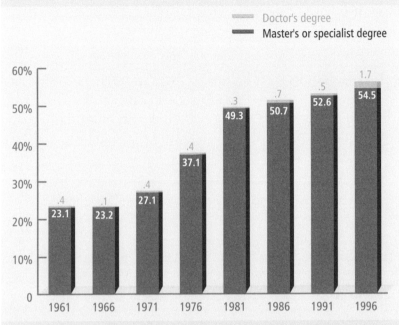

Doctor's degree
Master's or specialist degree

Source: Thomas D. Snyder, ed., *Digest of Education Statistics, 2001* (Washington, DC: U.S. Department of Education, National Center for Education Statistics, 2002), table 70, p. 81.
Note: Data are based upon sample surveys of public schoolteachers.
Data differ from figures appearing in other tables because of varying processing procedures and time period coverages.
Education specialists are defined as individuals who have had six years of college.

According to Richard Ingersoll's 1999 report in *Educational Researcher:*

- One-fifth of all public school students in English classes in grades 7–12 were taught by teachers who did not have even a minor in English, literature, communications, speech, journalism, English education, or reading education.

- About one-quarter of all public school students in mathematics classes in grades 7–12 were taught by teachers without a major or minor in mathematics or mathematics education.

- Nearly two-fifths of all public school students in life science or biology classes in grades 7–12 were taught by teachers without a minor in biology or life science.
- In addition, over half of all public school students in history or world civilization classes in grades 7–12 were taught by teachers who did not have a minor in history.
- More than half (56.5 percent) of all public school students in physical science classes in grades 7–12 were taught by teachers without at least a minor in physics, chemistry, geology, or earth science. (See figure 2.5.)[51]

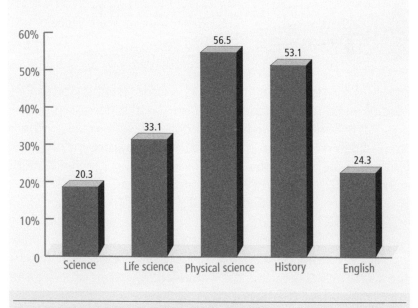

Figure 2.5: **Teachers without College Major or Minor in Their Teaching Field**
Grades 7–12, 1999

Source: Richard M. Ingersoll, "The Problem of Underqualified Teachers in American Schools," *Educational Researcher* 28, no. 2 (March 1999), available online at http://www.aera.net/pubs/er/arts/28-02/ingsoll01.htm.

Teacher education, as we know it, is not the sole solution to an improved education system. Whereas teachers' formal education levels have increased over the past 30 years, student achievement during that period has remained flat on a national level and has fallen in international comparisons.[52] Placing an even greater emphasis on teachers obtaining an academic major rather than a major in education might be a good starting point for increasing student performance in the technical fields.

PROPOSITION: SOME ARE CONCERNED THAT CHILDREN IN PUBLIC SCHOOLS ARE RECEIVING LESS INDIVIDUALIZED ATTENTION; THE NUMBERS TELL A DIFFERENT STORY.

Despite increasing enrollment, the public school system has become more consolidated, as shown by the decreasing numbers of schools and districts. Expected efficiencies, which would lead to a smaller administrative staff, however, have not followed. The educational staff has actually grown, with more instructional,[53] support,[54] and administrative[55] staff, presumably providing more individualized attention for students.

Elementary and secondary public education staff increased more than fourfold between 1950 and 1999, with the greatest increase occurring between 1950 and 1980. Yet, between 1950 and 1999, enrollment less than doubled. When considering the three categories of educational staff, each one has increased dramatically in contrast to enrollment. (See table 2.7 and figure 2.6.)[56]

- The student–educational staff ratio decreased from 19 to 1 in 1950 to 8 to 1 in 1999.
- The student–instructional staff ratio decreased from 26 to 1 in 1950 to 12 to 1 in 1999.
- Between 1950 and 1999, support staff increased more than fivefold. The ratio decreased from 83 to 1 to 27 to 1.
- Administrative staff nearly tripled; the ratio decreased from 746 to 1 to 499 to 1.[57]

Table 2.7: **Public School Staff**
By Functional Area, 1949–50—1999

	Number of educational staff							
	Total educational staff		District administrative staff		Instructional staff		Support staff	
School year	Number	Pupils per staff member	Number	Pupils per staff member	Number	Pupils per staff member	Number	Pupils per staff member
1949–50	1,300,031	19.3	33,642	746.4	963,110	26.1	303,280	82.8
1959–60	2,089,283	16.8	42,423	829.3	1,457,329	24.1	589,531	59.7
1969–70	3,360,763	13.6	65,282	697.7	2,285,568	19.9	1,009,913	45.1
Fall 1980	4,168,286	9.8	78,784	518.9	2,859,573	14.3	1,229,929	33.2
Fall 1990	4,494,076	9.2	75,868	543.3	3,051,404	13.5	1,366,804	30.2
Fall 1999	5,617,397	8.3	93,916	498.9	3,810,308	12.3	1,713,173	27.4

	Percent of educational staff			
	Total educational staff	District administrative staff	Instructional staff	Support staff
School year	Number	Percent of all staff	Percent of all staff	Percent of all staff
1949–50	1,300,031	2.6%	74.1%	23.3%
1959–60	2,089,283	2.0	69.8	28.2
1969–70	3,360,763	1.9	68.0	30.1
Fall 1980	4,168,286	1.9	68.6	29.5
Fall 1990	4,494,076	1.7	67.9	30.4
Fall 1999	5,617,397	1.7	67.8	30.5

Source: Thomas D. Snyder, ed., *Digest of Education Statistics, 2001* (Washington, DC: U.S. Department of Education, National Center for Education Statistics, 2002), table 82, p. 91.
Note: According to *Digest of Education Statistics, 2001,* data in the "Total" column from 1985 to the present are not comparable to figures for years prior. In addition, some data have been revised from previously published figures. Because of variations in data collection instruments, some categories are only roughly comparable over time.

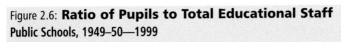

Figure 2.6: **Ratio of Pupils to Total Educational Staff**
Public Schools, 1949–50—1999

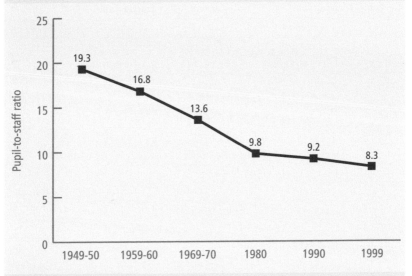

Source: Thomas D. Snyder, ed., *Digest of Education Statistics, 2001* (Washington, DC: U.S. Department of Education, National Center for Education Statistics, 2002), table 82, p. 91.
Note: Some data have been revised from previously published figures.
Because of variations in data collection instruments, category is only roughly comparable over time.

Not only has the size of the educational staff increased; its configuration has changed as well. Administrative and instructional staff have decreased as a percentage of total educational staff, while support staff has increased. The composition of instructional staff—those who have the most direct impact on students—has also changed; there are more instructional aides, librarians, and guidance counselors. It is difficult to compare changes in staff composition over time, due to changes in how jobs are classified; however, from the magnitude of the numbers, it is apparent there are more staff per pupil than ever.[58]

- In 1950, instructional staff made up 74 percent of total educational staff; in 1999, they made up 68 percent.

- In 1950, 70 percent of educational staff were teachers; in 1999, only 52 percent of public elementary and secondary educational staff were teachers.
- In 1950, the student-to-teacher ratio was 28 to 1; in 1999, it was 16 to 1.
- In 1970, less than 2 percent of educational staff were instructional aides.[59] In 1999, 16.4 percent were aides, an increase of more than 600 percent.
- The student–instructional aide ratio was 793 to 1 in 1970; in 1999, it was 75 to 1, a change by a factor of 10. (See table 2.8 and figures 2.7 & 2.8.)[60]

Table 2.8: **Public School Instructional Staff**
By Job Description, 1949–50—1999

Number of instructional staff

Year	Total instructional staff	Principals and assistant principals	Teachers	Instructional aides	Librarians	Guidance counselors	Psychological personnel	Other instructional staff
1949–50	963,110	43,137	913,671	a	a	a	a	6,302
1959–60	1,457,329	63,554	1,353,372	a	17,363	14,643	2,121	6,277
1969–70	2,285,568	90,593	2,016,244	57,418	42,689	48,763	6,168	23,693
Fall 1980	2,859,573	107,061	2,184,216	325,755	48,018	63,973	14,033	116,517
Fall 1990	3,051,404	127,417	2,398,169	395,959	49,909	79,950	b	b
Fall 1999	3,810,308	133,011	2,906,554	621,385	53,661	95,697	b	b

Instructional staff relative to total staff

Year	Total instructional staff	Principals and assistant principals	Teachers	Instructional aides	Librarians	Guidance counselors	Psychological personnel	Other instructional staff
1949–50	74.1%	3.3%	70.3%	a	a	a	a	0.5%
1959–60	69.8	3.0	64.8	a	0.8%	0.7%	0.1%	0.3
1969–70	68.0	2.7	60.0	1.7%	1.3	1.5	0.1	0.7
Fall 1980	68.6	2.6	52.4	7.8	1.2	1.5	0.3	2.8
Fall 1990	67.9	2.8	53.4	8.8	1.1	1.8	b	b
Fall 1999	67.8	2.4	51.7	11.1	1.0	a	b	b

Source: Thomas D. Snyder, ed., *Digest of Education Statistics, 2001* (Washington, DC: U.S. Department of Education, National Center for Education Statistics, 2002), table 82, p. 91.
Notes: According to *Digest of Education Statistics, 2001,* data in the "Total" column from 1985 to the present are not comparable to figures for years prior. In addition, some data have been revised from previously published figures. Because of variations in data collection instruments, some categories are only roughly comparable over time.
a. Data included in column entitled "Teachers."
b. Data included in "Support staff" totals, Table 2.7.

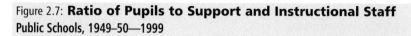

Figure 2.7: **Ratio of Pupils to Support and Instructional Staff**
Public Schools, 1949–50—1999

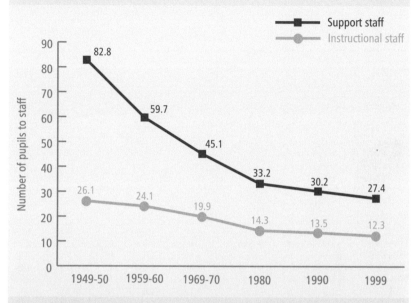

Source: Thomas D. Snyder, ed., *Digest of Education Statistics, 2001* (Washington, DC: U.S. Department of Education, National Center for Education Statistics, 2002), table 82, p. 91.
Note: Some data have been revised from previously published figures. Because of variations in data collection instruments, some categories are only roughly comparable over time. Because of rounding, details may not add to totals. *Instructional staff* includes principals, assistant principals, teachers, instructional aides, librarians, guidance counselors, psychological personnel, and other instructional staff. *Support staff* includes secretarial and clerical, transportation, food service, plant operation and maintenance, health, recreational, and other staff.

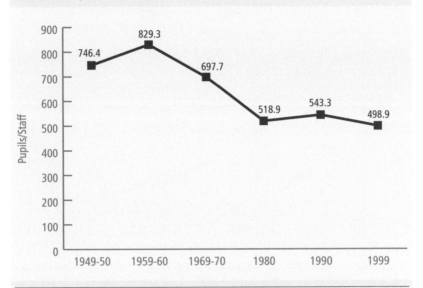

Figure 2.8: **Ratio of Pupils to Administrative Staff**
Public Schools, 1949–50—1999

Source: Thomas D. Snyder, ed., *Digest of Education Statistics, 2001* (Washington, DC: U.S. Department of Education, National Center for Education Statistics, 2002), table 82, p. 91.
Note: Some data have been revised from previously published figures.
Because of variations in data collection instruments, some categories are only roughly comparable over time. *Administrative staff* includes intermediate district staff, school district superintendents, officials and administrators, and instruction coordinators.

Looking at the current crisis in education, it seems apparent that more people providing more individualized attention does not necessarily guarantee a better outcome. Recent education reform advocates have recommended returning to instruction in the basics; perhaps this recommendation applies to staff, as well.

School Figures: The Data behind the Debate

► PROPOSITION: SECONDARY PUBLIC SCHOOL TEACHERS ARE SPENDING MORE TIME PERFORMING THEIR TEACHING DUTIES, YET THEY ARE TEACHING FEWER STUDENTS.

The public school teacher has not escaped the myriad of educational reform discussions. Many recommendations have been proposed to enhance the teaching profession and to better equip teachers in the classroom. Some believe that the public school teacher is ill-prepared, others are convinced that teachers are not paid enough, and another contingent contends that they simply do not have enough authority in the classroom to maintain order, let alone teach. Perhaps what has changed sheds some light on possible improvements, but it should be noted that many aspects of a teacher's job have remained constant over time.

- The average number of hours in a required school day has changed minimally. In 1961, the average was 7.4. In 1996, the average was 7.3.

- The average number of school days in a school year has hardly changed. Between 1966 and 1996, the number of days has decreased from 181 to 180.

- The average number of nonteaching days in a school year has not changed dramatically, increasing from 5 to 6.

- The average number of hours in a required school week was the same in 1996 as it was in 1966, 36.5 hours. (See table 2.9.)[61]

Table 2.9: **Average Workweek of Public School Teachers 1961–96**

| Date | Average hours in required school week | Average hours per week spent on all teaching duties | | | Average days in school year | |
		All teachers	Elementary teachers	Secondary teachers	Classroom teaching	Non-teaching
1961	37.0	47	49	46	na	na
1966	36.5	47	47	48	181	5
1971	36.5	47	46	48	181	4
1976	36.5	46	44	48	180	5
1981	36.5	46	44	48	180	6
1986	36.5	49	47	51	180	5
1991	36.0	47	44	50	180	5
1996	36.5	49	47	52	180	6

Source: Thomas D. Snyder, ed., *Digest of Education Statistics, 2001* (Washington, DC: U.S. Department of Education, National Center for Education Statistics, 2002), table 70, p. 81
Note: Data are based upon sample surveys of public school teachers.
Data differ from figures appearing in other tables because of varying processing procedures and time period coverages.

While the quantitative metrics have changed little, not all aspects of the teacher's job have remained as stable. At the secondary school level, for example, the decrease in the number of students taught per day is notable. In 1961, the average number of students a teacher taught per day was 138; in 1996, the average was 97, a decline of nearly one-third. During the same time period, the average number of pupils per class increased from 28 to 31. Furthermore, there was an increase in the number of reported hours per week spent on teaching duties by secondary school teachers, from 46 hours to 52 hours. (See figure 2.9.)[62]

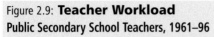

Figure 2.9: **Teacher Workload**
Public Secondary School Teachers, 1961–96

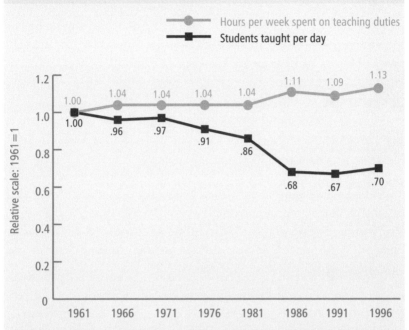

Hours per week spent on teaching duties
Students taught per day

Source: Thomas D. Snyder, ed., *Digest of Education Statistics, 2001* (Washington, DC: U.S. Department of Education, National Center for Education Statistics, 2002), table 70, p. 81.
Note: Data are based upon sample surveys of public school teachers.
Data differ from figures appearing in other tables because of varying processing procedures and time period coverages.

Combining these three facts—the increase in the number of students per class, the increase in the amount of time spent on teaching duties per week, and the decrease in the number of students taught per teacher—poses a conundrum: If there are more students per class and teachers are spending more time teaching, why are they not teaching more students per week? There are two possible explanations: Teachers may be spending more time on "teaching duties," but much of that time is spent performing nonclassroom activities—counseling, preparing, maintaining order, administrative functions, and so on; and there are far more teachers now, so the absolute student-teacher ratio has fallen.[63]

More teachers are spending more hours on teaching duties while teaching fewer students, yet student achievement at the secondary level has remained flat or declined over the last 30 years. This is contradictory to what one might expect, particularly when many of the aspects that might influence these changes have remained constant.

Students, however, might have changed, as well. Teachers and the general public have expressed consistent concern over the lack of discipline in the classroom. In a variety of surveys conducted between 1966 and 1996, after their heavy workload, discipline and negative attitudes were among the factors teachers most frequently mentioned as hindering them.[64] The general public agrees; lack of discipline was ranked first among "major problem(s) facing local public schools" over an extended period of time. (See figure 2.10.)[65]

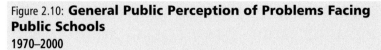

Figure 2.10: **General Public Perception of Problems Facing Public Schools**
1970–2000

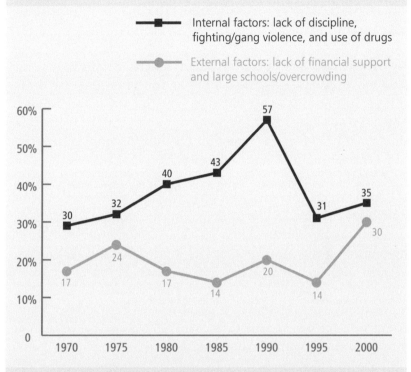

Internal factors: lack of discipline, fighting/gang violence, and use of drugs

External factors: lack of financial support and large schools/overcrowding

Source: Thomas D. Snyder, ed., *Digest of Education Statistics, 2001* (Washington, DC: U.S. Department of Education, National Center for Education Statistics, 2002), table 23, p. 29.

In addition to the fact that many certified teachers are not choosing to enter or stay in the profession, it appears teachers are actually spending less time in the classroom actually teaching and have less direct student contact. When considering education reform and the role teachers might play in it, the solution does not appear to be in the cumulative amount of time teachers spend on teaching duties but possibly in the use of their time.

▶ PROPOSITION: TEACHERS' UNIONS PROVIDE MORE THAN COLLECTIVE BARGAINING FOR TEACHERS.

At first glance, one would assume teachers' unions play a limited role in public education, fighting for better pay and working conditions for their members but having little influence beyond teacher needs. This, however, is not the case. Teachers' unions may have more impact on the public school system than any other group in American society.[66]

When it comes to influence, their impact is wielded via two mechanisms and in two directions: They shape from the bottom up through collective bargaining, and they shape from the top down through political activities. The combination of bottom-up and top-down strategies creates a powerful and far-reaching arm of influence that leaves few aspects of America's public schools untouched.[67]

A fundamental aspect of teachers' unions' power comes from their consistent growth in membership and hence funding. Nearly all K–12 public school teachers are a member of a local affiliate of either the AFT or the NEA. Through the late 1950s the AFT was the strongest teachers' union; however, only 5 percent of teachers were members.[68] In 1993, 80 percent of public school teachers were unionized, and 66.5 percent were covered by collective bargaining.[69]

When comparing teachers' unions and another major school-related organization, the National Parent-Teacher Association (PTA), union membership growth stands out. National PTA membership has decreased at nearly the same rate as teacher union membership has increased. In 1963, National PTA membership was at its peak, with 12,131,318 members nationwide; in 1999, its membership totaled 6,467,442, a decrease of nearly 47 percent.[70] Public school elementary and secondary enrollment increased from approximately 41,025,000 to 47,244,000 during the same time period, an increase of 15 percent. In 1961, the NEA and AFT claimed a joint membership total of 836,821; in the year 2000, joint membership was approximately 3.5 million, about 2.5 million of whom were K–12 teachers, a more than 300 percent increase. (See figure 2.11.)[71]

Figure 2.11: **NEA and PTA Membership and Public School Enrollment**
1960–99

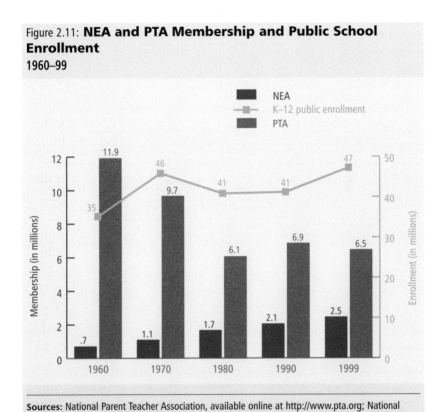

Sources: National Parent Teacher Association, available online at http://www.pta.org; National Education Association, available online at http://www.nea.org; Thomas D. Snyder, ed., *Digest of Education Statistics, 2001* (Washington, DC: U.S. Department of Education, National Center for Education Statistics, 2002), table 3, p. 12.

Contrary to the trend in other industries and professions, where unions lost power and influence, the NEA and AFT are still forces to be reckoned with. In the 20 years following the pivotal 1961 representation election, which gave the AFT the right to represent teachers in New York City, not only did teacher union membership skyrocket, as both the AFT and the NEA raced to recruit new members but collective bargaining became the norm.[72]

Teachers' unions make things happen through the collective bargaining process. Like most unions, the NEA and AFT seek to ensure job security and to base pay and promotion primarily on seniority. Restrictive contracts not only make it difficult to dismiss poorly performing teachers but make it impossible to reward teachers who are teaching well or to create incentives to attract teachers to teach in fields that have shortages.

Moreover, with substantial funds, the unions are also active and effective in local, state, and national politics. At the local level, teachers' unions greatly influence who sits on the school board and, therefore, whom they will be bargaining with.[73] At the state and national levels, teachers' unions spend tremendous amounts of money on political campaigns and lobbying. They regularly rank among the top spenders among interest groups at both the state and national levels, and in many states they are ranked number one.

In addition to their spending, the unions have millions of organized members working towards their stated objectives. A recent academic study of interest group politics at the state level asked experts to rank interest groups according to their influence on public policy. Teachers' unions were top on the list. They outranked general business organizations, trial lawyers, doctors, insurance companies, utilities, bankers, environmentalists, even the state AFL-CIO affiliates.[74] The NEA was among the top 20 PAC contributors to federal candidates in the 2001–2002 election year. Moreover, when the contributions of the NEA and the AFT were combined, they ranked second, at $2,023,140. (See table 2.10.)[75]

**Table 2.10: Top 20 PAC Contributors to Federal Candidates
2001–02 Contributions**

Association of Trial Lawyers of America	$2,136,253
Combined National Education Association and American Federation of Teachers	**2,023,140**
Machinists/Aerospace Workers Union	1,842,750
Laborers Union	1,815,500
International Brotherhood of Electrical Workers	1,758,450
American Federation of State, County, and Municipal Employees	1,723,000
National Auto Dealers Association	1,657,750
Carpenters & Joiners Union	1,625,000
National Association of Realtors	1,610,425
Teamsters Union	1,600,971
United Auto Workers	1,423,750
National Association of Home Builders	1,338,100
Service Employees International Union	1,321,499
Credit Union National Association	1,278,103
United Parcel Service	1,233,891
National Beer Wholesalers Association	1,197,750
SBC Communications	1,193,931
American Medical Association	1,130,666
Communications Workers of America	1,118,250
BellSouth Corporation	1,103,359
National Education Association	**1,092,500**

Source: The Center for Responsive Politics, *Top 20 PAC Contributors to Federal Candidates, 2001–2002* (Washington, DC: Center for Responsive Politics), available online at http://www.opensecrets.org/pacs/topacs.asp.

Surveying the last 50 years, the basic structure of the education system has not changed dramatically; however, one predominant change has been the impact and influence of teachers' unions. Their growth and political clout at all levels—local, state, and national—are a testament to this change.

The unions' impact prompted a *U.S. News and World Report* columnist to state, "The NEA, the giant dinosaur of educational policy, is the largest single reason why the public-school system seems almost impervious to real reform. Its clear goal is power over a monopolistic system."[76] If unions continue to shape public schools in their own image, it will be increasingly difficult to change how we educate our children. It may be time to include teachers' unions in discussions regarding education reform.

▶ **PROPOSITION: THE NATION'S LARGEST TEACHERS' UNIONS INVEST HEAVILY IN THE POLITICAL PROCESS, YET THEIR CONTRIBUTIONS DO NOT REFLECT THE POLITICAL VIEWS OF A LARGE SEGMENT OF THEIR MEMBERSHIP.**

The NEA and the AFT, the nation's largest teachers unions, are influential institutions not just in education but in politics, as well. Labor unions give more than 90 percent of their political contributions to Democratic candidates. The two teachers' unions are no different. Although the NEA consistently refers to its bipartisanship and has membership data to prove it, both NEA and AFT political contributions lean heavily toward the Democratic Party. In fact, of their 1999–2000 PAC contributions to federal candidates, nearly 97 percent went to Democrats, according to Federal Election Commission data.[77] Furthermore, in 1999, NEA and AFT soft-money contributions ranked sixth and seventh among the Democratic Party's 5,000 donors. (See table 2.11.)[78]

Table 2.11: **Contributions to Political Parties and Candidates**
NEA and AFT Combined, 1977–2000

Years[a]	Democrat	Republican	Other
1977–78	$428,780	$43,950	$0
1979–80	428,780	69,250	0
1981–82	1,824,975	77,708	0
1983–84	2,697,325	107,982	0
1985–86	2,828,526	141,226	0
1987–88	3,167,095	174,960	1,000
1989–90	3,305,847	106,025	29,000
1991–92	3,508,740	36,800	6,000
1993–94	3,894,446	31,600	15,617
1995–96	1,732,095	37,000	5,500
1997–98	3,145,540	120,750	9,500
1999–2000	3,057,405	93,150	5,000

Source: Common Cause, *The Soft Money Laundromat—Top Donors* (Washington, DC: Common Cause), available online at http://www.commoncause.org/soft-track/topdonors99_new.htm.
Note: a. Each double year reflects a 24-month congressional term, not a school year.

The political contributions, however, of both the NEA and the AFT are in sharp contrast to the voting records of their members. Talking about political affiliations in a National Public Radio interview, Bob Chase, president of the NEA, stated that his members are "not majority Democratic. Our membership breaks down very similar to the general public as far as percentage being Democratic, Republican, and independent."[79]

This is particularly relevant since at least 75 percent of public school teachers are members of the NEA or the AFT.[80] The data bear out Chase's claim; from 1971 to 1996, teachers' political affiliations have been relatively constant in their distribution among Democrats (about 40 percent), Republicans (about 30 percent), and "no affiliation/other" (the remaining 30 percent), according to NEA data. (See figure 2.12.)[81]

Figure 2.12: **Teacher Political Affiliation 1971–96**

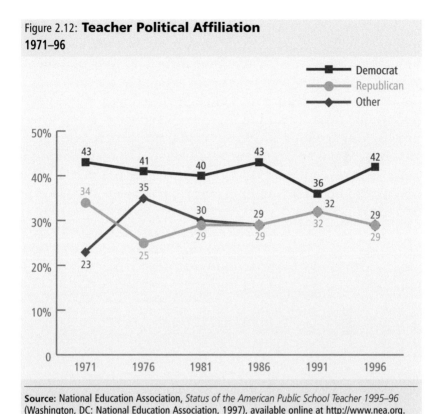

Source: National Education Association, *Status of the American Public School Teacher 1995–96* (Washington, DC: National Education Association, 1997), available online at http://www.nea.org.

Teachers' voting patterns are consistent with their voter registrations and show that they are in the American mainstream. The CBS/*New York Times* exit polls of the 1980 presidential elections revealed that 46 percent of teachers voted for Ronald Reagan, 41 percent for Jimmy Carter, and 10 percent for John Anderson. By comparison, 51 percent of nonteachers voted for Reagan, 40 percent for Carter, and 6 percent for Anderson—trivial differences between the two groups. The 1984 exit polls produced similar numbers.[82]

Teachers' voter registration data and voting patterns and the unions' political agenda are not consistent. The political record of the leadership may not represent that of the rank and file. It is instructive to note that when teachers are given a choice, they do not prefer to spend resources on politics, much less partisan politics. Between 1992 and 1997 in Washington state, where unions were required to obtain annual permission before collecting or using any portion of workers' salaries for political purposes, the number of teachers contributing to the education union's PAC declined by 82 percent. (See tables 2.12 & 2.13 and figure 2.13.)[83]

Table 2.12: **NEA Political Contributions 1977–2000**

Year[a]	Democratic		Republican		Other	
	Dollars	% of total	Dollars	% of total	Dollars	% of total
1977–78	$324,687	95.8%	$13,300	3.9%	$1,000	0.30%
1979–80	258,385	91.1	25,200	8.9	0	0.00
1985–86	1,969,276	95.6	90,157	4.4	0	0.00
1989–90	2,167,745	93.5	149,910	6.5	1,000	0.04
1995–96	2,303,980	99.0	11,850	0.5	11,000	0.50
1999–2000	1,583,125	95.2	76,250	4.6	4,000	0.20

Source: Common Cause, *The Soft Money Laundromat—Top Donors* (Washington, DC: Common Cause), available online at http://www.commoncause.org/soft-track/topdonors99_new.htm.
Note: a. Each double year reflects a 24-month congressional term, not a school year.

Table 2.13: **AFT (Teacher) Political Contributions 1977–2000**

Year[a]	Democratic		Republican		Other	
	Dollars	% of total	Dollars	% of total	Dollars	% of total
1977–78	$105,651	93.2%	$7,700	6.8%	$0	0.00%
1979–80	170,395	90.1	18,750	9.9	0	0.00
1985–86	728,049	97.6	17,925	2.4	0	0.00
1989–90	999,350	97.6	25,050	2.4	0	0.00
1995–96	1,590,466	98.5	19,750	1.2	4,617	0.29
1999–2000	1,471,580	98.8	16,900	1.1	1,000	0.07

Source: Education Policy Institute PAC Data available online at http://www.educationpolicy.org/data.htm and the Federal Election Commission.
Note: a. Each double year reflects a 24-month congressional term, not a school year.

Figure 2.13: **Teacher Political Affiliation and Union Political Contributions**
1995–96

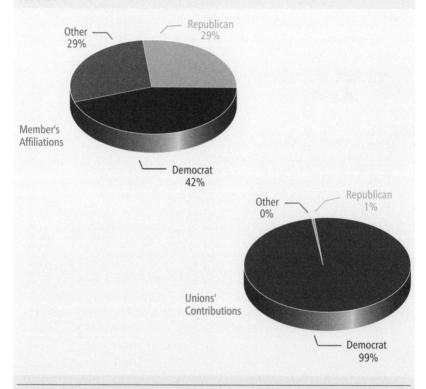

Member's
Affiliations

Other
29%

Republican
29%

Democrat
42%

Unions'
Contributions

Other
0%

Republican
1%

Democrat
99%

Sources: National Education Association, *Status of the American Public School Teacher 1995–96* (Washington, DC: National Education Association, 1997), available online at http://www.nea.org; Education Policy Institute, *PAC Data* (Washington, DC: Education Policy Institute), available online at http://www.educationpolicy.org/data.htm.

► CHAPTER NOTES

1. Thomas D. Snyder, ed., *Digest of Education Statistics, 2001* (Washington, DC: U.S. Department of Education, National Center for Education Statistics, 2002), table 4, p. 13.
2. Ibid., table 70, p. 81.
3. Ibid.
4. Ibid.
5. Ibid.
6. Ibid., table 82, p. 91.
7. Ibid., table 65, p. 76.
8. F. Howard Nelson, Rachel Drown, and Jewell C. Gould, *Survey & Analysis of Teacher Salary Trends 2001* (Washington, DC: Research & Information Services Department, American Federation of Teachers, AFL-CIO, 2002), available online at http://www.aft.org/research /salary01salarysurvey2001.pdf.
9. Ibid.
10. Snyder, *Digest of Education Statistics, 2001,* table 70, p. 81.
11. Robert W. Kasten, "An Oligopoly with a Unique Agenda: America's Major Teachers' Unions Are Out of Step with Their Counterparts Worldwide," *Education Week* 17, no. 23 (19 February 1997), available online at http://www.adti.net/teacherchoice/oligopoly.html.
12. Chester E. Finn, Jr., "Getting Better Teachers—and Treating Them Right?" in *A Primer on America's Schools*, ed. Terry M. Moe (Stanford, CA: Hoover Institution Press, 2001), pp. 127–150.
13. Lynn Olson, "Finding and Keeping Competent Teachers," *Education Week* 19, no. 18 (13 January 2000).
14. Finn, "Getting Better Teachers—and Treating Them Right?"
15. Snyder, *Digest of Education Statistics, 2001,* available online at http://www.ncei.com/MOT/Tables/table1.htm.
16. American Federation of Teachers, "Conditions Contributing to Teacher Shortage," *Survey & Analysis of Teacher Salary Trends 1998* (Washington, DC: Research Department, American Federation of Teachers, AFL-CIO, 1998), available online at http://www.aft.org.
17. Ibid.
18. Olson, "Finding and Keeping Competent Teachers."

19. American Federation of Teachers, "Conditions Contributing to Teacher Shortage"; Matthew Miller, "Wanted: Teachers," *The New Republic* (28 February 2000).

20. Miller, "Wanted: Teachers"; Nina Shrokraii Rees, "Education Achieving Results through Accountability," in *Issues 2000* (Washington DC: Heritage Foundation, 2000).

21. Snyder, *Digest of Education Statistics, 2001,* table 70, p. 81; Olson, "Finding and Keeping Competent Teachers."

22. Finn, "Getting Better Teachers—and Treating Them Right?"

23. Olson, "Finding and Keeping Competent Teachers."

24. John C. Bowman, *Teacher Compensation in Texas: Emerging Trends for Texas* (San Antonio: Texas Public Policy Foundation, July 2000), available online at http://www.tppf.org/education/report/report.html.

25. Ibid.

26. Nelson, Drown, and Gould, *Survey & Analysis of Teacher Salary Trends 2001.*

27. Ibid.

28. The number and percentage of teachers performing various additional duties is not mutually exclusive.

29. Bowman, *Teacher Compensation in Texas: Emerging Trends for Texas;* Mike Antonucci, "Teacher Salaries and Benefits," in *One Yard Below* (Sacramento, CA: Education Intelligence Agency), available online at http://www.calnews.com/Archives/1YB_II_sal.htm.

30. Ibid.

31. Ibid.

32. Public Agenda Online, *Education: Major Proposals* (New York, NY: Public Agenda Online), available online at http://www.publicagenda.org.

33. Finn, "Getting Better Teachers—and Treating Them Right?"

34. Rees, "Education Achieving Results through Accountability."

35. Ibid.

36. Finn, "Getting Better Teachers—and Treating Them Right?"

37. Ibid.

38. Ann Bradley, "The Gatekeeping Challenge," *Education Week* 19, no. 18 (13 January 2000).

39. Vartan Gregorian, "How to Train—and Retain—Teachers," *New York Times* (6 July 2001).

40. Ibid.

41. Margaret Raymond, Stephen Fletcher, and Javier Luque, *Teach for America: An Evaluation of Teacher Differences and Student Outcomes in Houston, Texas* (Stanford, CA: Hoover Institution Press, 2001).

42. Ibid.

43. Olson, "Finding and Keeping Competent Teachers."

44. C. Emily Feistritzer, *Alternative Routes to Teaching* (Washington, DC: Testimony before the Committee on Labor, Health and Human Services, Education and Related Agencies, Congress of the United States, House of Representatives, Committee on Appropriations, 22 May 2001), available online at http://www.ncei.com/Testimony010521.htm.

45. Feistritzer, *Alternative Routes to Teaching.*

46. C. Emily Feistritzer, "Introduction," in *Alternative Teacher Certification: An Overview, 2001* (Washington, DC: National Center for Education Information, 2001), available online at http://ncei.com/2001_Alt_Teacher_Cert.htm.

47. Feistritzer, *Alternative Routes to Teaching.*

48. Andrew S. Latham, Drew Gitomer, and Robert Ziomek, "What the Tests Tell Us about New Teachers," *Education Leadership* 56, no. 8 (May 1999), available online at http://www.ets.org/search97cgi/s97_cgi.

49. Richard M. Ingersoll, "The Problem of Underqualified Teachers in American Schools," *Educational Researcher* 28, no. 2 (March 1999), available online at http://www.aera.net/pubs/er/arts/28-02/ingsoll01.htm; U.S. Department of Education, *TIMSS-R Highlights Study* (Washington, DC: U.S. Department of Education, National Center for Education Statistics), available online at http://nces.ed.gov/timss/timss-r/highlights.asp.

50. Ibid.

51. Ibid.

52. U.S. Department of Education, *TIMSS-R Highlights Study.*

53. Instructional staff includes principals, assistant principals, teachers, instructional aides, librarians, guidance counselors, psychological personnel, and some others.

54. Support staff includes secretarial and clerical, transportation, food service, plant operation and maintenance, health, recreational, and other staff.

55. Administrative staff includes intermediate district staff, school district superintendents, officials and administrators, and instruction coordinators.

56. Snyder, *Digest of Education Statistics, 2001,* table 82, p. 91.

57. Ibid.

58. Ibid.

59. Before 1970, instructional aides were included in teacher tabulations.

60. Snyder, *Digest of Education Statistics, 2001*, table 82, p. 91.

61. Ibid., table 70, p. 81.

62. Ibid.

63. Ibid.

64. National Education Association, *Status of the American Public School Teacher 1995–96* (Washington, DC: National Education Association, 1997), available online at http://www.nea.org.

65. Snyder, *Digest of Education Statistics, 2001*, table 23, p. 29.

66. Terry M. Moe, "Teachers Unions and the Public Schools" in *A Primer on America's Schools*, ed. Terry M. Moe (Stanford, CA: Hoover Institution Press, 2001), pp. 151–183.

67. Ibid.

68. Ibid.

69. Kasten, *An Oligopoly with a Unique Agenda: America's Major Teachers' Unions Are Out of Step with Their Counterparts Worldwide.*

70. National Parent Teacher Association, available online at http://www.pta.org.

71. National Education Association, available online at http://www.nea.org; American Federation of Teachers, available online at http://www.aft.org. Note: The remaining membership consists of school support staff, higher education faculty and staff, health care professionals, and state and municipal employees.

72. Moe, "Teachers Unions and the Public Schools."

73. Ibid.

74. Ibid.

75. The Center for Responsive Politics, *Top 20 PAC Contributors to Federal Candidates, 2001–2002* (Washington, DC: Center for Responsive Politics), available online at http://www.opensecrets.org/pacs/topacs.asp.

76. The Alexis de Tocqueville Institution, "E Pluribus Union," *The Detroit News* (1 September 1996), available online at http://www.adti.net/html_files/education/detnedu.html.

77. Education Policy Institute, *PAC Data* (Washington, DC: Education Policy Institute), available online at http://www.educationpolicy.org/data.htm.

78. Common Cause, *The Soft Money Laundromat—Top Donors* (Washington, DC: Common Cause), available online at http://www.commoncause.org/soft-track/topdonors99_new.htm.

79. Kasten, *An Oligopoly with a Unique Agenda: America's Major Teachers' Unions Are Out of Step with Their Counterparts Worldwide.*

80. Ibid.

81. National Education Association, *Status of the American Public School Teacher 1995–96* (Washington, DC: National Education Association, 1997), available online at http://www.nea.org.

82. Sol Stern, "How Teachers' Unions Handcuff Schools," *City Journal* 7, no. 2 (Spring 1997).

83. Jami Lund, *Evergreen Freedom Foundation Takes Teachers Union to Court* (Washington, DC: Capital Research Center, June 1999), available online at http://www.capitalresearch.org/LaborWatch/lw-0699.htm.

Chapter 3:
Achievement

Propositions

▶ GOALS 2000 CALLED FOR AMBITIOUS CHANGE; WE
  ARE STILL AWAITING DELIVERY.

▶ SECONDARY STUDENTS' MATHEMATICS AND ENGLISH
  TEST SCORES ARE NOT COMMENSURATE WITH THE
  TIME SPENT ON THESE SUBJECTS.

▶ THE SHORTCOMINGS OF OUR K–12 EDUCATION
  SYSTEM HAVE LONG-TERM CONSEQUENCES.

▶ HOMEWORK PROVIDES CLEAR RESULTS FOR ALL
  STUDENTS AND COMPELLING RESULTS FOR HIGH
  SCHOOL STUDENTS.

▶ TELEVISION VIEWING IS A HOME-BASED HABIT THAT
  AFFECTS EDUCATIONAL ACHIEVEMENT.

▶ THE SAT I, ALTHOUGH IMPORTANT, IS NO LONGER
  AN ACCURATE BAROMETER FOR HISTORIC
  COMPARISONS.

▶ REMEDIAL EDUCATION AT POSTSECONDARY INSTITUTIONS IS EVIDENCE THAT THE K–12 EDUCATION SYSTEM IS FALLING SHORT.

▶ THE EMPHASIS ON COMMUNITY SERVICE IN K–12 EDUCATION HAS CLEARLY INCREASED; ITS IMPACT IS MORE DIFFICULT TO MEASURE.

Highlights

► In 1995 international comparisons of math achievement, American fourth-graders ranked 12th out of 26 nations, eighth-graders ranked 28th out of 41 nations; and twelfth-graders ranked 19th out of 21 nations.[1]

► In 1995 international comparisons of science achievement, American fourth-graders ranked 3rd out of 26 nations, eighth-graders ranked 17th out of 41 nations, and twelfth-graders ranked 16th out of 21 nations.[2]

► Between 1990 and 1999, student scores on the National Assessment of Educational Progress (NAEP) increased slightly (only 17-year-old reading and eleventh-grade writing decreased slightly).[3]

► In 1998, 38 percent of fourth-graders, 26 percent of eighth-graders, and 23 percent of twelfth-graders scored below basic levels in reading.[4]

► In the late 1990s, 77 percent of fourth-grade children in urban, high-poverty areas were reading below the basic level on the NAEP tests.[5]

► Between 1990 and 2000, there was a 19-point increase in average SAT scores. Between 1960 and 2000, however, there was a 56-point decrease.[6]

► Average SAT scores were at their highest level (980) in 1963–64. Between 1964 and 1980, when scores were at their lowest level, scores dropped 90 points.[7]

► Only 33 percent of college and university professors and 39 percent of employers believe that a high school diploma means that a student has "learned the basics," but 66 percent of parents, 74 percent of elementary and secondary school teachers, and 77 percent of students believe it does.[8]

▶ Four out of five seniors from the top 55 colleges and universities in the United States received a grade of D or F on a recent standardized American history test.[9]

Overview

t seems that every day we read in the newspapers and hear from the pundits how poorly American students are performing. International comparisons certainly sustain this claim. In standardized tests evaluating students from 21 countries, twelfth-grade American students rank 19th in math and 16th in science. American kids lag behind the traditional education power-houses of Asia, but they also trail Canada, Iceland, and Slovenia. In literacy comparisons, American children do better but still fall far short of the performances of non-U.S. children when measuring the degree of improved achievement over time.

The bad news is the current ranking of the American children on these international tests. The worse news is that the longer American kids stay in school, the further behind they fall. One should not miss the fact that children from third world countries, not just developed countries, often outperform American children.

Some question the validity of such international comparisons. Education in the United States is universal, so the full distribution of students takes these tests, thus dampening scores when comparisons are made to countries without universal, free education. However, time trends for scores within the United States have fallen as well. In the 1990s, we saw the first uptick in performance in more than 20 years. The question remains: Are the most recent scores aberrations, or have we turned the corner?

Moreover, what do we know about what works and what does not work when it comes to achievement? Does the amount of time dedicated to given subject matter, or the amount of television watched or homework completed, have any bearing? Theories abound as to why American children are not performing as well as in the past: too little time in school, too many distractions while away from school, lack of discipline while in school. We provide data that tests these theories and others.

PROPOSITION: GOALS 2000 CALLED FOR AMBITIOUS CHANGE; WE ARE STILL AWAITING DELIVERY.

In 1994, President Bill Clinton signed the Goals 2000: Educate America Act. This aggressive piece of legislation established eight national education goals affecting school readiness; school completion; student achievement and citizenship; teacher education and professional development; mathematics and science; adult literacy and lifelong learning; safe, disciplined, and alcohol- and drug-free schools; and parental participation. In regards to math and science achievement, the act stated, "By the year 2000, United States students will be first in the world in mathematics and science achievement."[10] The year 2000 has come and gone, and the United States not only has missed the mark but also appears to be slipping in international standings.

Student achievement is increasingly important. Test scores and rankings provide the simplest and most accurate measure of what students are learning and how well they are learning. Although parents and educators are often more concerned about student achievement as it relates to the quality of the education delivery system—types of classes and programs offered, school policies regarding conduct, safety, and so on— educational researchers, policy makers, and the business community focus on educational achievement because it is closely correlated with productive skills in the labor market. A highly literate and technologically skilled workforce possesses a competitive advantage in the global marketplace, and international comparisons of student achievement provide a way to evaluate various nations' competitive positions.

Available data allow us to measure achievement in mathematics, science, and reading in three ways. The absolute score method compares achievement of students, of various countries, in same-age groups, as measured by scale scores in the same year (the average percentage of questions students have answered correctly). Most data in this category measure achievement at the fourth- and ninth-grade levels. The second method is to examine changes in test scores between two grade levels and gauge the relative difference in scores over a given time period. This method is known as a value-added comparison. The third method, same-cohort/value-added, provides the most accurate measure by testing the exact same cohort of students and examining changes in test scores throughout their schooling.[11]

Relative to their peers in other nations, American students' math and science achievement decreases the longer they stay in school. The 1995 TIMSS data show that fourth-graders in the United States' performed fairly well compared to those in 25 other nations, ranking 12th in math and 3rd in science; about average among the 41 nations at the eighth-grade level, ranking 28th in math and 17th in science; and below the 21-nation average at the twelfth-grade level, ranking 19th in math and 16th in science. (See tables 3.1–3.4.)[12]

Table 3.1: **U.S. Student Ranking among TIMSS Countries 1995**

Grade	Math		Science		Countries in sample
	Rank	Percentile	Rank	Percentile	
4	12	54%	3	88%	26
8	28	32	17	59	41
12	19	10	16	24	21

Source: Harold W. Stevenson, "A TIMSS PRIMER: Lessons and Implications for U.S. Education," *Fordham Report* 2, no. 7 (Washington, DC: Thomas B. Fordham Foundation, July 1998).

Table 3.2: **National Student Performance**
TIMSS, Fourth Grade, 1995

Average math score		Average science score	
Country	Score	Country	Score
Significantly higher than U.S.			
Singapore	625	Korea	597
Korea	611		
Japan	597		
Hong Kong	587		
Netherlands[a]	577		
Czech Republic	567		
Austria[a]	559		
Not significantly different from U.S.			
Slovenia[a]	552	Japan	574
Ireland	550	**United States**	**565**
Hungary[a]	548	Austria[a]	565
Australia[a]	546	Australia[a]	562
United States	**545**	Netherlands[a]	557
Canada	532	Czech Republic	557
Israel[a]	531		
Significantly lower than U.S.			
Latvia[a]	525	England	551
Scotland	520	Canada	549
England	513	Singapore	547
Cyprus	502	Slovenia[a]	546
Norway	502	Ireland	539
New Zealand	499	Scotland	536
Greece	492	Hong Kong	533
Thailand[a]	490	Hungary[a]	532
Portugal	475	New Zealand	531
Iceland	474	Norway	530
Iran, Islamic Republic	429	Latvia[a]	512
Kuwait[a]	400	Israel[a]	505
		Iceland	505
		Greece	497
		Portugal	480
		Cyprus	475
		Thailand[a]	473
		Iran, Islamic Republic	416
		Kuwait[a]	401
Country average[b]	**529**		**524**

Source: Harold W. Stevenson, "A TIMSS PRIMER: Lessons and Implications for U.S. Education,"
Fordham Report 2, no. 7 (Washington, DC: Thomas B. Fordham Foundation, July 1998).
Notes: The standard error was calculated at a 95 percent confidence level. TIMSS 1995.
a. Nation not meeting international guidelines.
b. Average of the 26 national averages.

Table 3.3: **National Student Performance**
TIMSS, Eighth Grade, 1995

Average math score		Average science score	
Country	Score	Country	Score
Significantly higher than U.S.			
Singapore	643	Singapore	607
Korea	607	Czech Republic	574
Japan	605	Japan	571
Hong Kong	588	Korea	565
Belgium-Flemish	565	Bulgaria[a]	565
Czech Republic	564	Netherlands[a]	560
Slovac Republic	547	Slovenia[a]	560
Switzerland	545	Austria[a]	558
Netherlands[a]	541	Hungary	554
Slovenia[a]	541		
Bulgaria	540		
Austria[a]	539		
France	538		
Hungary	537		
Russian Federation	535		
Australia[a]	530		
Ireland	527		
Canada	527		
Belgium-French[a]	526		
Sweden	519		
Not significantly different from U.S.			
Thailand[a]	522	England	552
Israel[a]	522	Belgium-Flemish	550
Germany[a]	509	Australia[a]	545
New Zealand	508	Slovak Republic	544
England	506	Russian Federation	538
Norway	503	Ireland	538
Denmark[a]	502	Sweden	535
United States	**500**	**United States**	**534**
Scotland[a]	498	Germany[a]	531
Latvia	493	Canada	531
Spain	487	Norway	527
Iceland	487	New Zealand	525
Greece[a]	484	Thailand[a]	525
Romania[a]	482	Israel[a]	524
		Hong Kong	522
		Switzerland	522
		Scotland[a]	517

Continued on next page

School Figures: The Data behind the Debate

Table 3.3: **National Student Performance—Continued**
TIMSS, Eighth Grade, 1995

Average math score		Average science score	
Country	Score	Country	Score
Significantly lower than U.S.			
Lithuania	477	Spain	517
Cyprus	474	France	498
Portugal	454	Greece[a]	497
Iran, Islamic Republic	428	Iceland	494
Kuwait	392	Romania[a]	486
Colombia	385	Latvia	485
South Africa	354	Portugal	480
		Denmark[a]	478
		Lithuania	476
		Belgium-French[a]	471
		Iran, Islamic Republic	470
		Cyprus	463
		Kuwait[a]	430
		Colombia	411
		South Africa	326
Country average[b]	**513**		**516**

Source: Harold W. Stevenson, "A TIMSS PRIMER: Lessons and Implications for U.S. Education," *Fordham Report* 2, no. 7 (Washington, DC: Thomas B. Fordham Foundation, July 1998).
Notes: The standard error was calculated at a 95 percent confidence level.
a. Nation not meeting international guidelines.
b. Average of the 41 national averages.

Table 3.4: **National Student Performance**
TIMSS, Twelfth Grade, 1995

Average math score		Average science score	
Country	Score	Country	Score
Significantly higher than U.S.			
Netherlands[a]	560	Sweden	559
Sweden	552	Netherlands[a]	558
Denmark[a]	547	Iceland[a]	549
Switzerland	540	Norway[a]	544
Iceland[a]	534	Canada[a]	532
Norway[a]	528	New Zealand	529
France[a]	523	Australia[a]	527
New Zealand	522	Switzerland	523
Australia[a]	522	Austria[a]	520
Canada[a]	519	Slovenia[a]	517
Austria[a]	518	Denmark[a]	509
Slovenia[a]	512		
Germany[a]	495		
Hungary	483		
Not significantly different from U.S.			
Italy[a]	476	Germany[a]	497
Russian Federation[a]	471	France[a]	487
Lithuania[a]	469	Czech Republic	487
Czech Republic	466	Russian Federation[a]	481
United States[a]	**461**	**United States[a]**	**480**
		Italy[a]	475
		Hungary	471
		Lithuania[a]	461
Significantly lower than U.S.			
Cyprus[a]	446	Cyprus[a]	448
South Africa[a]	356	South Africa[a]	349
Country average[b]	**500**		**500**

Source: Harold W. Stevenson, "A TIMSS PRIMER: Lessons and Implications for U.S. Education," *Fordham Report* 2, no. 7 (Washington, DC: Thomas B. Fordham Foundation, July 1998).
Notes: The standard error was calculated at a 95 percent confidence level.
Because the standard errors average about 5 points, countries whose average scores are close to one another may not differ significantly.
a. Nation not meeting international guidelines.
b. Average of the 21 national averages.

In a value-added comparison of 17 nations, the United States made the least progress between the fourth and eighth grades in math and was 16th in science value-added comparisons. In both disciplines, the U.S. students were above the mean at the fourth grade but by the eighth grade had slipped below the 17-country averages. (See tables 3.5 and 3.6.)[13]

Table 3.5: **International Value-Added Comparisons**
TIMSS Mathematics, Fourth and Eighth Grades, 1995

Country	Fourth grade mean	Eighth grade mean	Difference
Iceland	338	487	149
Japan	457	605	148
New Zealand	362	508	146
Norway	365	503	138
Korea	471	607	137
Czech Republic	428	564	135
Canada	395	527	133
UK (England)	376	506	130
Greece	356	484[a]	128
Hungary	410[a]	537[a]	127
Australia	408[a]	530[a]	121
Austria	421[a]	539[a]	119
Ireland	412	527	116
Portugal	340	454	115
UK (Scotland)	383	498[a]	115
Netherlands	438[a]	541[a]	103
United States	**407**	**500[b]**	**93**
Country mean[c]	**399**	**526**	**127**

Source: Herbert J. Walberg, "Spending More while Learning Less," *Fordham Report* 2, no. 6 (Washington, DC: Thomas B. Fordham Foundation, July 1998).
Notes: The comparisons are based on a synthetic cohort and do not show the change of a specific group of students.
Fourth-grade average achievement scores and their standard errors for each country are adjusted to fit the eighth-grade achievement-scale.
The standard error was calculated at a 95 percent confidence level.
a. Country did not meet TIMSS sampling requirements, fourth grade.
b. Country only partially met TIMSS sampling requirements.
c. The country mean includes only those countries for which data are available at both levels of education.

Table 3.6: **International Value-Added Comparisons**
TIMSS Science, Fourth and Eighth Grades, 1995

Country	Fourth grade mean	Eighth grade mean	Difference
Hungary[a]	379	554	175
Portugal	314	480	165
Czech Republic	410	574	164
Greece[b]	336	497	161
Netherlands[a,b]	410	560	150
Norway	377	527	150
England[c,d]	404	552	149
Ireland	389	538	149
Iceland	345	494	148
New Zealand	378	526	147
Japan	431	571	140
Austria[a,b]	420	558	138
Scotland[b]	384	517	133
Canada	401	531	130
Australia[a,b]	417	545	127
United States[d]	**421**	**534**	**113**
Korea	460	565	105
Country mean[e]	**393**	**537**	**144**

Source: Herbert J. Walberg, "Spending More while Learning Less," *Fordham Report* 2, no. 6 (Washington, DC: Thomas B. Fordham Foundation, July 1998).
Notes: The comparisons are based on a synthetic cohort and do not show the change of a specific group of students.
Fourth-grade average achievement scores and their standard errors for each country are adjusted to fit the 8th-grade achievement-scale.
The standard error was calculated at a 95 percent confidence level.
a. Country did not meet TIMSS sampling requirements, fourth grade.
b. Country did not meet TIMSS sampling requirements, eighth grade.
c. Country met TIMSS sampling requirements only partially, fourth grade.
d. Country met TIMSS sampling requirements only partially, eighth grade.
e. The country mean includes only those countries for which data are available at both levels of education.

Percentage comparisons of students who scored in the top 10 percent of fourth-graders among the 26 TIMSS countries also show that the United States is lagging. In math, only 9 percent of U.S. fourth-graders were among the top 10 percent, compared to Singapore's 39 percent, Korea's 26 percent, and Japan's 23 percent. At the eighth-grade level, only 5 percent of U.S. students were included in this bracket, compared to Singapore's 45 percent, Korea's 34 percent, and Japan's 32 percent—once again confirming that U.S. students do not fare well in international comparisons and drop in rankings the further along they are in school.[14]

When comparing America's top students with other nations' top students in both advanced physics and advanced math, the U.S. once again falls short. In advanced physics, U.S. students ranked last among all nations taking the test. In advanced mathematics, U.S. students ranked 15th out of 16 nations. (See table 3.7.)[15]

Table 3.7: **Country Rankings in TIMSS Advanced Physics and Mathematics**
Twelfth-Grade Students, 1995

Rank	Advanced physics	Advanced mathematics
1	Norway	France
2	Sweden	Russia
3	Russia	Switzerland
4	Denmark	Australia
5	Slovenia	Denmark
6	Germany	Cyprus
7	Australia	Lithuania
8	Cyprus	Greece
9	Latvia	Sweden
10	Switzerland	Canada
11	Greece	Slovenia
12	Canada	Italy
13	France	Czech Republic
14	Czech Republic	Germany
15	Austria	**United States**
16	**United States**	Austria

Source: William J. Bennett, *The Index of Leading Cultural Indicators 2001* (Washington, DC: Empower.org, 2001), pp. 95, 96, available online at http://www.empower.org.

Comparing international achievement in reading, fourth-grade students in the United States excelled, ranking 2nd out of 18 nations in the fourth grade. By the eighth grade, however, the United States was tied with the 6th-ranking nation and ranked dead last in value-added comparisons. (See table 3.8.)[16]

Table 3.8: **International Value-Added Comparison**
Literacy, 9- and 14-Year-Old Students, 1991

Country	Age 9	Age 14	Difference
Denmark	291	500	209
East Germany (former)	322	501	180
Netherlands	304	486	178
Switzerland	340	516	172
Canada (BC)	325	494	168
West Germany (former)	329	498	164
Iceland	350	514	163
New Zealand	364	528	163
France	367	531	154
Spain	330	456	150
Sweden	379	529	150
Greece	332	482	147
Italy	365	488	146
Ireland	337	484	142
Norway	358	489	131
Belgium (Fr)	334	446	126
Finland	419	545	126
United States	**389**	**514**	**125**
Country mean	**346**	**500**	**154**

Source: Thomas D. Snyder, ed., *Elementary and Secondary Education: An International Perspective* (Washington, DC: U.S. Department of Education, National Center for Education Statistics, 2000), p. 127.
Note: The standard error was calculated at a 95 percent confidence level.

Finally, the 1999 TIMSS-Repeat test (a same-cohort/value-added comparison that provides the most up-to-date data) further supported such findings. When the same students were tested in fourth grade and then again in eighth grade, the U.S. students' performance declined in comparison to other nations.[17]

The United States has invested millions of dollars and a great deal of time and effort in the implementation of Goals 2000 and many other achievement-enhancing efforts. Year by year the United States has fallen short of its goals and, according to some, has jeopardized its future international standing. With relatively constant NAEP and SAT scores over the past 20 years, it is difficult to explain the United States' declining international achievement status.

▶ PROPOSITION: SECONDARY STUDENTS' MATHEMATICS AND ENGLISH TEST SCORES ARE NOT COMMENSURATE WITH THE TIME SPENT ON THESE SUBJECTS.

With concern regarding student achievement increasing and mounting attention given to the benefits of high standards and regular assessment, a renewed focus on what and how students are taught has also surfaced. A common impression is that students are receiving less and less instruction in the basics; presumably, more time spent on the basics would mean better test results and higher achievement overall. This may not be supported by the facts—right now, although more time has been dedicated to the basics, students' test scores do not reflect the renewed focus.

Between 1966 and 1996, the percentage of time teachers spent in given teaching fields has remained relatively constant in some subjects and changed dramatically in others. Since the lengths of the school day and school year have remained nearly the same over the last 30 years, the amount of time spent teaching specific subjects is easily compared. For example, of the 13 available fields or subjects taught in secondary public schools over the last 30 years, 3 of the 5 showing increased emphasis (math, science, and English) were in "required" subjects. In contrast, 8 subjects—agriculture, business education, foreign languages, health and physical education, home economics, industrial arts, music, and social studies—mostly elective, have had less actual teaching time. (See table 3.9.)[18]

Table 3.9: **Designated Teaching Time in Subject Areas**
Public Secondary School, 1966–96

Field	1966	1971	1976	1981	1986	1991	1996
Agriculture	1.6%	0.6%	0.6%	1.1%	0.6%	3.0%	0.5%
Art	2.0	3.7	2.4	3.1	1.5	2.6	3.3
Business education	7.0	5.9	4.6	6.2	6.5	3.5	4.1
English	18.1	20.4	19.9	23.8	21.8	25.0	23.9
Foreign language	6.4	4.8	4.2	2.8	3.7	3.8	5.2
Health and physical education	6.9	8.3	7.9	6.5	5.6	7.5	5.9
Home economics	5.9	5.1	2.8	3.6	2.6	3.1	2.2
Industrial arts	5.1	4.1	3.9	5.2	2.2	2.1	0.5
Mathematics	13.9	14.4	18.2	15.3	19.2	14.5	17.2
Music	4.7	3.8	3.0	3.7	4.8	4.2	4.3
Science	10.8	10.6	13.1	12.1	11.0	13.3	12.6
Social studies	15.3	14.0	12.4	11.2	13.6	11.0	13.4
Special education	0.4	1.1	3.0	2.1	3.5	5.2	1.7
Other	1.9	3.1	4.0	3.3	3.4	3.9	5.2

Source: Thomas D. Snyder, ed., *Digest of Education Statistics, 2001* (Washington, DC: U.S. Department of Education, National Center for Education Statistics, 2002), table 71, p. 82. **Note:** U.S. public secondary schools. Data are based upon sample surveys of public school teachers. Because of rounding, columns may not add to 100 percent.

Looking at college prep subjects as a whole—English, foreign languages, mathematics, science, and social studies—the percentage of time spent teaching these subjects in public schools has increased steadily since 1966. The increase is substantial; in aggregate, from 65 percent to 72 percent. This amounts to an 11 percent increase in time spent on these subjects over a generation.[19]

Comparing test scores from the NAEP should provide a barometer for tracking performance. Seventeen-year-old NAEP test scores, however, have remained relatively flat or decreased slightly over time. (See table 3.10.)[20]

Table 3.10: NAEP Average Scale Scores
17-Year-Olds, 1970–99

Subject	1970s	1980s	1992	1999
Mathematics	304.0 (1973)	298.5 (1982)	306.7	308.2
Science	305.0 (1970)	283.3 (1982)	294.1	295.3
Reading	285.2 (1971)	288.8 (1984)	289.7	287.8
Writing (11th grade)	na	290.0 (1984)	287.0	283.0 (1996)

Source: William J. Bennett, *The Index of Leading Cultural Indicators 2001* (Washington, DC: Empower.org, 2001), pp. 97–99, available online at http://www.empower.org.

Comparing SAT I test scores appears to support the same conclusions. With additional instruction time dedicated to college prep courses, SAT I[21] test scores should improve. In comparing scores, however, we see that despite the increase in time spent in math and English, test scores overall are decreasing. Ironically, in both subjects, some of the lowest SAT I scores were recorded during the years in which relatively more instruction time was designated to them. (See figures 3.1 and 3.2.)[22]

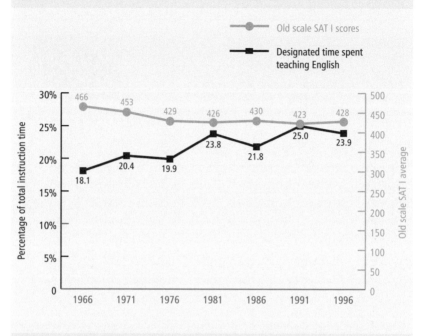

Figure 3.1: **English Instruction Time and SAT I Verbal Scores 1966–96**

Old scale SAT I scores

Designated time spent teaching English

Source: Thomas D. Snyder, ed., *Digest of Education Statistics, 2001* (Washington, DC: U.S. Department of Education, National Center for Education Statistics, 2002), tables 70, 135, pp. 81, 153.
Notes: Old-scale SAT I scores are used due to data availability and accuracy. Old-scale scores have not been recentered.
a. SAT scores for 1996 are actually 1994–95 scores.

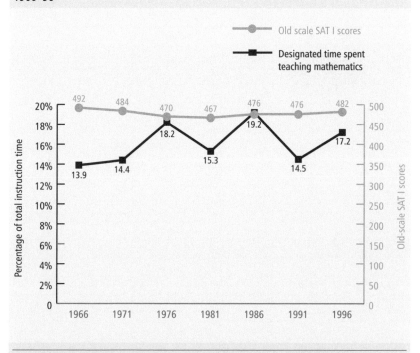

Figure 3.2: **Mathematics Instruction Time and SAT I Math Scores**
1966–96

- Old scale SAT I scores
- Designated time spent teaching mathematics

Source: Thomas D. Snyder, ed., *Digest of Education Statistics, 2001* (Washington, DC: U.S. Department of Education, National Center for Education Statistics, 2002), tables 70, 135, pp. 81, 153.
Notes: Old-scale SAT I scores are used due to data availability and accuracy. Old-scale scores have not been recentered.
a. SAT scores for 1996 are actually 1994–95 scores.

The results show that comparing SAT I data from the recentered scale, average total scores decreased from 1,039 to 1,017, a total of 22 points over a 26-year period. Comparing the old scale SAT I data, average total scores decreased from 958 to 910, a total of 48 points over a slightly different but generally overlapping 28-year period. (See table 3.11.)[23]

Table 3.11: **Average SAT Scores**
Old Scale and Recentered Scale, College-Bound High School Seniors, 1966–2001

	Scholastic Assessment Test I Score (recentered scale)			Scholastic Aptitude Test Score (old scale)		
Year	Total	Verbal	Math	Total	Verbal	Math
1966–67	na	na	na	958	466	492
1967–68	na	na	na	958	466	492
1968–69	na	na	na	956	463	493
1969–70	na	na	na	948	460	488
1970–71	na	na	na	943	455	488
1971–72	1,039	530	509	937	453	484
1972–73	1,029	523	506	926	445	481
1973–74	1,026	521	505	924	444	480
1974–75	1,010	512	498	906	434	472
1975–76	1,006	509	497	903	431	472
1976–77	1,003	507	496	899	429	470
1977–78	1,001	507	494	897	429	468
1978–79	998	505	493	894	427	467
1979–80	994	502	492	890	424	466
1980–81	994	502	492	890	424	466
1981–82	997	504	493	893	426	467
1982–83	997	503	494	893	425	468
1983–84	1,001	504	497	897	426	471
1984–85	1,009	509	500	906	431	475
1985–86	1,009	509	500	906	431	475
1986–87	1,008	507	501	906	430	476
1987–88	1,006	505	501	904	428	476
1988–89	1,006	504	502	903	427	476
1989–90	1,001	500	501	900	424	476
1990–91	999	499	500	896	422	474
1991–92	1,001	500	501	899	423	476
1992–93	1,003	500	503	902	424	478
1993–94	1,003	499	504	902	423	479
1994–95	1,010	504	506	910	428	482
1995–96	1,013	505	508	na	na	na
1996–97	1,016	505	511	na	na	na
1997–98	1,017	505	512	na	na	na
1998–99	1,016	505	511	na	na	na
1999–2000	1,019	505	514	na	na	na
2000–01	1,020	506	514	na	na	na

Source: Thomas D. Snyder, ed., *Digest of Education Statistics, 2001* (Washington, DC: U.S. Department of Education, National Center for Education Statistics, 2002), table 135, p. 153.
Notes: Scholastic Assessment Test, formerly known as the Scholastic Aptitude Test.
Averages of college-bound high school seniors. Possible scores on each part of the SAT range from 200 to 800.
Data for 1972 to 1986 were converted to the recentered scale by using a formula applied to the original mean and standard deviation. For 1987 to 1995, individual student scores were converted to the recentered scale and recomputed. For 1996 and 1997, most students received scores on the recentered scale score. Any score on the original scale was converted to the recentered scale prior to recomputing the mean.
Data for the years 1966–67 through 1970–71 are estimates derived from the test scores of all participants. Test was recentered in 1995.

Using the SAT I as a barometer for achievement is not without controversy. Some consider the SAT I an excellent predictor of college preparedness but not an accurate gauge of academic achievement. The SAT I does, however, provide largely comparable scores from the mid-1950s through 1995, prior to its recentering. Also, perhaps more than with any other test, extensive studies regarding the SAT I's relevance and validity have been done. On the other hand, the SAT I has several weaknesses: the test is self-selecting, it lacks comparable scores from a variety of grade levels, and the range of subjects covered is limited (verbal and math). Furthermore, the number of SAT I test takers has increased dramatically.[24] For example, in 1972, only 34.1 percent of high school graduates took the SAT I; by 1995, 41.8 percent were taking it.[25] The larger number of students taking the test dips deeper into the pool and will tend to affect the overall average adversely. Despite these caveats, most experts feel that the SAT I is one basis for achievement comparison.

Using the NAEP and SAT I scores as measures, the increased emphasis on math, science, and English has not been reflected in improved performance. Although many factors influence test scores, assuming that increased instruction time leads to better test scores may be presumptuous.

PROPOSITION: THE SHORTCOMINGS OF OUR K–12 EDUCATION SYSTEM HAVE LONG-TERM CONSEQUENCES.

In the United States, educational excellence has always been important. Many consider it a gauge for determining the vibrancy and health of our nation and an indicator of potential economic growth and development. In 1989, for example, the nation's governors set a goal that U.S. students be first in the world in math and science by the turn of the century; in 1994, Congress enacted the Goals 2000: Educate America Act, which set the same goal.[26] This goal was not achieved. Moreover, according to then-Secretary of Education Richard W. Riley, "American children continue to learn, but their peers in other countries are learning at a higher rate."[27]

The results of the TIMSS-Repeat are discouraging. This 1999 follow-up study to the first TIMSS (1995) tested the same cohorts that had done well as fourth-graders in international comparisons, scoring in the top 25 percent in 1995. By 1999, as eighth-graders, these students had dropped dramatically in their rankings, confirming that the further along in school one looks, the further behind U.S. students fall in math and science. The only American group that showed improvement since the 1995 survey were black students, whose achievement rose in math but not in science.[28]

These shortcomings in our elementary and secondary educational system affect higher education, as well. For example, the five highest-performing countries in eighth-grade mathematics in the TIMSS-Repeat were all Asian—Singapore, Korea, China, Hong Kong, and Japan. In science, four out of the top five were Asian countries—China, Singapore, Japan, and Korea.[29] Not surprisingly, the highest percentages of foreign students enrolled in institutions of higher education in the United States represent Asia. Furthermore, the percentage of Asian students has grown relative to foreign enrollment from 30.3 percent in the 1980–81 school year to 54.4 percent in the 1999–2000 school year.[30]

In the United States, the number of bachelor's, master's, and doctoral degrees in science and math awarded to U.S. citizens compared to non-U.S. citizens has decreased over time. In the 1979–80 school year, for example, of the total number of Ph.D. degrees conferred in the physical sciences, U.S. students received nearly 76 percent and foreign students received nearly 22 percent. (The percentages do not total 100 because some students' citizenship status was unknown.) In the 1998–99 school year, 54 percent of doctoral degrees in physical sciences were conferred on U.S. citizens versus 41 percent on foreign citizens. The trend is exhibited in all fields. Furthermore, in that same year, of those receiving Ph.D.s in mathematics and engineering, only 49.6 and 46.4 percent, respectively, were U.S. citizens. In mathematics, of those reporting, there are now more noncitizens than U.S. citizens receiving Ph.D.s. (See table 3.12 and figures 3.3 and 3.4.)[31]

Table 3.12: **Proportions of Ph.D. Degrees Conferred on Non-U.S. Citizens**

Field	1979–80	1998–99
Engineering	46.3%	48.6%
Physical sciences	21.6	40.7
Life sciences	17.6	33.4
Social sciences	11.6	17.5
Humanities	8.8	17.4
Education	8.2	10.6

Source: Thomas D. Snyder, ed., *Digest of Education Statistics, 2001* (Washington, DC: U.S. Department of Education, National Center for Education Statistics, 2002), tables 302–304, 306–308, pp. 349–352.

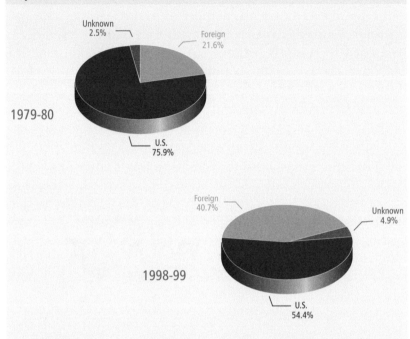

Unknown
2.5%

Foreign
21.6%

1979-80

U.S.
75.9%

Foreign
40.7%

Unknown
4.9%

1998-99

U.S.
54.4%

Source: Thomas D. Snyder, ed., *Digest of Education Statistics, 2001* (Washington, DC: U.S. Department of Education, National Center for Education Statistics, 2002), table 307, p. 352.

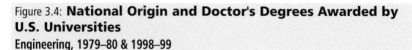

Figure 3.4: **National Origin and Doctor's Degrees Awarded by U.S. Universities**
Engineering, 1979–80 & 1998–99

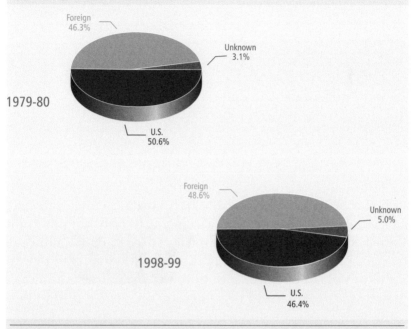

Foreign
46.3%

Unknown
3.1%

1979-80

U.S.
50.6%

Foreign
48.6%

Unknown
5.0%

1998-99

U.S.
46.4%

Source: Thomas D. Snyder, ed., *Digest of Education Statistics, 2001* (Washington, DC: U.S. Department of Education, National Center for Education Statistics, 2002), table 304, p. 350.

The number of foreign students enrolled in institutions of higher education in the United States continues to grow at the undergraduate, as well as the graduate, level. In 1980, some 311,880 foreign students were enrolled in institutions of higher education in the United States, 2.6 percent of total enrollment. In the 1999–2000 school year, a total of 514,723 foreign students were enrolled, 3.5 percent of enrollment, an increase of more than 35 percent during this time period. Most of the growth came from two regions, Asia and Europe, both of which nearly tripled in enrollment; enrollment of students from Middle East countries, in contrast, fell by more than half. (See table 3.13.)[32]

Table 3.13: **Foreign Students Enrolled in U.S. Higher Education**

Home region	1980–81		1999–2000		
	Number	% of total	Number	% of total	19-year growth
Asia	94,640	30.3%	280,146	54.4%	196%
Europe	25,330	8.1	78,485	15.2	201
Latin America	49,810	16.0	62,098	12.1	25
Middle East	84,710	27.2	34,897	6.8	−58
Africa	38,180	12.2	30,292	5.9	−21
North America	14,790	4.7	24,128	4.7	63
Oceania	4,180	1.3	4,676	0.9	12
Total	311,640	100.0	514,722	100.0	65

Source: Thomas D. Snyder, ed., *Digest of Education Statistics, 2001* (Washington, DC: U.S. Department of Education, National Center for Education Statistics, 2002), table 416, p. 486.

The United States' postsecondary education is still considered the best in the world, but its elementary and secondary education is slipping in international rankings. Although the United States has benefited in many ways from the influx of foreign students when they stay in the United States, participating as a part of American society and contributing to economic growth and research and development, they don't all stay. And those who choose to stay may not do so for their entire lifetimes. In 1995, for example, only 53.6 percent of foreign Ph.D. recipients stayed in the United States.[33]

As the world economy becomes more globalized, the United States has become increasingly dependent on the skills of the international students who gain advanced degrees in the hard sciences. The ramifications of poor achievement in elementary and secondary schools extend far beyond twelfth grade.

PROPOSITION: HOMEWORK PROVIDES CLEAR RESULTS FOR ALL STUDENTS AND COMPELLING RESULTS FOR HIGH SCHOOL STUDENTS.

In 1983, the nationally commissioned report *A Nation At Risk* recommended that homework requirements be increased to improve student achievement. Today, however, experts disagree on the value of homework. While some still feel that this is an area where schools, teachers, and parents have become too lax, others feel that too much homework can create excessive amounts of stress and allow for too little free time. Interestingly, the amount of homework the average American tenth-grader is assigned has not changed dramatically over time. In 1982, it was just under 1 hour per day; in 2000, the amount was just a few minutes less.

The purpose of homework is to develop intellectual discipline, establish good study habits, balance classroom workload, and supplement and reinforce material covered in class. It also serves as a link between home and school. Moreover, recent studies have strengthened the case for a positive relationship between homework and achievement.

The amount of time spent on homework is easily measured; however, using time as the only barometer for success can be deceptive. Quality is not easy to measure. An exhaustive analysis of numerous studies regarding homework provided by the School Improvement Research Series concluded that homework is most effective when it is

- relevant to learning objectives
- appropriate to students' learning ability and maturity
- assigned regularly
- collected, corrected, and reviewed in class

- assigned in reasonable amounts
- well explained
- supported by parents

Homework may also be used to close achievement gaps between students, resulting in more homework for some.[34]

In the School Improvement Research Series, a comprehensive study also asked the following questions: Does homework improve achievement? Does the amount of homework matter? When comparing the achievement of students who were given homework to those who were not, 14 of 20 studies showed effects favoring homework. Interestingly, grade level played a dramatic role. High school students in a class with assigned homework outperformed fellow students who did not receive assigned homework by about 70 percent. In junior high school, the difference was only 35 percent. In elementary school, there was no discernible difference. Also, out of 50 independent studies, 43 (86 percent) indicated that students who did more homework had better test scores or class grades. Once again, a strong correlation with grade level was apparent, and the patterns were consistent over time. (See tables 3.14 and 3.15 and figures 3.5 and 3.6.)[35]

Table 3.14: **Homework and NAEP Reading Scores**
1984–99

Daily time spent on homework	9-year-olds			13-year-olds			17-year-olds		
	1984	1994	1999	1984	1994	1999	1984	1994	1999
None									
Average proficiency	212	213	210	254	250	251	276	273	275
Percentage	36%	32%	26%	23%	23%	24%	22%	23%	26%
Did not do assignment									
Average proficiency	199	200	204	247	243	249	287	285	282
Percentage	4%	5%	4%	4%	6%	5%	11%	11%	13%
Less than 1 hour									
Average proficiency	218	212	214	261	261	262	290	288	291
Percentage	42%	48%	53%	36%	34%	37%	26%	27%	26%
1 to 2 hours									
Average proficiency	216	214	215	266	268	269	296	297	296
Percentage	13%	12%	12%	29%	28%	26%	27%	26%	23%
More than 2 hours									
Average proficiency	201	193	197	265	270	269	303	306	300
Percentage	6%	4%	5%	9%	9%	8%	13%	13%	12%

Source: Thomas D. Snyder, ed., *Digest of Education Statistics, 2001* (Washington, DC: U.S. Department of Education, National Center for Education Statistics, 2002).
Note: NAEP scale scores. Percentages of all in a given year's age group.
Because of rounding, columns may not add to 100 percent.

Table 3.15: **Homework and NAEP U.S. History Scores**
1994

Daily time spent on homework	Grade 4	Grade 8	Grade 12
Usually do not have it			
Average proficiency	209	245	272
Percentage	13%	7%	13%
Usually do not do it			
Average proficiency	180	244	279
Percentage	3%	8%	8%
1/2 hour or less			
Average proficiency	204	279	287
Percentage	39%	22%	23%
1 hour			
Average proficiency	209	262	287
Percentage	30%	36%	29%
More than 1 hour			
Average proficiency	200	266	295
Percentage	16%	27%	26%

Source: U.S. Department of Education, *The Condition of Education 1996,* Supplemental table 18-3, available online at http://nces.ed.gov/pubsold/ce96/c9618d03.html.
Note: NAEP scale scores, 1994. Percentages of all in grade group.
Because of rounding, columns may not add to 100 percent.

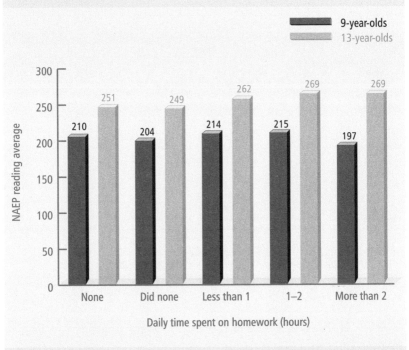

Figure 3.5: **Homework and NAEP Reading Scores**
9- and 13-Year-Olds, 1999

Sources: U.S. Department of Education, National Center for Education Statistics; *NAEP 1999 Long-Term Trend Reading Summary,* Data Tables for Age 9 Student Data, available online at http://llnces.ed.gov/nationsreportcard/tables/Ltt1999/NTR11012.asp; *NAEP 1999 Long-Term Trend Reading Summary,* Data Tables for Age 13 Student Data, available online at http://llnces.ed.gov/nationsreportcard/tables/Ltt1999/NTR21012.asp.

School Figures: The Data behind the Debate

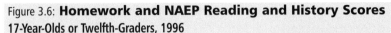

Figure 3.6: **Homework and NAEP Reading and History Scores**
17-Year-Olds or Twelfth-Graders, 1996

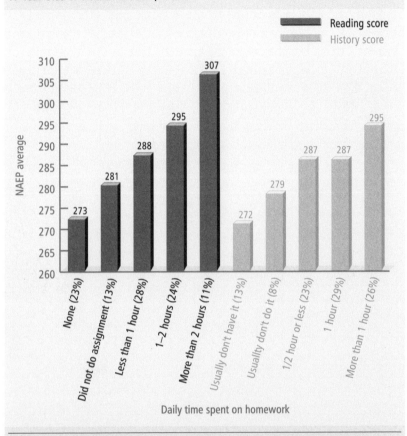

Daily time spent on homework

Sources: Thomas D. Snyder, ed., *Digest of Education Statistics, 1999* (Washington, DC: U.S. Department of Education, National Center for Education Statistics, 2000), table 114, p. 132; U.S. Department of Education, *The Condition of Education 1996*, Supplemental table 18-3, available at http://nces.ed.gov/pubsold/ce96/c9618d03.html.

Furthermore, in another comprehensive study by the International Association for the Evaluation of Educational Achievement, a significant and positive correlation was found between the amount of time spent a week on homework and grades. In addition, "low-ability" students who spent 10 or more hours a week on homework got higher grades than "high-ability" students who did not.[36]

Many factors contribute to the quality and effectiveness of homework, including a commitment by the teacher, parent, and student. Although the older the student, the greater the impact, what cannot be measured is the impact homework in early grades has on formulating good study habits, academic discipline, and basic preparation for later years. Homework for elementary students may not produce higher test scores, but it may lay the foundation for future success.

PROPOSITION: TELEVISION VIEWING IS A HOME-BASED HABIT THAT AFFECTS EDUCATIONAL ACHIEVEMENT

Numerous changes to enhance academic achievement have been recommended, but few have been applicable outside of school; decreased television viewing may be an exception. Studies show that the amount of time students spend watching television affects achievement. If a student spends several hours a night watching television, less time is available for homework, reading, or other instructional activities; it may also be that there is less time for needed sleep. By monitoring and limiting their children's television viewing, parents can be more actively involved in improving their children's achievement.

The television has become a centerpiece of American home life. Over the past 50 years, the amount of television watched steadily increased, and only recently has the number of hours plateaued or decreased slightly. According to the Advisory Panel on the Scholastic Aptitude Test (SAT) Score Decline, "By age 16 most children [in America] have spent 10,000 to 15,000 hours watching television, more time than they have spent in school. When they reach first grade, their watching time is between 20 and 35 hours per week; this usually peaks at about age 12. The average time per child per day increased by approximately an hour between 1960 and 1970."[37] According to one intensive study, in 1982, high school seniors, on average, watched television 31.0 hours per week but spent only 4.4 hours doing homework.[38]

During the 1990s, however, the amount of time spent by students watching television declined. (See table 3.16 and figure 3.7.)

- Between 1992 and 1998, fourth-graders' television viewing decreased from an average of 3.39 hours per day to 3.04.

- Between 1992 and 1998, eighth-graders' television viewing decreased from an average of 3.34 hours per day to 3.20.
- Between 1992 and 1998, twelfth-graders' television viewing decreased from an average of 2.60 hours per day to 2.46. [39]

Table 3.16: **Time Watching Television and Reading Performance**
1992–98

Daily time spent watching TV	Grade 4			Grade 8			Grade 12		
	1992	1994	1998	1992	1994	1998	1992	1994	1998
6 hours or more									
Average proficiency	199	194	198	241	239	244	271	264	260
Percentage	20%	21%	16%	14%	14%	12%	6%	7%	6%
4–5 hours									
Average proficiency	216	216	216	258	257	259	284	280	281
Percentage	22%	22%	19%	27%	27%	26%	20%	18%	17%
2–3 hours									
Average proficiency	224	222	223	265	265	269	293	289	292
Percentage	40%	38%	41%	46%	45%	47%	47%	46%	46%
1 hour or less									
Average proficiency	221	220	222	270	270	271	301	297	300
Percentage	19%	19%	24%	13%	14%	15%	27%	29%	31%
Average hours daily									
	3.39	3.4	3.04	3.34	3.32	3.2	2.6	2.56	2.46

Source: National Center for Education Statistics, "Television Viewing," *The Nation's Report Card* (Washington, DC: Department of Education, National Center for Education Statistics, 1999), available online at http://nces.ed.gov/NAEP/policy/pol_use_recent_tv.asp.
Note: NAEP scales scores. Percentages of all in a given year's age group. Because of rounding, columns may not add to 100 percent.

Average Hours of Television Watched per Day 1992–98

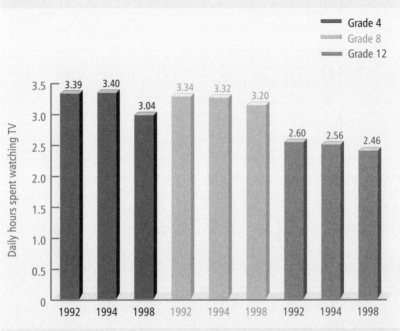

Source: Educational Testing Service, *America's Smallest School: The Family* (Princeton, NJ: Educational Testing Service, Policy Information Center, Educational Testing Service Network, 1999), available online at http://www.ets.org/research/pic/ssfig12.html.

One caveat to this trend, however, is the increasing amount of time students spend playing video games and on the Internet. An NCES study showed a decrease between 1982 and 1992 in the percentage of high school seniors who watched 5 or more hours of television on weekdays. In 1992, the study introduced a new category defining use of time: video game playing. According to the data, 13 percent of seniors spent more than an hour a day playing video games. This activity was not even presented as an option in the 1982 questionnaire.[40]

Moreover, in 1995, 77 percent of children reported sometimes playing video games at home, and 24 percent reported playing every day. Internet and video game playing may make up for the decrease in television viewing.[41] When comparing these data, one must be cautious. Time spent on the Internet may be education-enhancing; clearly, one of the great benefits of the World-Wide Web is the accessibility to a wide knowledge base. Just as all television is not "bad" and distracting, neither is all time spent on the Internet.

Large amounts of television viewing, however, appear to lower test scores. Although one study's assessment did not establish a causal relationship, NAEP scores in 1998 revealed that students who watch long hours of television have lower proficiencies in school. For example, fourth-grade students who watched 1 hour or less of television had an average scale reading score of 222. In contrast, those who watched 6 or more hours had an average score of 198. Eighth- and twelfth-grade scores were similar. In fact, the older the students, the greater the achievement gap between those students who watched 1 hour or less of television and those who watched 6 hours or more. These patterns are remarkably consistent over time. (See table 3.16.)[42]

NAEP math and science proficiency scores for twelfth-grade students exhibit the same pattern. Seventeen-year-olds who watched between 0 and 2 hours of television a day averaged a score of 312 in math. Students who watched between 3 and 5 hours scored 300 on average; those who watched 6 or more hours averaged 287. (See table 3.17 and figure 3.8.)[43]

Table 3.17: **Time Watching Television and Science Performance 2000**

Daily time spent watching TV	Grade 8 scale scores	Grade 12 scale scores
6 hours or more	131	127
5 hours	142	135
4 hours	148	140
3 hours	153	144
2 hours	158	150
1 hour or less	160	155
None	152	152

Source: National Center for Education Statistics, *National Assessment of Educational Progress: 2000 Science Assessment,* available online at http://nces.ed.gov/naep3/science/results/television-g8.asp. **Note:** NAEP science scale scores, 2000.

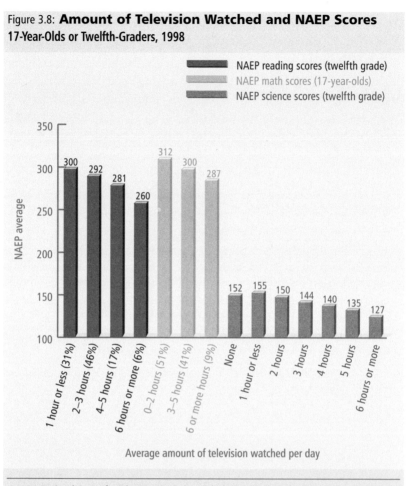

Figure 3.8: **Amount of Television Watched and NAEP Scores**
17-Year-Olds or Twelfth-Graders, 1998

NAEP reading scores (twelfth grade)
NAEP math scores (17-year-olds)
NAEP science scores (twelfth grade)

Source: National Center for Education Statistics, "Television Viewing," *The Nation's Report Card* (Washington, DC: Department of Education, National Center for Education Statistics, 1999), available online at http://nces.ed.gov/NAEP/policy/pol_use_recent_tv.asp.

An earlier state-by-state assessment of math proficiency among eighth-graders demonstrated that, in general, the higher the percentage of students watching long hours of television, the lower the math proficiency. For example, North Dakota and Montana have the lowest percentages of eighth-grade students who watch 6 or more hours of television per day (6 percent each), and their NAEP scores were the highest among state averages. In contrast, in Washington, D.C., one in three eighth-graders watched 6 or more hours of television each day, and their scores were the lowest in the sample. Statistics show a strong correlation between more hours spent watching television and lower test scores even when accounting for parental education levels and population size. In statistical terms, the uncontrolled correlation between television viewing and test scores is –0.87—the more time spent watching television, the lower the test score. Controlling for parental education levels does not change the relationship; however, the correlation coefficient does drop to –0.75 (although still statistically significant) when the data are weighted by population size. (See table 3.18 and figure 3.9.)[44]

Table 3.18: **Extensive Television Viewing and Mathematics Proficiency**
Eighth Grade, 1990

State[a]	Average NAEP math proficiency	Percentage of students watching at least 6 hours or more of TV daily
North Dakota	281	6%
Montana	280	6%
Iowa	278	7%
Nebraska	276	7%
Minnesota	276	7%
Wisconsin	274	7%
New Hampshire	273	8%
Idaho	272	9%
Wyoming	272	8%
Oregon	271	9%
Connecticut	270	9%
New Jersey	269	10%
Indiana	267	11%
Colorado	267	11%
Pennsylvania	266	11%
Virginia	264	12%
Michigan	264	12%
Ohio	264	11%
Oklahoma	263	12%
Delaware	261	14%
New York	261	13%
Maryland	260	14%
Illinois	260	14%
Rhode Island	260	14%
Arizona	259	15%
Georgia	258	16%
Texas	258	16%
Arkansas	256	19%
West Virginia	256	18%
Kentucky	256	18%
California	256	17%
New Mexico	256	17%
Florida	255	19%
Alabama	252	19%
Hawaii	251	20%
North Carolina	250	21%
Louisiana	246	23%
District of Columbia	231	33%

Source: Educational Testing Service, *America's Smallest School: The Family* (Princeton, NJ: Educational Testing Service, Policy Information Center, Educational Testing Service Network, 1999), available online at http://www.ets.org/research/pic/ssfig12.html.
Note: a. Some states provided insufficient data or did not participate.

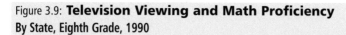

Figure 3.9: **Television Viewing and Math Proficiency By State, Eighth Grade, 1990**

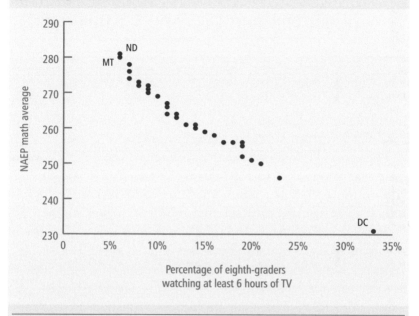

Source: Educational Testing Service, *America's Smallest School: The Family* (Princeton, NJ: Educational Testing Service, Policy Information Center, Educational Testing Service Network, 1999), available online at http://www.ets.org/research/pic/ssfig12.html.

No school reform recommendation can stand alone; however, curbing the amount of television students watch each day may play an important role in achievement. Many recommendations for improving achievement are directly connected to the classroom—teachers, class size, curriculum, spending—but television viewing is based in the home.

PROPOSITION: THE SAT I, ALTHOUGH IMPORTANT, IS NO LONGER AN ACCURATE BAROMETER FOR HISTORIC COMPARISONS.

The College Board's Scholastic Assessment Test was once a consistent predictor of college preparedness and an easy gauge for academic comparisons. It was also viewed as a way to compare one cohort of students against another.

In April 1995, however, this changed. The SAT I[45] score scale was recentered to reestablish the original mean score of 500 on the 200–800 scale in an effort to maintain the SAT I's statistical integrity and predictive validity.[46] The scale had not been recalibrated since 1941, when it reflected the norm of approximately 10,000 students (less than 1 percent of secondary school enrollment), of whom 62 percent were male and 41 percent attended independent or private schools.[47] Compare that to the 1,260,278 students (nearly 9 percent of total secondary school enrollment), 46 percent male and 17 percent attending religious or independent schools, who took the SAT I in 2000. As mean scores fell below 500, the score distribution became stretched in the upper half and compressed in the lower half. The old scale no longer reflected the normal curve distribution of scores, as originally envisioned. The new recentered scale reflects a normal curve distribution of scores that accounts for a larger, more diverse population and boosts average scores by 100 points. (See table 3.19 and figure 3.10.)[48]

Table 3.19: **Scholastic Aptitude Test**
1972–95

Year	High school graduates (thousand)[a]	SAT test takers Number (thousand)[a]	SAT test takers % of graduates[b]	SAT test takers % minority	Combined Mean	Verbal Mean score	Verbal % scoring at least 600	Math Mean	Math % scoring at least 600
1972	3,001	1,023	34.1%	na	937	453	11%	484	17%
1973	3,036	1,015	33.4	na	926	445	10	481	16
1974	3,073	985	32.1	na	924	444	10	480	17
1975	3,133	996	31.8	na	906	434	8	472	15
1976	3,148	1,000	31.8	15.0%	903	431	8	472	17
1977	3,155	979	31.0	16.1	899	429	8	470	16
1978	3,127	989	31.6	17.0	897	429	8	468	15
1979	3,117	992	31.8	17.1	894	427	7	467	15
1980	3,043	992	32.6	17.9	890	424	7	466	15
1981	3,020	994	32.9	18.1	890	424	7	466	14
1982	2,995	989	33.0	18.3	893	426	7	467	15
1983	2,888	963	33.3	18.9	893	425	7	468	16
1984	2,767	965	34.9	19.7	897	426	7	471	17
1985	2,677	977	36.5	20.0	906	431	7	475	17
1986	2,643	1,001	37.9	na	906	431	8	475	17
1987	2,694	1,080	40.1	21.8	906	430	8	476	18
1988	2,773	1,134	40.9	23.0	904	428	7	476	17
1989	2,727	1,088	39.9	25.3	903	427	8	476	18
1990	2,588	1,026	39.7	26.6	900	424	7	476	18
1991	2,493	1,033	41.4	28.0	896	422	7	474	17
1992	2,483	1,034	41.6	28.5	899	423	7	476	18
1993	2,481	1,044	42.1	30.0	902	424	7	478	19
1994	2,479	1,050	42.4	31.0	902	423	7	479	18
1995	2,553	1,068	41.8	31.0	910	428	8	482	21

Source: U.S. Department of Education, *The Condition of Education 1996,* Supplemental table 22-1, available online at http://nces.ed.gov/pubsold/ce96/c9622d01.html.
Notes: Old-scale SAT.
Some data revised from previously published figures.
a. Includes both public and private schools.
b. High school grads who took the SAT at any time while in high school.

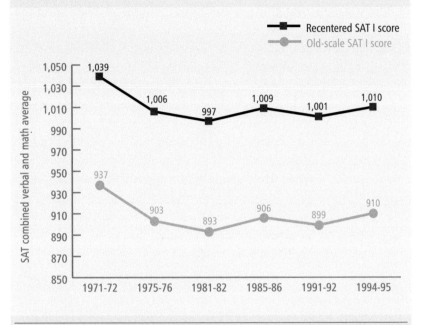

Figure 3.10: **SAT I Scores**
1971–95

Recentered SAT I score
Old-scale SAT I score

SAT combined verbal and math average

1,039
1,006
997
1,009
1,001
1,010

937
903
893
906
899
910

1971-72 1975-76 1981-82 1985-86 1991-92 1994-95

Source: Thomas D. Snyder, ed., *Digest of Education Statistics, 2001* (Washington, DC: U.S. Department of Education, National Center for Education Statistics, 2002), table 135, p. 153.

Intentional or not, however, the recentering changed several things. It is now easier to score a 1600 on the SAT I. The College Board's conversion chart shows that a pre-1995 verbal score of 730 or above and a math score of 780 or above are equivalent to a perfect 800 score on the tests today. The minimum verbal score today, 230, is 30 points higher than it was pre-1995. The minimum math score has remained the same.[49] It is now possible for a student to obtain a perfect score of 1,600 even with up to four wrong answers; this was not the case before 1995.[50] Critics say the test has been further diluted—difficult sections of the verbal portion have been

School Figures: The Data behind the Debate

removed; students now have an additional 30 minutes to take the test, and they are allowed to use calculators.[51]

Many argue that the decline in SAT I scores is primarily a result of more students and more diversity among test takers; this is not accurate. Of the test takers in 2000, 66 percent were white, 9 percent Asian, 11 percent black, and 9 percent Hispanic. The number of minorities taking the SAT I has increased, and so have their scores. In fact, minorities are the only subset making distinctive gains on their SAT I scores. For example, minorities made up 31 percent of SAT I test takers in 1995, double the proportion of minorities taking the SAT I in 1976, the first year this statistic was recorded. During this period (1976–95), black students' SAT I scores increased 24 points in verbal and 34 points in math, whereas white students' scores declined 3 points in verbal and increased only 5 points in math. (See table 3.20 and figures 3.11 through 3.13.)[52]

Table 3.20: **SAT I Scores of College-Bound Seniors By Race/Ethnicity, 1976–95**

Year[a]	White	Black	Hispanic	Asian	Native American
1976	944	686	773	932	808
1977	937	687	766	919	811
1978	931	686	755	911	806
1979	927	688	757	907	807
1980	924	690	765	905	816
1981	925	694	770	910	816
1982	927	707	779	911	812
1983	927	708	777	909	813
1984	932	715	780	917	817
1985	939	722	793	922	820
1986[b]	na	na	na	na	na
1987	936	728	794	926	825
1988	935	737	796	930	828
1989	937	737	801	934	812
1990	933	737	797	938	825
1991	930	736	794	941	830
1992	933	737	795	945	837
1993	938	741	798	950	847
1994	938	740	798	951	837
1995	946	744	804	956	850

Source: U.S. Department of Education, *The Condition of Education 1996,* Supplemental table 22-2, available online at http://nces.cd.gov/pubsold/ce96/c9622d02.html.
Notes: College-bound seniors, including graduating seniors participating in the college Board Admissions Testing Program, not including all first-year college students or all high school seniors. Old scale scores.
a. The first year for which SAT scores by racial/ethnic group are available is 1976.
b. Data were not collected by racial/ethnic group in 1986.

Figure 3.11: **SAT I Scores and SAT I Test Takers**

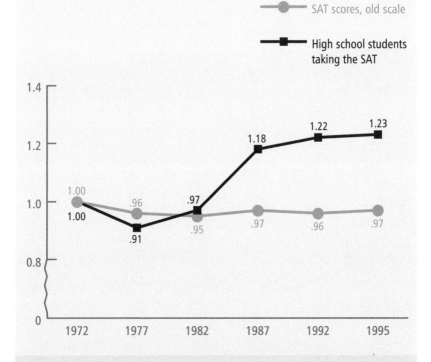

Source: U.S. Department of Education, *The Condition of Education 1996,* Supplemental table 22-1, available online at http://www.nces.ed.gov/pubsold/ce96/c9622d01.html.
Note: Old SAT scoring scale.
Re-scaled: 1972 data = 1.0.

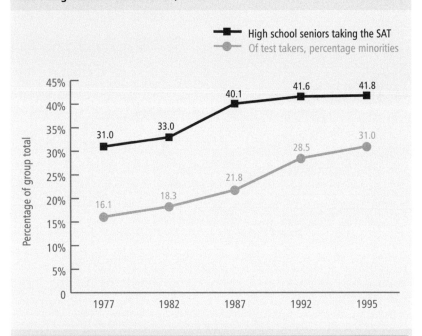

Figure 3.12: **SAT I Test Takers**
Graduating Seniors and Minorities, 1977–95

High school seniors taking the SAT
Of test takers, percentage minorities

Source: U.S. Department of Education, *The Condition of Education 1996,* Supplemental table 22-1, available online at http://www.nces.ed.gov/pubsold/ce96/c9622d01.html.
Note: Old SAT scoring scale.

School Figures: The Data behind the Debate

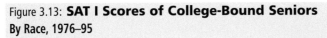

Figure 3.13: **SAT I Scores of College-Bound Seniors By Race, 1976–95**

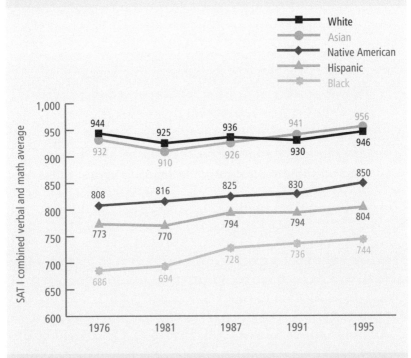

Source: U.S. Department of Education, *The Condition of Education 1996,* Supplemental table 22-2, available online at http://www.nces.ed.gov/pubsold/ce96/c9622d02.html.
Note: Old SAT scoring scale.

Although there were periods of modest improvement in the mid-1980s and then again in the mid- and late 1990s, overall SAT I scores still have not reached the levels they were at in the early 1970s.[53] If students were maintaining achievement levels, the number of students scoring above 600 on the verbal portion should increase as the number of students taking the test increases; this is not the case. In 1972, 112,530 of students (11 percent) scored above 600 on the verbal section of the SAT I; in 1995, only 85,440 (8 percent) scored above 600. In mathematics, the percentage of students scoring 600 or higher did increase, from 17 to 21 percent.[54]

Has the value of the SAT I dissipated as a useful means of student assessment? Yes, according to Chester Finn and Diane Ravitch:

> The College Board's decision to 'recenter' the SAT I scores has considerably reduced the utility of those scores as a national barometer of the educational performance of college bound students. For some two decades, the SAT I has served this function, mainly because of its stable scale. The recentering however magically ... gives the impression that the nation's educational deficit has been eliminated.[55]

In spite of drawbacks (the test is self-selective, lacks comparable scores from a variety of grade levels, and the range of subjects covered is limited to verbal and math), most experts feel that the SAT I is one basis for achievement comparison.[56]

A host of critics further argue that the SAT I should be dismissed because it is unfair to able students who do not perform well on fill-in-the-bubble tests, to those who belong to ethnic and minority groups and so are on uneasy terms with the cultural assumptions of the verbal SAT I, and to those whose parents are not rich enough to pay for the expensive SAT preparation courses that claim to raise scores.[57] Despite the SAT I's dissipated value, it is still one of the most useful tools colleges employ during the admissions process a 1997 study by the College Board showed that a combination of SAT scores and grades is a better indicator of student success in college than grades alone. Furthermore, records of 46,379 students at 55 colleges and universities across the country found that "for most ethnic groups the SAT alone is a better predictor of course grades than are high school grades alone." Of significance, for blacks, Hispanics, and Native Americans, "the SAT tends to predict a slightly higher GPA than the students actually earn." A 1997 University of California study confirmed that if SAT scores were eliminated as admissions criteria, "white student eligibility would rise by 17 percent, Hispanic eligibility would rise only slightly, and black eligibility would fall by 18 percent."[58]

SAT I data now confuse many who make intertemporal comparisons in secondary education achievement. Moreover, potentially misleading conclusions may have been drawn and may have long-term consequences. If it appears students are doing better when they're actually doing worse, it may be doing students and the education system more harm than good. Claiming a score of 1010 when the old score would have been 910 provides a false sense of security when it comes to achievement.[59]

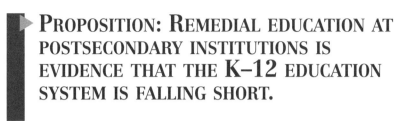

PROPOSITION: REMEDIAL EDUCATION AT POSTSECONDARY INSTITUTIONS IS EVIDENCE THAT THE K–12 EDUCATION SYSTEM IS FALLING SHORT.

Remedial education at the collegiate level has become a topic of concern for many. Alarming reports of high enrollment in remedial courses are at the fore, as are discussions as to why such enrollment percentages are high and how to reduce the numbers. The data, however, are confusing. Nationwide remedial course offerings at the collegiate level peaked in the 1996–97 school year and have since begun a steady decline. Despite these reported "improvements," postsecondary remedial enrollment is still high. In 1998, an average of 36 percent of students new to higher education were enrolled in at least one remedial course. High remedial enrollment rates are evidence that our K–12 education system is not preparing students adequately for future education opportunities. (See table 3.21.)[60]

Table 3.21: **Degree-Granting Institutions Offering Remedial Services**
1990–91—2000–01

	1990–91	1996–97	2000–01
All 4-year colleges	70.6%	80.0%	75.1%
Public	83.5	85.1	81.7
Private	65.6	68.6	67.9
All 2-year colleges	88.4	91.0	80.4
Public	98.9	99.2	99.7
Private	65.5	68.4	48.8
Total	77.7	80.0	75.1

Source: Thomas D. Snyder, ed., *Digest of Education Statistics, 2001* (Washington, DC: U.S. Department of Education, National Center for Education Statistics, 2002), table 313, p. 356.

What's being said and done about postsecondary remedial education? Many states are concerned about their high remediation rates and have begun aggressive campaigns to reduce them. California is one example. California's state university system, one of the nation's largest university systems (with more than 350,000 students), has pledged to reduce the proportion of entering freshmen who require remediation to 10 percent by 2007; in 2001, more than 50 percent of its incoming freshmen required remediation in mathematics or English. The Cal State system's numbers are high when compared to the national average of approximately 35 percent; however, when the number of students whose second language is English are accounted for, the Cal State University remediation rates are more in line with national figures.[61]

In fall 2000, based on placement exams that determine who is assigned to remedial education classes, 62 percent of first-time freshmen required remediation, 20,890 students out of 33,822. In the Cal State system, 81 percent of those enrolled in remediation class had gained full proficiency before the second year.[62]

Cal State's remedial education students do confirm theories of K–12 shortcomings. According to university statistics, those needing remediation typically graduated from high school with a B average (3.2 GPA) and in the top third of their class. The Cal State system is now working with high schools statewide to reach its goal. Although improvements can be seen, reducing the percentage of freshmen who require remediation to 10 percent by 2007 seems optimistic. (See table 3.22.)[63]

Table 3.22: **California State University Freshman Remediation Rates**
1997–2001

Ethnicity	Math remediation		English remediation	
	1997	2001	1997	2001
American Indian	55.0%	49.5%	34.0%	39.4%
Black	80.0	74.5	64.0	64.4
Mexican-American	71.0	64.8	65.0	64.6
Other Latino	68.0	64.5	57.0	58.1
Asian-American	43.0	35.5	66.0	63.5
Pacific Islander	51.0	47.1	41.0	51.4
Filipino	54.0	46.4	56.0	53.8
White non-Latino	47.0	36.7	28.0	27.8
Nonresident	35.0	34.7	80.0	76.5
Unknown	51.0	44.8	37.0	39.7
Total	**54.0**	**46.2**	**47.0**	**46.2**

Sources: U.S. Department of Education, *Remedial Education at Higher Education Institutions in Fall 1995* (Washington, DC: U.S. Department of Education, National Center for Education Statistics, October 1996), available online at http:/www.nces.ed.gov/pubs/97584.html; Christopher Shults, *Remedial Education: Practices and Policies in Community Colleges* (Washington, DC: American Association of Community Colleges, January 2001), available online at http://www.aacc.nche.edu/initiatives/issues/Remedial.pdf.

▶ PROPOSITION: THE EMPHASIS ON COMMUNITY SERVICE IN K–12 EDUCATION HAS CLEARLY INCREASED; ITS IMPACT IS MORE DIFFICULT TO MEASURE.

Involving America's students in community service activities is one of the objectives established under the third National Education Goal for the year 2000, which seeks to prepare students for responsible citizenship.

> All students will be involved in activities that promote and demonstrate good citizenship, good health, community service, and personal responsibility.[64]

Over the past 10 years, legislative initiatives have responded to and galvanized a growing national emphasis on increasing students' involvement with their local communities and linking this service to academic study. This is service-learning, curriculum-based community service that integrates classroom instruction with community service activities, and it may be mandatory. In addition to their study of soil and water composition, for example, students in a science class preserve the natural habitat of animals living at a local lake by keeping the area clean and by posting signs educating the public. Community service is defined as community service activities that are not curriculum based and are recognized by or arranged through the school. It may be mandatory or voluntary.[65] Examples of initiatives that have mandated support for service-learning activities in elementary and secondary schools include the National and Community Service Act of 1990, the Serve America program, the National and Community Service Trust Act of 1993, and the Learn and Serve America program.[66] Proponents of service-learning and community service argue that involvement in service-learning enhances education, revitalizes communities, and teaches the importance of community participation and democratic values.[67]

While community involvement is clearly an important aspect of good citizenship, it is not apparent that this emphasis and participation make for a better education. The opportunities for involvement may have increased, but the academic benefits are less obvious.

- In 1984, approximately 9 percent of all high schools offered some form of service-learning; in 1999, roughly 46 percent of public high schools had incorporated some service-learning activities.
- In 1984, 27 percent of high schools offered community service opportunities to their students; in 1999, 83 percent of public high schools were doing so.
- In 1999, 32 percent of students in grades 6 through 12 reported that at least part of their community service experience was incorporated into their curriculum in some way. Of the 32 percent, 49 percent stated some components were mandatory, and 79 percent stated some components were voluntary. (The percentages of students reporting mandatory and voluntary student participation do not sum to 100 because many schools had both mandatory and voluntary student participation. (See figure 3.14.)[68]
- In the year 2001, the total number of students engaged in community service in North America was roughly 13 million.[69]

Figure 3.14: **Public Schools with Service-Learning**
1998–99

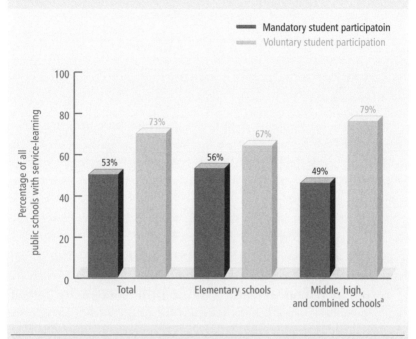

Source: Chris Chapman and Rebecca Skinner, *Service-Learning and Community Service in K–12 Public Schools* (Washington, DC: U.S. Department of Education, Office of Educational Research and Improvement, National Center for Education Statistics, September 1999).
Notes: Data presented in the chart are based upon the number of schools having service-learning, which is 32 percent of sixth- through twelfth-grade public schools. Many schools had both mandatory and voluntary student participation.
a. Combined schools contain both elementary and secondary grades. The highest grade in such schools must be at least ninth grade.

Findings indicate that the propensity for sixth-through twelfth-grade public school students to participate in community service remained relatively flat from the 1970s through the early 1990s but has increased slightly in the mid- to late 1990s, perhaps due to the strong emphasis from legislators and others.[70]

- In 1999, 52 percent of sixth-through twelfth-graders had participated in community service within the previous year; in 1996, 49 percent had participated.[71]
- Some 56 percent of students who participated regularly in community service said that their service was incorporated into the school curriculum in some way (service-learning).[72]

It is difficult to gauge whether voluntary community service has actually increased because of the large influx of school programs that now have mandatory community service. Evidence suggests, however, that students are more likely to participate when the opportunity is provided but less likely to voluntarily seek out opportunities of their own accord. For example, students' participation rates in schools that required and also arranged community service were higher than participation rates in schools that only required it.[73]

Does community involvement contribute to a better-educated populace, or are we cheating our students by not spending enough time on the basics? Achievement over the last decade has remained flat, and students' community involvement has increased marginally, despite the heavy emphasis. Most would agree that community involvement is important; however, the proper context for participation might be less obvious. One of the primary purposes of K–12 education is to make sure that students are well equipped to contribute as citizens; however, students must also know the basics—reading, writing, and arithmetic—if they are to be prepared to contribute to their communities.

▶ CHAPTER NOTES

1. William J. Bennett, *The Index of Leading Cultural Indicators 2001* (Washington, DC: Empower.org, 2001), p. 91, available online at http://www.empower.org.
2. Ibid., p. 93.
3. Ibid., p. 97.
4. Ibid., p. 103.
5. Ibid., p. 104.
6. Ibid., p. 102.
7. Ibid., p. 103.
8. Ibid., p. 104.
9. Ibid.
10. *Goals 2000: Educate America Act, Sec. 102,* available online at http://www.ed.gov/legislation/GOALS2000/TheAct/sec102.html.
11. Thomas D. Snyder, ed., *Elementary and Secondary Education: An International Perspective* (Washington, DC: U.S. Department of Education, National Center for Education Statistics, 2000), p. 50.
12. Harold W. Stevenson, "A TIMSS PRIMER: Lessons and Implications for U.S. Education," *Fordham Report* 2, no. 7 (Washington, DC: Thomas B. Fordham Foundation, July 1998).
13. Stevenson, "A TIMSS PRIMER: Lessons and Implications for U.S. Education"; Herbert J. Walberg, "Achievement in American Schools," in *A Primer on America's Schools*, ed. Terry M. Moe (Stanford, CA: Hoover Institution Press, 2001), pp. 43–67; Organisation for Economic Co-operation and Development, *Education at a Glance: OECD Indicators, 1998* (Paris: Organisation for Economic Co-operation and Development, 1998), available online at http://www.oecd.org//els/stats/eag97/chapterf.htm; Herbert J. Walberg, "Spending More while Learning Less," *Fordham Report* 2, no. 6 (Washington, DC: Thomas B. Fordham Foundation, July 1998); Snyder, ed., *Elementary and Secondary Education: An International Perspective,* pp. 50–71.
14. Stevenson, "A TIMSS PRIMER: Lessons and Implications for U.S. Education."
15. Bennett, *The Index of Leading Cultural Indicators 2001*, pp. 95–96.
16. Snyder, ed., *Elementary and Secondary Education: An International Perspective,* pp. 55–56.

17. U.S. Department of Education, *Trends in International Mathematics and Science Study* (Washington, DC: U.S. Department of Education, National Center for Education Statistics, 2002), available online at http://nces.ed.gov/timss/results.asp.

18. Thomas D. Snyder, ed., *Digest of Education Statistics, 2001* (Washington, DC: U.S. Department of Education, National Center for Education Statistics, 2002), table 70, p. 81.

19. Ibid., table 71, p. 82.

20. Bennett, *The Index of Leading Cultural Indicators 2001*, pp. 97–101.

21. In April 1995, the SAT I was recentered. "Old-scale" scores are scores that have not been recentered. The SAT I tests general verbal and math skills. The SAT II test is subject specific by design.

22. Snyder, *Digest of Education Statistics, 2001*, table 135, p. 153.

23. Ibid.

24. Congress of the United States, Congressional Budget Office, *Trends in Educational Achievement* (Washington, DC: Congressional Budget Office, April 1996).

25. Ibid.

26. *Goals 2000: Educate America Act, Sec. 102.*

27. Diana Jean Schemo, "Worldwide Survey Finds U.S. Students Are Not Keeping Up," *New York Times* (6 December 2000).

28. U.S. Department of Education, *Trends in International Mathematics and Science Study.*

29. Ibid.

30. Snyder, *Digest of Education Statistics, 2001*, table 416, p. 486.

31. Ibid., tables 302, 304, 306, 307, pp. 349–352.

32. Ibid., table 416, p. 486.

33. U.S. Department of Education, *Degrees Earned by Foreign Graduate Students: Fields of Study and Plans after Graduation* (Washington, DC: U.S. Department of Education, Office of Educational Research and Improvement, November 1997).

34. Kathleen Cotton, *Educational Time Factors*, School Improvement Research Series (Portland, OR: Northwest Regional Educational Laboratory, November 1989), available online at http://www.nwrel.org/scpd/sirs/4/cu8.html.

35. Cotton, *Educational Time Factors*; Debbie Reese, "Homework: What Does the Research Say?" *Parent News for 1997* (Champaign, IL: ERIC Clearinghouse on Elementary and Early Childhood Education and the

National Parent Information Network, 1997), available online at http://ericps.crc.uiuc.edu/npin/pnews/pnewn97/pnewn97e.html.

36. Richard A. NeSmith, "Research Findings Regarding Homework," in *Developing Homework Policies* (April 2000), available online at http://members.tripod.com/~bioscience/homeworkpolicy.html.

37. Educational Testing Service, *America's Smallest School: The Family* (Princeton, NJ: Educational Testing Service, Policy Information Center, Educational Testing Service Network, 1999), available online at http://www.ets.org/research/pic/ssfig12.html.

38. Herbert J. Walberg and Timothy Shanahan, "High School Effects on Individual Students," *Education Researcher* 12, no. 7 (1983), pp. 4–9.

39. National Center for Education Statistics, "Television Viewing," *The Nation's Report Card* (Washington, DC: Department of Education, National Center for Education Statistics, 1999), available online at http://nces.ed.gov/NAEP/policy/pol_use_recent_tv.asp.

40. Snyder, *Digest of Education Statistics, 2001,* table 145, p. 163.

41. Bernard Cesarone, "Video Games: Research, Ratings, Recommendations," *ERIC Digest* (Washington, DC: U.S. Department of Education, November 1998), available online at http:ericeece.org/pubs/digests/1998/cesar1998.html.

42. National Center for Education Statistics, "Television Viewing."

43. Educational Testing Service, *America's Smallest School: The Family.*

44. Ibid. Note: In statistical terms, the uncontrolled correlation between television viewing and test scores is –0.87. The more time spent watching television, the lower the test score. Controlling for parental education levels does not change the correlation; however, the correlation does drop to –0.75 (although still statistically significant) when the data is weighted by population size.

45. The SAT I tests general verbal and math skills. The SAT II test is subject specific by design.

46. The College Entrance Examination Board, *What You Need to Know about Recentering SAT Scores* (New York: College Entrance Examination Board, 1994), available online at http://www.collegeboard.org.

47. Donald M. Stewart, letter to the editor, *Washington Post* (15 September 1996).

48. The College Entrance Examination Board, *National Background Information, 2000* (New York: College Board Online, 2000), available online at http://www.collegeboard.org.

49. The Center for Education Reform, *SAT Increase—The Real Story, Part II* (Washington, DC: Center for Education Reform, August 1996), available online at http://edreform.com/press/960822sa.htm.

50. The College Entrance Examination Board, *National Background Information, 2000*.

51. The Center for Education Reform, *SAT Increase—The Real Story, Part II*.

52. The Center for Education Reform, *The SAT Myth* (Washington, DC: Center for Education Reform, spring 1997), available online at http://edreform.com/elc/opmag/spr97op.htm.

53. Snyder, *Digest of Education Statistics, 2001*, table 135, p. 153.

54. The Center for Education Reform, *SAT Increase—The Real Story, Part II*.

55. Ibid.

56. Ibid.

57. E.D. Hirsch, Jr., "The SAT: Blaming the Messenger," *The Weekly Standard* 6, no. 35 (28 May 2001).

58. Lance T. Izumi, "Does SAT Discriminate against Minorities?" *School Reform News* 5, no. 5 (May 2001).

59. The College Entrance Examination Board, *What You Need to Know about Recentering SAT Scores*.

60. U.S. Department of Education, *Remedial Education at Higher Education Institutions in Fall 1995* (Washington, DC: U.S. Department of Education, National Center for Education Statistics, October 1996), available online at http:/www.nces.ed.gov/pubs/97584.html; Christopher Shults, *Remedial Education: Practices and Policies in Community Colleges* (Washington, DC: American Association of Community Colleges, January 2001), available online at http://www.aacc.nche.edu/initiatives/issues/Remedial.pdf; Snyder, *Digest of Education Statistics, 2001*, table 313, p. 356.

61. California State University, *Freshman Remediation Rates 1997* (Long Beach: California State University, 1997), available online at http://www.calstate.edu; California State University, *Freshman Remediation Rates 2001* (Long Beach: California State University, 2001), available online at http://www.calstate.edu; Tennessee Higher Education Commission, *An Analysis of Remedial and Developmental Education* (Nashville: Tennessee Higher Education Commission, May 2001), available online at http://www.state.tn.us/thec/.

62. California State University, *Freshman Remediation Rates 1997;* California State University, *Freshman Remediation Rates 2001.*

63. California State University, *Freshman Remediation Rates 1997;* California State University, *Freshman Remediation Rates 2001*; Jeffrey Selingo, "Cal State Puts Remediation on an 'Or Else' Basis," *The Chronicle of Higher Education* (4 August 2000), available online at http://chronicle.com/free/v46/i48a02701.htm.

64. National Education Goals Panel, "Goal 3," in *National Education Goals* (Washington, DC: National Education Goals Panel), available online at http://www.negp.gov/page3-7.htm.

65. Chris Chapman and Brian Kleiner, *Youth Service-Learning and Community Service among 6th- through 12th-Grade Students in the United States, 1996 and 1999* (Washington, DC: U.S. Department of Education Office of Educational Research and Improvement, National Center for Education Statistics, November 1999).

66. Ibid.

67. The National Student Service-Learning and Community Service Survey defines service-learning as "curriculum-based community service that integrates classroom instruction with community service activities." Community service is defined as activities that are non–curriculum-based and are recognized by and/or arranged through the school. Community service may be mandatory or voluntary.

68. Chapman and Kleiner, *Youth Service-Learning and Community Service among 6th- through 12th-Grade Students in the United States, 1996 and 1999*; Chris Chapman and Rebecca Skinner, *Service-Learning and Community Service in K–12 Public Schools* (Washington, DC: U.S. Department of Education, Office of Educational Research and Improvement, National Center for Education Statistics, September 1999). Note: Percentages of schools reporting mandatory and voluntary student participation in service-learning do not sum to 100 because many schools had both mandatory and voluntary student participation in service-learning.

69. Joel Westheimer and Joseph Kahne, "Service Learning Required," *Education Week* 19, no. 20 (26 January 2000), available online at http://www.edweek.org/ew/ewstory.cfm?slug=20westheimer.h19.

70. Ibid.

71. U.S. Department of Education, *The Condition of Education 2001* (Washington, DC: U.S. Department of Education, National Center for Education Statistics, Office of Educational Research and Improvement, 2001), indicator 16, p. 30.

72. Chapman and Skinner, *Service-Learning and Community Service in K–12 Public Schools.*

73. U.S. Department of Education, *The Condition of Education 2001,* indicator 16, p. 30.

Chapter 4:
Expenditures

Propositions

▶ PUBLIC SCHOOLS AT ONE TIME WERE LOCALLY CONTROLLED; THIS IS CHANGING. FUNDING PROVIDES ONE PIECE OF EVIDENCE.

▶ INCREASED PER-PUPIL EXPENDITURES HAVE NOT BEEN MATCHED BY IMPROVED STUDENT PERFORMANCE.

▶ EXPENDITURES MAY NOT MATTER AS MUCH AS ALLOCATION.

▶ SPECIAL EDUCATION IS AN EXPENDITURE, STAFFING, AND CLASSROOM CONUNDRUM.

▶ WHEN IT COMES TO ACHIEVEMENT, THE LARGEST SOURCE OF FEDERAL AID TO ELEMENTARY AND SECONDARY SCHOOLS HAS NOT MADE A BIT OF DIFFERENCE.

Highlights

In the 2000–2001 school year, total expenditures for elementary and secondary education in the United States amounted to more than $420 billion—fully 4.3 percent of GDP. In the 1949–50 school year, total expenditures for elementary and secondary education were $6.2 billion, only 2.3 percent of GDP.[1]

In the 2000–2001 school year, average per-pupil expenditures were approximately $7,079; in the 1949–50 school year, they were approximately $1,380, in constant dollars.[2]

In 1999, the United States was ranked 3rd out of 26 nations in public expenditures per pupil at the elementary level; the U.S. was also ranked 3rd at the secondary level.[3]

In the 1920s, less than 1 percent of public K–12 education funding came from the federal government. States provided 17 percent, and local government provided the vast majority, 83 percent. In the 1930s, state funding increased dramatically, contributing more than 30 percent, and local funding decreased to less than 70 percent; there was little change in the federal contribution.[4]

By the late 1970s, the largest source of funding was the state, more than 45 percent. Since the '70s, state funding has fluctuated between 45 and 50 percent. Federal funding reached a high of nearly 10 percent in the late 1970s and wavered between 6 and 7 percent through the '90s.[5]

In 1999, 56 percent of public education expenditures were spent on compensation for teachers, 26 percent on compensation of other staff, and 18 percent on other costs.[6]

There is a wide variance when comparing current per-pupil expenditures in fall enrollment by state. In the 1998–99 school year, Utah spent less than $4,000 per pupil, while New Jersey spent close to $10,000.[7]

According to a recent survey, 76 percent of Americans feel that expenditures on education should increase, 18 percent think they should remain the same, and only 5 percent think they should decrease.[8]

Overview

n the 2000–2001 school year, the cost of public education for K–12 students in the United States amounted to more than $420 billion—fully 4.3 percent of GDP. No doubt, this is a tremendous amount of money; however, some say it is too little. When surveyed, for example, Americans put education near the top of spending priorities, and the vast majority feels more should be spent.

As remarkable as this expenditure number is, equally and possibly more dramatic is the relative increase in the costs of education during the 20th century. Using the 2000–2001 school year as a base year, per pupil expenditures in the 1919–20 school year were $367; since then, costs have increased nearly 20-fold. In the 2000–2001 school year, per pupil expenditures were estimated at $7,079.

Understanding the full cost of public education and how money is spent are among the greatest challenges facing education researchers. Finding a consistent set of data that all parties—politicians, school boards, school administrators, unions, school reformers, teachers, and parents—will agree to is virtually impossible. Those advocating reform of the public school system claim that the administrators, sympathetic politicians, and unions understate the true costs in an effort to get more money. Their antagonists say costs are up. First, teachers are doing more than they were asked to do in previous decades, they are more educated and experienced, and hence are paid more. Second, costly regulations have been imposed by federal, state, and local governments. Third, there have been great changes in American public education. However, explaining how costs have risen so precipitously is a challenge.

The federal government has assumed an increasing role in education, historically a function controlled almost exclusively by local government and school boards. Initially, federal dollars preceded federally mandated programs and regulations. As time has passed, however, growing concern over U.S. students' performance has led to a greater federal role—with associated higher costs and levels of bureaucracy without commensurate funding—not a diminished role.

Across states, there is great variability in how education funds are spent. Student achievement also varies widely from state to state and even district to district. From all appearances, however, there does not appear to be a direct correlation between the expenditures and performance. No matter which data one uses, one phenomenon is inescapable: Over the past 30 years, costs are up while performance is down. To follow the money, one embarks on a serpentine path. In this chapter, we provide some guidance.

PROPOSITION: PUBLIC SCHOOLS AT ONE TIME WERE LOCALLY CONTROLLED; THIS IS CHANGING. FUNDING PROVIDES ONE PIECE OF EVIDENCE.

Throughout U.S. history, local school boards governed public schools, and local control, parental involvement, and accountability were pillars of public education. Local organization allowed for more community involvement; decision making could be tailored specifically to meet local needs and desires.

The setting, however, of public education has changed. In government, function often follows funding; the current status of public education is not exempt from this causal relationship. Over time, the source of public school funding has increasingly shifted from primarily local funding toward state and national funding. FDR's New Deal and LBJ's Great Society, far-reaching domestic programs, both contributed to the swing from local to state and national involvement. During the 1920s, less than 1 percent of public K–12 education funding came from the federal government. States provided 16.9 percent, and local governments provided the vast majority, 82.7 percent. In the 1930s states began to play a much more active role, contributing 30.3 percent, while the local share was reduced to 68 percent. Although the federal role was still small, it increased through the 1960s. By the 1970s local government funding had been replaced by state funding, which provided a plurality of funding, more than 45 percent. The federal government's support rose to 9.8 percent, an all-time high. In the early 1990s federal funding was scaled back, hovering around 6 percent; by the end of the decade, however, federal funding had climbed back into the 7 percent range. (See table 4.1 and figure 4.1.)[9]

Table 4.1: **Public Elementary and Secondary School Funding 1919–20—1998–99**

Year	Federal government (millions $)	State governments (millions $)	Local sources, including intermediate[a] (millions $)
1919–20	$2	$160	$808
1929–30	7	354	1,728
1939–40	40	684	1,536
1949–50	156	2,166	3,116
1959–60	652	5,768	8,327
1969–70	3,220	16,063	20,985
1979–80	9,504	45,349	42,029
1989–90	12,701	98,239	97,608
1990–91	13,776	105,325	104,240
1995–96	19,104	136,671	131,928
1996–97	20,081	146,434	138,537
1997–98	22,202	157,645	146,129
1998–99	24,522	169,298	153,510

Percent of funding

Year	Federal government	State governments	Local sources, including intermediate[a]
1919–20	0.3%	16.5%	83.2%
1929–30	0.4	16.9	82.7
1939–40	1.8	30.3	68.0
1949–50	2.9	39.8	57.3
1959–60	4.4	39.1	56.5
1969–70	8.0	39.9	52.1
1979–80	9.8	46.8	43.4
1989–90	6.1	47.1	46.8
1990–91	6.2	47.2	46.7
1995–96	6.6	47.5	45.9
1996–97	6.6	48.0	45.4
1997–98	6.8	48.4	44.8
1998–99	7.1	48.7	44.2

Source: Thomas D. Snyder, ed., *Digest of Education Statistics, 2001* (Washington, DC: U.S. Department of Education, National Center for Education Statistics, 2002), table 157, p. 178.
Note: a. Includes a relatively small amount from nongovernmental private sources (gifts and tuition and transportation fees from patrons). These sources accounted for 2.5% of total revenues in 1998–99.

Figure 4.1: **Public School Funding Sources**
1919–20—1998–99

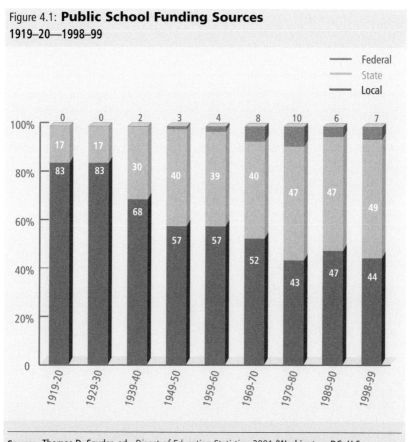

Source: Thomas D. Snyder, ed., *Digest of Education Statistics, 2001* (Washington, DC: U.S. Department of Education, National Center for Education Statistics, 2002), table 157, p. 178.

With their increased funding, federal and state agencies have become more involved with administrative and legislative decision making—as one would expect. Supervision is gradually moving from the local community to state capitals and the U.S. Department of Education. Coincident with the reduction in local funding has come a reduction in the number of school districts.[10] One disadvantage, however, is that top-down imposition of rules leads to less flexibility and less ability to mold, shape, on the part of local school boards, families, and the community. Furthermore, a distant locus of decision making often requires extensive reporting and paperwork, adding to administrative costs.

Efficiency and economies of scale are clearly important in a large education system. The decline in local funding distances families from involvement in their children's education, and the added bureaucracy associated with state and federal funding draws school boards' and educators' attention away from teaching, as they must be more responsive to legislators and administrators in state capitals and Washington, D.C.

▶ PROPOSITION: INCREASED PER-PUPIL EXPENDITURES HAVE NOT BEEN MATCHED BY IMPROVED STUDENT PERFORMANCE.

There is a common perception that the way to improve our failing public schools is simply to spend more money on them. According to many public school administrators, the amount we spend per pupil is an excellent way to predict student performance, yet a review of the data for the last 80 years shows clearly that there is not a strong correlation between increased spending and improvements in student performance. In fact, increases in per-pupil expenditures in the past have often not been matched by better student performance. In short, the evidence suggests that we cannot simply buy better schools.

Spending per student has increased markedly over time. According to the U.S. Department of Education, in the 1919–20 school year, expenditures per pupil, in constant 2000–2001 dollars, were $367. By 1960, real expenditures had more than quintupled. In the 2000–2001 school year, per pupil expenditures were approximately $7,000—nearly 20 times as high as in the 1919–20 school year. (See table 4.2.)[11]

Table 4.2: **Per-Pupil Expenditures**
1919–20—2000–01

School year	Current expenditures per pupil in fall enrollment[a]
1919–20	$367
1929–30	734
1939–40	957
1949–50	1,380
1959–60	2,088
1969–70	3,482
1979–80	4,710
1989–90	6,402
1999–00	7,045[b]
2000–01	7,079[b]

Source: Thomas D. Snyder, ed., *Digest of Education Statistics, 2001* (Washington, DC: U.S. Department of Education, National Center for Education Statistics, 2002), table 167, p. 191.
Notes: Data for 1919–20 to 1949–50 are based on school-year enrollment.
a. Constant 2000–2001 dollars, based on the Consumer Price Index, prepared by the Bureau of Labor Statistics, U.S. Department of Labor, adjusted to a school-year basis.
b. Estimated.

Where have the resources gone, and what are the results? Special education is often cited as a primary contributor to increased per-pupil costs. Although special education has grown rapidly in recent years (approximately 13 percent of students are now designated as special education students) and per-pupil expenditures for special education are more than twice the cost of regular education, these expenditures and their growth still do not explain the majority of the increase in school spending. Cost data on special education are difficult to track, but according to recent estimates, special education student expenditures explained less than 20 percent of expenditure growth between 1980 and 1990.[12]

However, it is clear that there are three additional factors that have contributed to increased expenditures: (1) falling pupil-teacher ratios (i.e., more teachers), (2) rising teacher salaries, and (3) growth in expenditures for things other than instructional salaries.[13]

Between 1970 and 1995, per-pupil expenditures increased by more than three-fourths. During that time period, the pupil-teacher ratio decreased by one-quarter, the percentage of teachers with advanced degrees doubled, and the median number of years of a teacher's experience nearly doubled. With more teachers in the system, and with teacher pay linked to increases in credentials and experience, higher per-pupil spending resulted. Furthermore, between the 1969–70 school year and 1995–96 school year, "administration expenditures" increased by more than 80 percent, and "other school services" accounted for nearly 18 percent of total public education expenditures, nearly tripling. (See table 4.3.)[14]

Table 4.3: **Descriptive Statistics, U.S. Public Schools 1970 & 1995**

Aspect	1970	1995
Real expenditure per pupil (2000–2001 $)	$3,713.00	$6,447.00
Pupil-teacher ratio	22.3	17.3
Teachers with at least a master's degree	27.5%	56.2%
Median teacher experience	8 years	15 years
Administration expenditures (as % of total education $)	3.9%	7.1%
Other school services (as % of total education $)	6.3%	17.4%

Sources: Eric Hanushek, "Spending on Schools," in *A Primer on America's Schools,* ed. Terry M. Moe (Stanford, CA: Hoover Institution Press, 2001); Thomas D. Snyder, ed., *Digest of Education Statistics, 2001* (Washington, DC: U.S. Department of Education, National Center for Education Statistics, 2002), tables 167, p. 191.

More teachers with advanced degrees and more experience and more teachers per student should lead to better educational outcomes. The evidence, however, does not support that conclusion. During the same quarter-century that these educational resources were being increased, student achievement remained flat. (See table 4.4.)

Table 4.4: **Student Achievement**
U.S. Public Schools, 1970s & 1996

	1970s	1996
Average NAEP reading score, 17-year-olds (1971)	285.2	287.6
Average NAEP math score, 17-year-olds (1973)	304.0	307.2
Average NAEP science score, 17-year-olds (1970)	305.0	295.7

Sources: Eric Hanushek, "Spending on Schools," in *A Primer on America's Schools,* ed. Terry M. Moe (Stanford, CA: Hoover Institution Press, 2001); Thomas D. Snyder, ed., *Digest of Education Statistics, 2001* (Washington, DC: U.S. Department of Education, National Center for Education Statistics, 2002), tables 112, 124, 130, pp. 133, 143, 149.

The contradiction of increasing resources and flat achievement suggests that resource shortages may not have been the sole culprit for low levels of student performance. This is not to say that resources do not matter, but that there is no simple cause-and-effect relationship between resources and results.

Recent studies reinforce the disconnect between spending and achievement. For example, the American Legislative Exchange Council's (ALEC) *Report Card on American Education: A State-by-State Analysis 1976–2000,* concluded, "It is clear after studying the data and results that the policies of the past have failed to meet the educational needs of our country's children. If we continue to spend more money on the existing educational system in an attempt to buy our way to better student achievement, we will condemn another generation of students to mediocrity."[15]

The ALEC study showed no significant correlation between conventional measures of educational inputs (such as expenditures per pupil and teacher salaries) and educational outputs (such as scores on standardized tests). Stated simply, increased funding does not translate into improved achievement. (See figure 4.2.)[16]

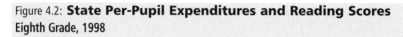

Figure 4.2: **State Per-Pupil Expenditures and Reading Scores** Eighth Grade, 1998

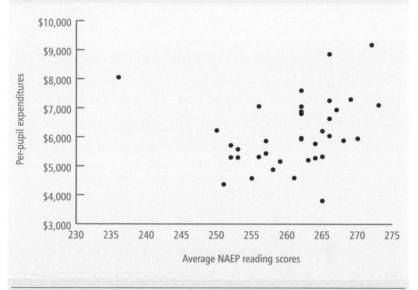

Average NAEP reading scores

Source: National Center for Policy Analysis, "Alec Study: Increased Education Spending Doesn't Improve Performance," *Daily Policy Digest* (23 April, 2001), available online at http://www.ncpa.org. **Note:** Some states not indicated due to data inavailability.

An analysis of per-pupil expenditures on a state-by-state basis is illuminating. There is little evidence to suggest that equalizing resources between any two states would equalize achievement. For example, in the 1998–99 school year, Utah spent $3,807 per pupil (ranking 51st, the least of any state plus D.C.), whereas Maryland spent $7,059 (ranking 13th). In the 1998 National Assessment of Educational Progress, 31 percent of Utah's eighth-graders scored at "proficient" or better in reading; despite the large discrepancy in per-pupil expenditures, Maryland had the same percentage of eighth-graders who scored at or above proficient, 31 percent.[17]

Also, based on several standardized tests, the ALEC report rated Iowa (ranked 32nd in per-pupil expenditures) as having the top-performing public elementary and secondary schools in the nation, followed by Minnesota (ranked 14th in spending) and Wisconsin (ranked 9th). At the bottom of the achievement ratings were Mississippi (ranked 50th in per-pupil expenditures), Washington, D.C. (ranked 5th), and Louisiana (ranked 39th). (See table 4.5.)[18]

Table 4.5: **Achievement Rankings and Per-Pupil Expenditures**
Selected States, 1998

State	Achievement ranking	Expenditure ranking	Actual per-pupil expenditure[a]	Average NAEP reading score (eighth grade)
Low expenditure states				
Utah	12	51	$3,807	265
Mississippi	35	50	4,377	251
Alabama	31	49	4,584	255
North Dakota	na	48	4,597	na
Arizona	23	47	4,598	261
High expenditure states				
District of Columbia	37	5	8,055	236
Alaska	na	4	8,842	na
New York	7	3	8,860	266
Connecticut	2	2	9,184	272
New Jersey	na	1	9,703	na

Source: National Center for Policy Analysis, "Alec Study: Increased Education Spending Doesn't Improve Performance," *Daily Policy Digest* (23 April, 2001), available online at http://www.ncpa.org.
Notes: District of Columbia counted as though a state.
Iowa had the highest NAEP eighth-grade math scores in 1992 and 1996. Iowa's 1998 per-pupil expenditures were $5,725.
There were no data available for eighth-grade reading scores in 1998.
a. Adjusted to 1998–99 dollars.

Expenditures per student have increased over time, and the distribution of the expenditures has been according to popular emphasis: The level of teacher education has increased, teacher experience has increased, and student-teacher ratios have fallen. The last 3 decades, however, do not reflect the desired outcomes—as noted, student achievement has remained flat.

If increased resources are not at the heart of improved student achievement, what is? One possible answer is that resources need to be allocated differently rather than simply increased. Spending more money on teaching and less on other things might be a step in the right direction. Severing the link between teacher compensation and their resumes may be another. For example, the present teacher pay system provides no way to distinguish between a good teacher and a bad teacher. Both can expect the same salary and promotion pattern, regardless of whether the performance of their students is mediocre or outstanding. This is true for most everyone currently employed in the public education system. The evidence suggests that additional resources alone are not the sole solution to poor student achievement; a reallocation of those resources is necessary, as well.

▶ PROPOSITION: EXPENDITURES MAY NOT MATTER AS MUCH AS COST ALLOCATION.

Of late, focus on the amount of resources invested in education has increased. The spotlight is due, in part, to growing economic competition between nations. To compete globally, a well-educated workforce is essential. Nations seek to ensure that they invest sufficient resources in their educational systems to create a workforce that is educated and technically sophisticated.

Investment in education is measured by aggregate investment in education, spending per student, and sources and uses of education funds. Measuring education expenditures as a percentage of gross domestic product (GDP) is often used to determine a country's "fiscal effort" in support of education or, put differently, a country's financial commitment to education relative to other functions and activities in the economy. Compared to other developed nations, in 1999, the United States fell in the middle of the total public direct expenditures on education distribution, allocating 3.5 percent of GDP for public and private primary and secondary education. (See table 4.6.)[19]

Table 4.6: **Educational Expenditures**
Primary, Secondary, and Postsecondary Nontertiary Education, Selected Countries, 1999

Country	Education expenditure as percentage of GDP
Australia	3.8%
Austria	4.1
Belgium	3.5
Canada[a]	3.5
Czech Republic	3.0
Denmark	4.8
Finland	3.8
France	4.2
Germany	3.0
Greece	2.4
Hungary	2.9
Ireland	3.1
Italy	3.2
Japan[b]	2.7
Korea	3.2
Mexico	3.1
Netherlands	3.1
New Zealand	4.8
Norway	4.3
Poland	3.6
Portugal	4.2
Slovak Republic	3.0
Spain	3.3
Sweden	5.1
Switzerland	4.0
Turkey	2.9
United Kingdom	3.3
United States[a]	**3.5**
28-country mean	**3.5**

Source: Organisation for Economic Co-operation and Development, *Education at a Glance: OECD Indicators, 2002* (Paris: Organisation for Economic Co-operation and Development, 2002), available online at http://www.oecd.org/EN/document/0,,EN-document-604-5-no-27-35364-604,00.html.
Notes: a. Postsecondary nontertiary is counted as tertiary education and excluded from figures for primary, secondary, and postsecondary nontertiary education.
b. Excludes public subsidies to the private sector. Postsecondary nontertiary is counted as both upper secondary and tertiary education.

Education expenditures per student measure the quantity of resources that a country devotes, on average, to each student's education.[20] The United States is ranked near the top in expenditures per pupil in public and private primary and secondary grades. Expenditures per pupil for primary grades averaged

$6,582 in 1999, 3rd out of 26 countries. Expenditures per pupil for secondary grades averaged $8,157 in 1999, 3rd out of 26 nations. (See table 4.7 and figure 4.3.)[21]

Table 4.7: **Educational Expenditures per Student**
Selected Countries, Public and Private Institutions, 1999

Country	Primary	Secondary
Australia	$4,858	$6,850
Austria	6,568	8,504
Belgium	3,952	6,444
Canada	5,981	5,981
Czech Republic	1,769	3,449
Denmark	6,721	7,626
Finland	4,138	5,863
France	4,139	7,152
Germany	3,818	6,603
Greece[a]	2,176	2,904
Hungary[a]	2,179	2,368
Ireland	3,018	4,383
Italy[a]	5,354	6,518
Japan	5,240	6,039
Korea	2,838	3,419
Mexico	1,096	1,480
Netherlands[b]	4,162	5,670
Norway[a]	5,920	7,628
Poland[a]	1,888	1,583
Portugal	3,478	5,181
Slovak Republic	1,811	2,163
Spain	3,635	4,864
Sweden	5,736	5,911
Switzerland[a]	6,663	9,756
United Kingdom	3,627	5,608
United States[c]	**6,582**	**8,157**
26-country mean	**4,129**	**5,465**

Source: Organisation for Economic Co-operation and Development, *Education at a Glance: OECD Indicators, 2002* (Paris: Organisation for Economic Co-operation and Development, 2002), available online at http://www.oecd.org/EN/document/0,,EN-document-604-5-no-27-35364-604,00.html.
Notes: Annual expenditure on educational institutions per student, based on full-time equivalents in U.S. dollars converted using PPPs.
a. Public institutions only.
b. Public and government-dependent private institutions only.
c. Public and independent private institutions only.

Figure 4.3: **Per-Pupil Expenditures**
Public and Private Institutions, Selected Countries, 1999

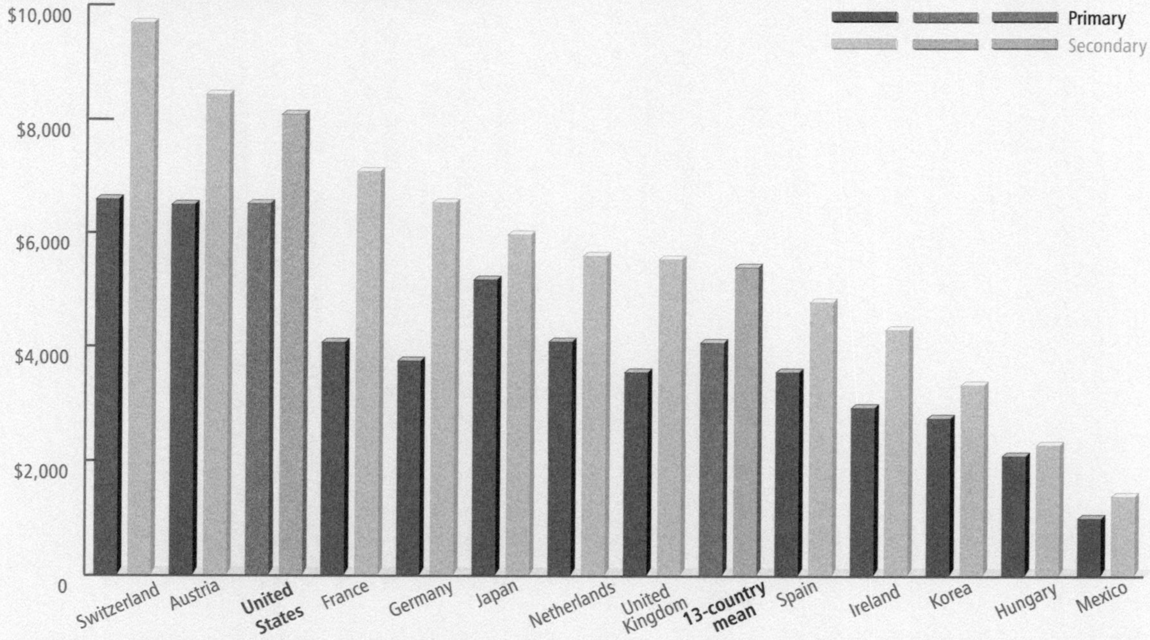

Source: Organisation for Economic Co-operation and Development, *Education at a Glance: OECD Indicators, 2002* (Paris: Organisation for Economic Co-operation and Development, 2002), available online at http://www.oecd.org/EN/document/0,,EN-document-604-5-no-27-35364-604,00.html.
Note: Both public and private institutions.

In the United States, debate has raged over the extent to which education expenditures are related to educational outcomes. Research linking school expenditures to student outcomes has been mixed. The United States' fourth-grade students are ranked in the top third in math and science, according to the 1995 TIMSS results. Eighth-grade students are ranked just below the top 50 percent. By the twelfth grade, U.S. students have fallen to the bottom quartile in rankings. Compared to other nations, on average, the United States actually spends more per pupil at the secondary level, yet its achievement ranking there is far lower than its ranking at the fourth- or eighth-grade levels.[22]

One element that may shed some light on the relationship between expenditures and achievement is the apportionment of resources. Denmark and the United States allocate more than 20 percent of staff expenditures to personnel other than teachers. At the other extreme, Belgium and Iceland allocate only 2 percent and 4 percent, respectively. This difference most likely reflects the degree to which educational personnel specialize in nonteaching activities (guidance counselors, bus drivers, school nurses, maintenance workers, etc.), as well as the relative salaries of teaching and nonteaching personnel. At times, the distinction between teaching and nonteaching personnel can be difficult to define; therefore, differences between nations should be interpreted with caution.[23] However, in the United States, there has been a clear shift in allocation. In 1950, 70 percent of instructional staff were teachers. By 1980, only 52 percent of public elementary and secondary instructional staff were teachers; percentages have remained relatively flat since 1980.[24] If it is agreed that teachers are the most important input to students' performance in the classroom, then when it comes to expenditures, perhaps a more important question is not how much is spent but how it is spent. (See table 4.8 and figure 4.4.)

Table 4.8: **Educational Expenditures**
By Resource Category, Selected Countries, Public and Private Institutions, 1999

| Country | % of total expenditures | | % of current expenditures | |
	Current	Capital	Staff compensation, all	Other current
Australia	93.7%	6.3%	71.9%	28.1%
Austria	93.5	6.5	81.2	18.8
Belgium	97.2	2.8	79.1	20.9
Canada[a]	96.4	3.6	76.8	23.2
Czech Republic	91.9	8.1	62.1	37.9
Denmark	95.1	4.9	75.3	24.7
Finland	92.9	7.1	68.9	31.1
France	91.4	8.6	78.6	21.4
Germany	92.3	7.7	88.8	11.2
Greece[b]	85.8	14.2	96.4	3.6
Hungary[b]	92.6	7.4	75.2	24.8
Ireland[b]	92.2	7.8	84.9	15.9
Italy[b]	94.8	5.2	80.2	19.8
Japan[a]	87.6	12.4	88.1	11.9
Korea	85.6	14.4	83.8	16.2
Mexico[b]	97.6	2.4	94.9	5.1
Netherlands[c]	95.7	4.3	75.9	24.1
Norway	86.3	13.7	82.3	17.7
Poland[b]	92.7	7.3	74.9	25.1
Portugal	95.4	4.6	93.7	6.3
Slovak Republic	96.8	3.2	77.4	22.6
Spain	93.9	6.1	85.6	14.4
Sweden	na	na	61.8	38.2
Switzerland[b]	90.4	9.6	85.3	14.7
Turkey[b]	80.6	19.4	96.8	3.2
United Kingdom	93.9	6.1	67.2	32.8
United States[a,b]	88.1	11.9	82.3	17.7
Country mean	92.1	7.9	80.3	19.7

Source: Organisation for Economic Co-operation and Development, *Education at a Glance: OECD Indicators, 2002* (Paris: Organisation for Economic Co-operation and Development, 2002), available online at http://www.oecd.org/EN/document/0,,EN-document-604-5-no-27-35364-604,00.html.
Notes: a. Postsecondary nontertiary counted as both upper secondary and tertiary education.
b. Public institutions only.
c. Public and government-dependent private institutions only.

Figure 4.4: **Distribution of Current Expenditures**
Selected Countries, 1999

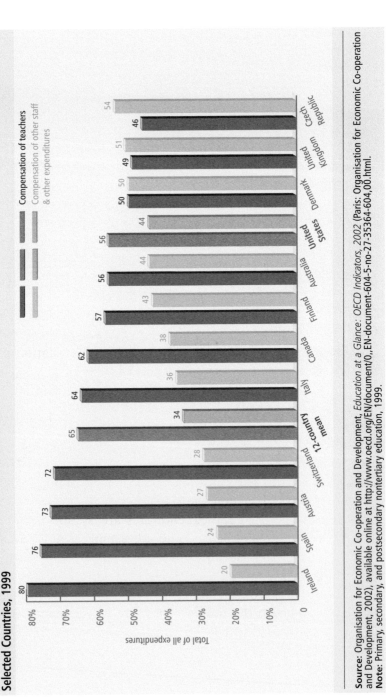

Source: Organisation for Economic Co-operation and Development, *Education at a Glance: OECD Indicators, 2002* (Paris: Organisation for Economic Co-operation and Development, 2002), available online at http://www.oecd.org/EN/document/0,,EN-document-604-5-no-27-35364-604,00.html.
Note: Primary, secondary, and postsecondary nontertiary education, 1999.

▶ PROPOSITION: SPECIAL EDUCATION IS AN EXPENDITURE, STAFFING, AND CLASSROOM CONUNDRUM.

Special education is an emotional, controversial issue in education politics today. Special education legislation, which traditionally includes the Individuals with Disabilities Education Act (IDEA) of 1968 and the Education for All Handicapped Children Act (EAHCA) of 1975, sought to ensure that all children have available to them an appropriately free education designed to meet their unique and special needs. Disagreements regarding who is responsible for providing special education, however—local, state, or national government—have made it difficult to evaluate and determine special education's effectiveness.

A look at the origins of special education legislation provides some insight into current ambiguities. When the EAHCA became public law on November 29, 1975, for example, the maximum federal grant to which a state was entitled for special education costs was 40 percent of per pupil expenditures. The starting multiplier, however, was 5 percent; the maximum, 40 percent, was to be reached by 1982. The grant was computed as a predetermined percentage of the average per-pupil expenditure in public elementary and secondary schools.[25] If, for example, average per-pupil expenditures are $7,000 per pupil, then the federal government would contribute at most $2,800 per child. Many feel that the federal government has not lived up to its commitment; the federal government multiplier for the year 2001 was approximately 15 percent, not even close to 40 percent.[26] Although the funding structure was amended in the 1997 renewal of IDEA, the commitment to maximize the multiplier at 40 percent was not removed. (See figure 4.5.)[27]

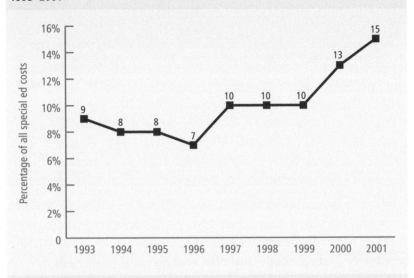

Figure 4.5: **Proportional Special Education Expenditures Paid by the Federal Government**
1993–2001

Source: American Association of School Administrators, AASA Leadership for Learning, *AASA Proposal to Make IDEA Funding Mandatory* (Arlington, VA: American Association of School Administrators, 2001), available online at http://www.aasa.org.

In contrast, even after signing the EAHCA in 1975, President Ford made this statement:

> Unfortunately, this bill promises more than the Federal Government can deliver, and its good intentions could be thwarted by the many unwise provisions it contains. Even the strongest supporters of this measure know as well as I that they are falsely raising the expectations of the groups affected by claiming authorization levels which are excessive and unrealistic. Despite my strong support for full educational opportunities for our

School Figures: The Data behind the Debate

handicapped children, the funding levels proposed in this bill will simply not be possible. There are many features in the bill which I believe to be objectionable and which should be changed. It contains a vast array of detailed, complex, and costly administrative requirements which would unnecessarily assert Federal control over traditional State and local government functions. Fortunately, since the provisions of this bill will not become fully effective until fiscal year 1978, there is time to revise the legislation and come up with a program that is effective and realistic.[28]

Revisions have been made to the bill; however, they have not been the revisions that President Ford considered necessary. President Ford's fears were not unfounded; the very same debates regarding scope and effectiveness still exist today.

Designations

Since the mid-'70s, there has been a marked increase in the number of students classified as needing special education. As general public school enrollment decreased, special education designations increased. Between 1977 and 2000, the number of disabled students[29] increased as a percentage of total public school enrollment from 8.3 percent to more than 13 percent.[30] More specifically, the number of students with learning disabilities, a specific classification of special education, increased markedly. In the 1976–77 school year, nearly 22 percent of all students with disabilities served by federally supported programs were classified as having specific learning disabilities; in 2000, nearly half were classified as such, more than doubling the percentage of students with specific learning disabilities. (See table 4.9 and figures 4.6 and 4.7.)[31]

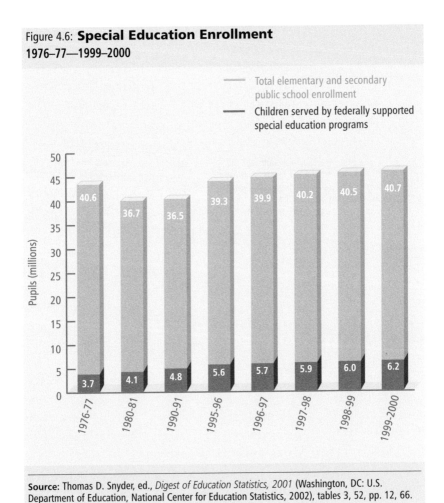

Figure 4.6: **Special Education Enrollment** 1976–77—1999–2000

——— Total elementary and secondary public school enrollment

——— Children served by federally supported special education programs

Source: Thomas D. Snyder, ed., *Digest of Education Statistics, 2001* (Washington, DC: U.S. Department of Education, National Center for Education Statistics, 2002), tables 3, 52, pp. 12, 66.

School Figures: The Data behind the Debate

Table 4.9: **Special Education**
By Disability Category, 1977 & 2000

Disability	% of total public school enrollment (K–12)	
	1977[a]	2000[b]
All disabilities	**8.32%**	**13.22%**
Specific learning disabilities	1.80	6.05
Speech impairments	2.94	2.30
Mental retardation	2.17	1.28
Serious emotional disturbances	0.64	1.00
Physical	0.81	1.35
Preschool designations	na	1.24

Source: Thomas D. Snyder, ed., *Digest of Education Statistics, 2001* (Washington, DC: U.S. Department of Education, National Center for Education Statistics, 2002), table 52, p. 66.
Notes: Percentages may not sum to totals due to rounding.
Numbers are based on the enrollment in public schools, kindergarten through 12th grade, including a relatively small number of prekindergarten (preschool) students.
Includes students served under Chapter 1 and IDEA, formerly the Education of the Handicapped Act. Prior to October 1994, children and youth with disabilities were served under IDEA, Part B, and Chapter 1 of the ESEA. In October 1994, Congress passed the Improving America's Schools Act, in which funding for children and youth with disabilities was consolidated under IDEA, Part B.
a. Data include children ages 0–21 served under Chapter 1.
b. Data reflect children ages 3–21 served under IDEA, Part B.

Figure 4.7: **Proportion of Students with Disabilities**
1976–77—1999–2000

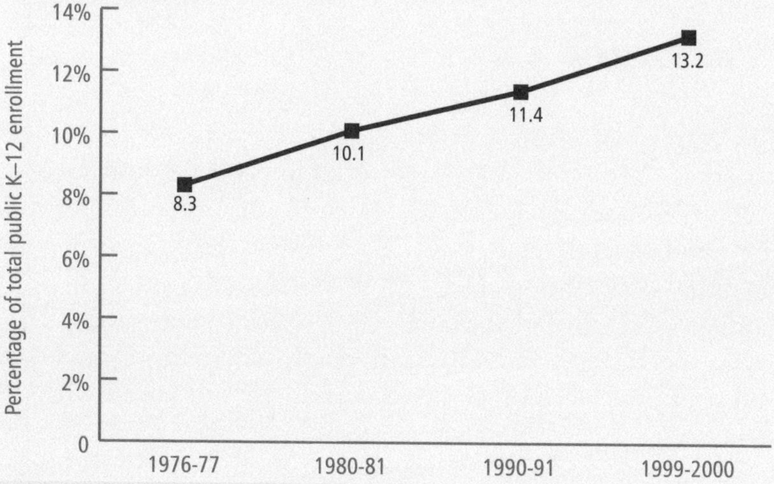

Source: Thomas D. Snyder, ed., *Digest of Education Statistics, 2001* (Washington, DC: U.S. Department of Education, National Center for Education Statistics, 2002), table 52, p. 66.
Note: Includes a relatively small number of prekindergarten students.

The reason for the overall increases in special education designations has been hotly debated. Some critics have questioned whether the number of students being labeled "disabled" has increased substantially in order for school districts to obtain extra funding or to provide an excuse for poorly performing students. Studies have shown that among some children with reading disabilities, for example, there are severe discrepancies between their IQs and achievement; that is, their IQs indicate they should be performing substantially better.[32] Others practitioners have proposed that two primary factors have contributed to the documented increases in learning disabilities, (1) The field of learning disabilities is relatively new, and with each new year, experts become more adept at recognizing learning disabilities; and (2) higher levels of poverty and substance abuse among pregnant women lead to more children born with disabilities.[33]

Personnel

The implementation of IDEA and subsequent laws often required a structural overhaul of administrative and teaching systems, in addition to expanded staff and programs, to meet more and stricter regulations. As a result, the relative number of special education teachers grew much more rapidly than the number of children classified as disabled. For example, in 1977, there were 331,453 staff employed to provide special education and related services for children and youth with disabilities; in 1997 there were nearly 808,000, a 144 percent increase.[34] In contrast, the number of children served in federally supported programs for the disabled increased from 3,692,000 to 5,904,000.[35] Although a marked increase

(60 percent), it certainly does not match the growth in personnel over the same time period. The ratio of the number of students with disabilities per special education teacher serving them has consistently decreased, as well, of course; in 1977, it was 21.0 to 1 (versus 19.7 to 1 mainstream); in 1997, it was less than 16.0 to 1 (versus 16.8 mainstream).[36] Furthermore, the primary growth in personnel for special education students has occurred in staff other than teachers,[37] a 44 percent increase between 1992 and 1997 alone. In comparison, the number of special education teachers increased 11 percent during the same time period.[38]

Expenditures

Since the passage of IDEA, the costs of special education have risen consistently. The average cost per student for special education is approximately 2.3 times the cost for a regular education.[39] The average per-pupil expenditures for a traditional public school student in the 2000–2001 school year was more than $7,000, which translates to per-pupil special education expenditures of approximately $16,000.[40] Nationwide expenditures are difficult to determine; however, in 1977, nationwide special education funding was estimated at $5 billion; in the 2000–2001 school year, local education agencies, state education agencies, and Congress spent an estimated $54.4 billion on special education, a whopping tenfold increase.[41]

Some critics of special education growth have actually argued that special education expenditures are to blame for overall public school expenditure increases. It is important to remember that although increases in special education funding have been significant at the federal level, between the period of

1980 and 1990, the increases explain less than 20 percent of total public school expenditure growth; it is not the sole source of public school expenditure increases.[42]

Special education presents many questions and few quick answers. The diverging viewpoints surrounding legislation at inception are a foreshadowing of current confusion and disagreement. Few comprehensive assessments of special education programs exist, therefore leaving the question of effectiveness unanswered. For example, there are presently no comprehensive and accurate data sources that indicate what public schools in the United States are spending on special education services and what corresponding measurable outcomes there are.[43] Without proper substantiation, special education will continue to be a conundrum wrought with confusing results.

School Figures: The Data behind the Debate

PROPOSITION: WHEN IT COMES TO ACHIEVEMENT, THE LARGEST SOURCE OF FEDERAL AID TO ELEMENTARY AND SECONDARY SCHOOLS HAS NOT MADE A BIT OF DIFFERENCE.

Title I of the Elementary and Secondary Education Act (ESEA), 1965, is at the heart of the federal government's role in education. Its annual appropriation of approximately $9.5 billion makes up more than one-third (38 percent)[44] of the Department of Education's elementary and secondary education budget each year.[45] It is by far the largest source of federal aid to elementary and secondary schools. With an ambitious goal to close the achievement gap between advantaged and disadvantaged students, Title I has sent more than $130 billion to local school districts over the past 3 decades.

Despite this extensive investment, there is scant evidence that these specially designated funds have helped the department achieve its stated goals. Title I is far reaching in scope. The program provides support services to students in schools under two basic models: (1) targeted assistance, which provides specific students with instructional or support services, (2) and the schoolwide approach, which provides funds to an individual school when at least 50 percent of the students in that school are eligible for a free or reduced-price lunch under the U.S. Department of Agriculture's Child Nutrition Program. In the 1997–98 school year, more than 12.3 million public school students were recipients of Title I funds. In the same year, 48,000 schools participated in the Title I program either as schoolwide participants or through targeted assistance. This was more than 50 percent of public schools nationwide. Some 19,000 schools reported operating schoolwide programs, a

28 percent increase from the previous school year. (See table 4.10 and figures 4.8 and 4.9.)[46]

Table 4.10: **Title I Participation**
Public Schools, 1979–80—1997–98

Year	Total student recipients[a]	Schoolwide programs[b]
1979–80	4,973,708	na
1980–81	4,862,308	na
1981–82	4,434,447	na
1982–83	4,270,424	na
1983–84	4,381,975	na
1984–85	4,528,177	na
1985–86	4,611,948	na
1986–87	4,594,761	na
1987–88	4,808,030	na
1988–89	4,777,643	na
1989–90	5,014,617	na
1990–91	5,252,141	na
1991–92	5,594,718	na
1992–93	6,042,849	2,806
1993–94	6,198,095	3,903
1994–95	6,392,372	5,050
1995–96[c]	na	na
1996–97	11,050,384	14,982
1997–98	12,306,900	19,000[d]

Sources: U.S. Department of Education, Planning and Evaluation Service, *High Standards for All Students: A Report from the National Assessment of Title I on Progress and Challenges since the 1994 Reauthorization* (Washington, DC: U.S. Department of Education, January 2001); Beth Sinclair, *State ESEA Title I Participation Information for 1996–97: Summary Report* (Rockville, MD: U.S. Department of Education, 2000); U.S. Department of Education, Planning and Evaluation Service, *State ESEA Title I Participation Information for 1997–98: Summary Report* (Washington, DC: U.S. Department of Education, 1998), available online at http://www.ed.gov/offices/OUS/PES/esed/eseatitleI.html.
Notes: a. Receiving support through either targeted assistance or schoolwide. Students in schoolwide programs are included in the "Total student recipients" column.
b. Schools receiving support through schoolwide approach.
c. No state performance report was collected for the 1995–96 school year.
d. Estimate.

School Figures: The Data behind the Debate

Figure 4.8: **Title I Recipients**
Public School Students, 1980–81—1997–98

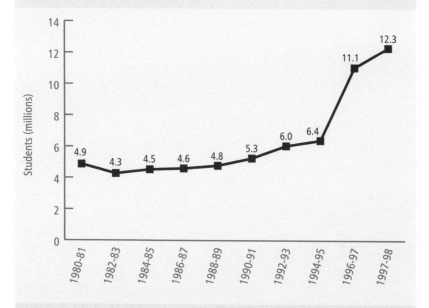

Sources: U.S. Department of Education, Planning and Evaluation Service, *High Standards for All Students: A Report from the National Assessment of Title I on Progress and Challenges since the 1994 Reauthorization* (Washington, DC: U.S. Department of Education, January 2001); Beth Sinclair, *State ESEA Title I Participation Information for 1996–97: Summary Report* (Rockville, MD: U.S. Department of Education, 2000); U.S. Department of Education, Planning and Evaluation Service, *State ESEA Title I Participation Information for 1997–98: Summary Report* (Washington, DC: U.S. Department of Education, 1998), available online at http://www.ed.gov/offices/OUS/PES/esed/eseatitlel.html.

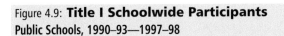

Figure 4.9: **Title I Schoolwide Participants**
Public Schools, 1990–93—1997–98

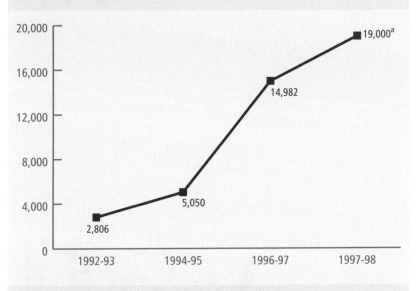

Sources: U.S. Department of Education, Planning and Evaluation Service, *High Standards for All Students: A Report from the National Assessment of Title I on Progress and Challenges since the 1994 Reauthorization* (Washington, DC: U.S. Department of Education, January 2001); Beth Sinclair, *State ESEA Title I Participation Information for 1996-97: Summary Report* (Rockville, MD: U.S. Department of Education, 2000); U.S. Department of Education, Planning and Evaluation Service, *State ESEA Title I Participation Information for 1997–98: Summary Report* (Washington, DC: U.S. Department of Education, 1998), available online at http://www.ed.gov/offices/OUS/PES/esed/eseatitleI.html.
Note: a. Estimate.

The most recent report prepared by the U.S. Department of Education's Planning and Evaluation Services stated that "trends in NAEP scores depict a widening achievement gap between high- and low-poverty schools (Title I recipients vs. non-recipients) from the late 1980s to 1999."[47] Between the period of 1973 and 1977, the same students were measured first at 9 years of age and then again at 13. The average score of the 9-year-olds compared with the average score of the same group when they reached 13 showed a 50-point improvement on the mathematics scale. Nineteen years later, a new group was tested, again first at 9 years of age and then at 13; this test group improved only 44 points.[48] Moreover, the data show, there was no marginal improvement in science or writing during the same time period; only modest improvement was recorded in reading scores. (See figure 4.10.)

Figure 4.10: **NAEP Score Value-Added Comparisons**
Public Schools, 1973–77 & 1992–96

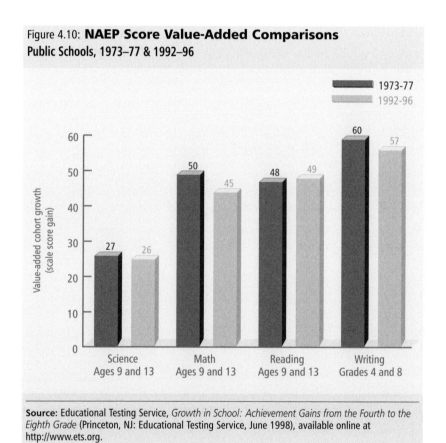

Source: Educational Testing Service, *Growth in School: Achievement Gains from the Fourth to the Eighth Grade* (Princeton, NJ: Educational Testing Service, June 1998), available online at http://www.ets.org.

The Department of Education's 2001 report revealed that the achievement gap between low- and high-poverty schools is substantial, equal to several grade levels.[49] In fact, between 1988 and 1999, the gap in reading and math NAEP scores between 9-year-old public school students in low- and high-poverty schools increased. Although high-poverty students' scores may have shown improvement, they did not improve by as much as low-poverty schools. In reading, the gap increased from 29 points to 40 points; in math, the gap increased from 20 to 29 points. (See table 4.11 and figures 4.11 and 4.12.)[50]

Table 4.11: **NAEP Scale Score Differences between Low-Poverty and High-Poverty Public Schools 1988–99**

Year	Reading	Math
1988	29	20[a]
1990	32	24
1992	30	28
1994	36	24
1996	36	21
1999	40	29

Source: U.S. Department of Education, Planning and Evaluation Service, *High Standards for All Students: A Report from the National Assessment of Title I on Progress and Challenges since the 1994 Reauthorization* (Washington, DC: U.S. Department of Education, January 2001). **Note:** a. 1986.

Figure 4.11: **Reading Performance**
By Poverty Level of Public Schools, 1988–99

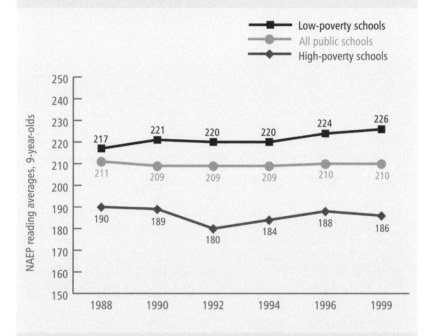

Source: U.S. Department of Education, Planning and Evaluation Service, *High Standards for All Students: A Report from the National Assessment of Title I on Progress and Challenges since the 1994 Reauthorization* (Washington, DC: U.S. Department of Education, January 2001).

Figure 4.12: **Math Performance**
By Poverty Level of Public Schools, 1988–99

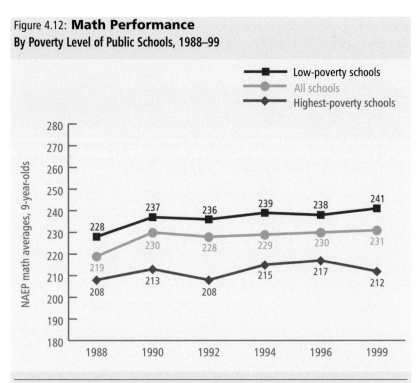

Source: U.S. Department of Education, Planning and Evaluation Service, *High Standards for All Students: A Report from the National Assessment of Title I on Progress and Challenges since the 1994 Reauthorization* (Washington, DC: U.S. Department of Education, January 2001).

The Title I program has fallen short of its achievement goals, yet it has still played a role in transforming state and local priorities. Title I has sensitized superintendents, principals, and teachers to the importance of educating the disadvantaged and proved to be a substantial source of supplemental school funding. For example, the highest-poverty districts received an average of $692 Title I funds per pupil in the 1997–98 school year. While a seemingly small percentage of total funds, Title I funds are flexible and play a significant role in supporting local education improvement efforts.[51] In 1982, Marshall Smith, former U.S. undersecretary of education, and historian Carl Kaestle wrote, "After almost two decades of intervention, the Title I program stands primarily as a symbol of national concern for the poor rather than as a viable response to their needs."[52]

In sum, the effectiveness of Title I funds remains questionable. The number of participants and the amount of funding has consistently grown, while the achievement gap between advantaged and disadvantaged students has not diminished.

▶ CHAPTER NOTES

1. Thomas D. Snyder, ed., *Digest of Education Statistics, 2001* (Washington, DC: U.S. Department of Education, National Center for Education Statistics, 2002), table 29, p. 33.
2. Ibid.
3. Organisation for Economic Co-operation and Development, *Education at a Glance: OECD Indicators, 2002* (Paris: Organisation for Economic Co-operation and Development, 2002), available online at http://www.oecd.org/EN/document/0,,EN-document-604-5-no-27-35364-604,00.html.
4. Snyder, *Digest of Education Statistics, 2001*, table 157, p. 178.
5. Ibid.
6. Organisation for Economic Co-operation and Development, *Education at a Glance: OECD Indicators, 2002.*
7. Andrew T. LeFevre and Rea S. Herman, Jr., *Report Card on American Education: A State-by-State Analysis, 1976–2000* (Washington, DC: American Legislative Exchange Council, April 2001), available online at http://www.alec.org.
8. Public Agenda Online, *Education: Major Proposals* (New York: Public Agenda Online), available online at http://www.publicagenda.org.
9. Snyder, *Digest of Education Statistics, 2001*, table 157, p. 178.
10. Ibid., table 89, p. 98.
11. Ibid., table 167, p. 191.
12. Snyder, *Digest of Education Statistics, 2001*, table 52, p. 66; Eric Hanushek and Steven Rivkin, "Understanding the Twentieth-Century Growth in U.S. School Spending," *Journal of Human Resources* 32, no. 1 (June 1996).
13. Eric Hanushek, "Spending on Schools," in *A Primer on America's Schools*, ed. Terry M. Moe (Stanford, CA: Hoover Institution Press, 2001), pp. 69–86.
14. Ibid.
15. LeFevre and Herman, *Report Card on American Education: A State-by-State Analysis, 1976–2000.*
16. Ibid.

17. National Center for Policy Analysis, "Alec Study: Increased Education Spending Doesn't Improve Performance," *Daily Policy Digest* (23 April, 2001), available online at http://www.ncpa.org.

18. Ibid.

19. Organisation for Economic Co-operation and Development, *Education at a Glance: OECD Indicators, 2002.*

20. Per-pupil expenditures are calculated by dividing total expenditures for education in the national currency by the number of full-time-equivalent (FTE) students enrolled at that education level. The result is then converted to U.S. dollars by dividing expenditures by the purchasing power parity (PPP) index between that country's currency and the U.S. dollar.

21. Organisation for Economic Co-operation and Development, *Education at a Glance: OECD Indicators, 2002.*

22. Harold W. Stevenson, "A TIMSS Primer: Lessons and Implications for U.S. Education," *Fordham Report* 2, no. 7 (Washington, DC: Thomas B. Fordham Foundation, July 1998), available online at http://www.edexcellence.net/library/stevenso.pdf.

23. Organisation for Economic Co-operation and Development, *Education at a Glance: OECD Indicators, 2002.*

24. Snyder, *Digest of Education Statistics, 2001,* table 82, p. 91.

25. Public Law 94-142, available online at http://www.thomas.loc.gov; Public Law 105-17, available online at http://www.ed.gov/offices/OSERS/IDEA/the_law.html.

26. American Association of School Administrators, AASA Leadership for Learning, *AASA Proposal to Make IDEA Funding Mandatory* (Arlington, VA: American Association of School Administrators, 2001), available online at http://www.aasa.org.

27. As of July 2000, states now receive a base allocation consisting of the amount of Section 611 funds that the state received in Federal Fiscal Year 1999. After base allocations are made, 85 percent of the remaining funds are distributed to states based on the relative populations of children ages 3 through 21 who are of the same ages as children with disabilities for whom the states ensure the availability of free appropriate public education (FAPE) under IDEA. Fifteen percent of the remaining funds are distributed to states based on the relative populations of children that fall within the age range for which the states ensure the availability of FAPE under IDEA who are living in poverty. Section 611 states, "The maximum amount of the grant a state may receive under this section for any fiscal year is ... 40 percent of the average per-pupil

expenditure in public elementary and secondary schools in the United States."

28. President Gerald R. Ford, "President Gerald R. Ford's Statement on Signing the Education for All Handicapped Children Act of 1975," speech delivered December 2, 1975, available online at http://www.ford.utexas.edu/library/speeches/750707.htm.

29. "Disabled students" includes students classified with the following: specific learning disabilities, speech or language impairments, mental retardation, serious emotional disturbance, hearing impairments, orthopedic impairments, other health impairments, visual impairments, multiple disabilities, deaf-blindness, autism and dramatic brain injury, and preschool disabled.

30. Snyder, *Digest of Education Statistics, 2001,* table 82, p. 91; U.S. Department of Education, Office of Special Education Programs, Data Analysis System (DANS), *Number of Children Served under IDEA by Disability and Age Group* (Washington, DC: U.S. Department of Education, September 2000), table AA12, available online at http://www.ideadata.org/tables/ar_aa12.htm.

31. G. Reid Lyon and Jack M. Fletcher, "Early Warning System," *Education Matters* 1, no. 2 (Stanford, CA: Hoover Institution Press, summer 2001), pp. 23–29.

32. Ibid.

33. U.S. Department of Education, *Seventeenth Annual Report to Congress on the Implementation of the Individuals with Disabilities Education Act* (Washington, DC: U.S. Department of Education, 1995), available online at http://www.ed.gov/pubs/OSEP95AnlRpt/ch1b.html.

34. U.S. Department of Education, *Twenty-second Annual Report to Congress on the Implementation of the Individuals with Disabilities Education Act* (Washington, DC: U.S. Department of Education, 2000), available online at http://www.ed.gov/offices/OSERS/OSEP2000AnlRpt/ExecSumm.html.

35. Thomas D. Snyder, ed., *Digest of Education Statistics, 1999* (Washington, DC: U.S. Department of Education, National Center for Education Statistics, 2000), table 53, p. 66.

36. U.S. Department of Education, National Center for Education Statistics, *The Condition of Education 1998* (Washington, DC: U.S. Department of Education, 1998), supplemental table 45-6, available online at http://www.nces.ed.gov/pubs98/condition98/c9845d06.html; Snyder, *Digest of Education Statistics, 1999,* table 83, p. 90.

37. "Other staff" includes school social workers, occupational therapists, recreation specialists, teacher aides, physical education teachers, supervisors, psychologists, work-study coordinators, audiologists, vocational education teachers, counselors, interpreters, speech pathologists, non-professional staff, and other professional staff.

38. U.S. Department of Education, *Seventeenth Annual Report to Congress on the Implementation of the Individuals with Disabilities Education Act*; U.S. Department of Education, *Twenty-second Annual Report to Congress on the Implementation of the Individuals with Disabilities Education Act.*

39. Hanushek, "Spending on Schools."

40. Snyder, *Digest of Education Statistics, 2001*, table 167, p. 191.

41. National Center for Policy Analysis, "Alec Study: Increased Education Spending Doesn't Improve Performance"; National Center for Policy Analysis, "Education," *Policy Digest* (January 1996), available online at http://www.ncpa.org; American Association of School Administrators, AASA Leadership for Learning, "AASA Proposal to Make IDEA Funding Mandatory."

42. Hanushek, "Spending on Schools."

43. Jay Chambers, Tom Parrish, and Joanne Lieberman, "What Are We Spending on Special Education in the U.S.?" *CSEF Brief,* no. 8 (Palo Alto, CA: Center for Special Education Finance, February 1998), available online at http://www.csef-air.org.

44. $8.6 billion goes to Part A of Title I.

45. U.S. Department of Education, Planning and Evaluation Service, *High Standards for All Students: A Report from the National Assessment of Title I on Progress and Challenges since the 1994 Reauthorization* (Washington, DC: U.S. Department of Education, January 2001).

46. U.S. Department of Education, Planning and Evaluation Service, *High Standards for All Students: A Report from the National Assessment of Title I on Progress and Challenges since the 1994 Reauthorization;* Beth Sinclair, *State ESEA Title I Participation Information for 1996–97: Summary Report* (Rockville, MD: U.S. Department of Education, 2000); U.S. Department of Education, Planning and Evaluation Service, *State ESEA Title I Participation Information for 1997–98: Summary Report* (Washington, DC: U.S. Department of Education, 1998), available online at http://www.ed.gov/offices/OUS/PES/esed/eseatitleI.html. Note: The number of schoolwide participants dramatically increased due to more lax eligibility criteria. Currently, only 50 percent of

students, instead of 75 percent, have to qualify for a free or reduced-price lunch to be eligible.

47. U.S. Department of Education, Planning and Evaluation Service, *High Standards for All Students: A Report from the National Assessment of Title I on Progress and Challenges since the 1994 Reauthorization.*

48. Educational Testing Service, *Growth in School: Achievement Gains from the Fourth to the Eighth Grade* (Princeton, NJ: Educational Testing Service, June 1998), available online at http://www.ets.org.

49. A 10-point difference in NAEP scale scores can be considered roughly equivalent to one grade level. "High-poverty schools" are defined as schools where more than 75 percent of students receive a free or reduced-price lunch. "Low-poverty schools" are defined as schools where 25 percent or fewer students receive a free or reduced-price lunch.

50. U.S. Department of Education, Planning and Evaluation Service, *High Standards for All Students: A Report from the National Assessment of Title I on Progress and Challenges since the 1994 Reauthorization.*

51. Ibid.

52. Carl Kaestle and Marshall Smith, "The Federal Role in Elementary and Secondary Education, 1940–1980," *Harvard Educational Review* 52, p. 400.

Chapter 5:
School Reform

Propositions

CRITICS OF SCHOOL CHOICE FEAR THAT THE MOST DISADVANTAGED STUDENTS WILL BE LEFT BEHIND; PRELIMINARY DATA CONTRADICT THIS ASSUMPTION.

VOUCHERS ARE BECOMING MORE POPULAR BY THE DAY, AND THEY ARE NOT A SOLUTION SOLELY SUPPORTED BY THE RICH.

CATHOLIC SCHOOLS PROVIDE HIGH MARKS AT LOW COSTS.

HOME EDUCATION IS THE FASTEST-GROWING ALTERNATIVE TO PUBLIC SCHOOLING, AND A GOOD ONE AT THAT.

THE PUSH FOR INCREASED ACCOUNTABILITY IS APPARENT, BUT BETTER SCHOOLS ARE STILL TO COME.

▶ SUMMER SCHOOL PROVIDES EVIDENCE THAT ACCOUNTABILITY IS CHANGING THE WAY WE EDUCATE.

▶ CALIFORNIA'S CLASS SIZE REDUCTION APPEARS TO BE AN EDUCATION REFORM INITIATIVE GONE BAD.

Highlights

In 1978, public school enrollment made up 89 percent of total elementary and secondary enrollment; private schools, 11 percent; and home school students, 0.03 percent. In 2000, public school enrollment made up 86 percent; private schools, 11 percent; and home school students, 3 percent.[1]

In the 2000–2001 school year, there were more than 2,300 charter schools enrolling nearly 580,000 students.[2]

Nationwide, slightly more than 50 percent of charter school students are white, compared with almost 60 percent in public schools. Charter schools are more likely to serve black, Hispanic, and Native American students than traditional public schools.[3]

In 2000, an estimated 61,525 vouchers were used in private schools, accounting for more than 1 percent of private school enrollment.[4]

A 1999 survey showed that 60 percent of African-Americans favored vouchers, a higher figure than the general public. Moreover, support swelled to 72 percent among African-Americans earning less than $15,000 a year.[5]

In New York City, Catholic high schools graduated 95 percent of their senior class each year, while the public schools graduated slightly more than 50 percent of their seniors.[6]

Attending a Catholic high school raised an inner-city student's probability of finishing high school and entering college by 17 percentage points.[7]

- Home school students' numbers are growing at an estimated 15–25 percent annually; in the year 2000, approximately 1.7 million elementary and secondary students were home-educated.[8]

- In 2000, approximately 20 states had enacted legislation requiring students to pass an assessment test with a minimum score in order to graduate from high school.[9]

- More students than ever before were enrolled in summer school in the year 2000; approximately one in five students in the nation's 53 largest urban districts attended summer school.[10]

Overview

string of presidents and major events over the past half-century have kept elementary and secondary education at the forefront of American public policy. The launch of *Sputnik* in 1957 shocked American citizens into realizing that their kids were lagging in the sciences; 25 years later, the release of *A Nation at Risk* by a blue-ribbon panel of education experts put the United States on notice for education reform; in 1994, *Goals 2000,* an aggressive piece of legislation, established eight education goals to be achieved by the year 2000—but by 2002, virtually none had been met. George Herbert Walker Bush talked of "one thousand points of light," Bill Clinton sought to become the "education President," and George W. Bush pledged to "leave no child behind." These concerns and promises, however, have led to little change in the American education system.

Sputnik no doubt shook us out of the complacency of the 1950s and made us pay more attention to teaching science. However, despite open classrooms, "modern math," whole learning, and the promises of leading politicians, performance has remained flat and in some cases has fallen. And, at the end of the day, little has changed in the classroom or in the schools.

Reform became the buzzword of the 1990s, mostly in response to the lack of progress in achievement. Parents, educators, politicians, and advocacy groups say they have waited long enough—it is time for change now.

Although not new in concept, the most highly publicized and politically polarizing reforms of the last decade have been charter schools, vouchers, and home education, particularly as they have found their way into mainstream education discussions. Nobel laureate economist Milton Friedman first proposed school vouchers in 1955. The charter school movement began in 1992. In 2000, there were more than 500,000 students enrolled in charter schools and more than 61,000 publicly and privately funded school vouchers. School choice, as these alternatives are loosely termed, is a venue for parents and schools to partner in the education process, and it is a catalyst for increased family involvement.

In the public schools, a working relationship between school and parent, however, has become increasingly difficult due to the growing education bureaucracy. The greater the bureaucracy is, the less autonomous the school and its administration. When schools and districts are too large, parents have little or no direct access to voice their concerns, and schools are less able to work with and respond to parents directly and personally. Parents have very little incentive to be involved in their children's schools when they feel they will not be heard. Many elements of school choice, however, encourage a more decentralized education style, and hence a chance for parents to be heard. Parents are voting with their feet and their dollars. Enrollment in private schools, and other alternatives to public schools where the individual schools are smaller, is at an all-time high.

Among the most telling statistics is the rise in home schooling. The number of students home schooled in 2000 was an estimated 1.7 million, a figure that dwarfs the number of students taking advantage of either publicly or privately funded vouchers or charter school enrollees. Moreover, traditional public school enrollment has decreased as a percentage of total enrollment from 89 percent to 86 percent over the last 2 decades. The percentage of home-educated students has increased as a percentage of total enrollment from virtually zero to 3 percent during the same time period.

Despite the growth of these alternatives, they have not touched many children; in fact, they have affected a surprisingly small number. In this chapter, we look to provide data on the most promising school reform options: vouchers, charter schools, and home schooling, as well as other alternatives implemented in this education reform era. We look at class size reduction, for example, an eagerly anticipated California initiative, fully within the public school system, that has cost much, yet, according to early results, accomplished little.

▶ Proposition: Critics of school choice fear that the most disadvantaged students will be left behind; preliminary data contradict this assumption.

The two most common school choices available to parents are charter schools and vouchers. In 1992, the charter school movement began. Today there are more than 2,300 charter schools, enrolling more than 575,000 students. This is nearly 1 percent of total elementary and secondary enrollment. In 1990, there were 341 public and private vouchers provided, an insignificant percentage; in 2000, there were 61,525 vouchers used in private schools, totaling more than 1 percent of private school enrollment.[11]

Critics of school choice programs invoke a two-pronged attack. First, they claim that only the best students with the most motivated parents will take advantage of charter schools and voucher programs. Presumably, the best students come from families in which parents are involved at home and at school and who partner with the school in their children's education. Second, critics contend that the flight of the best students leaves behind disproportionately large groups of chronically underperforming, special-needs, and other problem children who will drag down the rest of the students in the public schools. Teachers will thus spend inordinate amounts of time on discipline and basic skills, and administrators will be obliged to devote excessive amounts of resources to meet special needs. Some contend these two effects of choice will doom the traditional public school system to failure.

Indirect evidence to the contrary, however, has been uncovered. These data may be preliminary, but they are compelling.

Charter Schools and Demographics

Enrollment data on charter schools in the 1997–98 school year show that the demographic mix of students enrolling in charter schools is remarkably like that of students in the rest of the school system—the flight of the best and brightest, the affluent, and nonminorities is not apparent. The striking similarity of these enrollment patterns and their performance rebuts arguments that only the privileged will choose charter schools.[12]

Students' eligibility for a free or reduced-price lunch under the National School Lunch program (a measure of economic disadvantage) allows comparisons of poverty levels between students in charter schools and those in public schools. Overall, in the states that have charter schools, the total percentage of students eligible for a free or reduced-price lunch is nearly identical: 37 percent in charter schools and 38 percent in traditional public schools. (See table 5.1 and figure 5.1.)[13]

Table 5.1: **Students Eligible for Free and Reduced-Price Lunch Programs**
Selected States

| State | Charter schools (1997–98) | | All public schools (1994–95) | |
	Eligible students	Percent of all students	Eligible students	Percent of all students
Alaska	60	7.0%	32,340	25.7%
Arizona	9,640	39.4	284,357	40.1
California	17,820	35.4	2,257,008	42.4
Colorado	1,967	18.1	174,023	27.8
Connecticut	521	49.6	113,221	22.8
Florida	1,080	37.7	895,510	43.9
Georgia	3,803	29.4	501,824	40.6
Illinois	1,396	88.5	583,238	30.8
Louisiana	344	74.3	474,608	59.3
Massachusetts	2,490	45.1	225,110	25.6
Michigan	5,540	34.1	459,747	28.7
Minnesota	1,502	52.5	217,376	26.8
New Jersey	201	43.1	326,022	28.3
New Mexico	1,167	30.1	159,740	49.6
North Carolina	1,465	40.1	413,729	36.5
Pennsylvania	399	69.3	541,793	31.1
Texas	3,456	68.7	1,662,900	46.1
Wisconsin	438	27.6	210,011	24.9
Total	**53,970**	**36.7**	**10,146,087**	**37.6**

Source: National Center for Education Statistics, *The State of Charter Schools Third-Year Report* (Washington, DC: U.S. Department of Education, National Center for Education Statistics, May 1999). **Note:** The total number of students eligible for free and reduced-price lunch is based on 566 of the 619 open charter schools that responded to the survey. Of the 566 schools, 9 schools in the District of Columbia and 5 states (Delaware, Hawaii, Kansas, Rhode Island, and South Carolina) are not displayed in the table because each state has 3 or fewer charter schools and percentages are not meaningful. The "Total" row includes data from all 24 charter states, including the 6 states not included in the table.

School Figures: The Data behind the Debate

Figure 5.1: **Selected Characteristics of Charter School and Traditional Public School Students** 1997–98

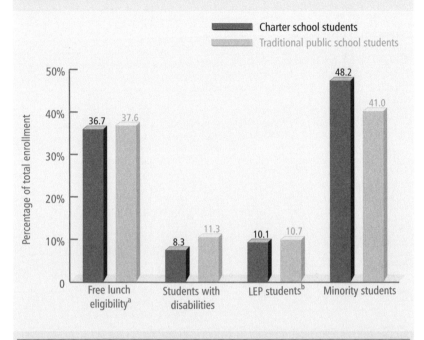

Charter school students
Traditional public school students

Percentage of total enrollment

	Charter	Traditional
Free lunch eligibility[a]	36.7	37.6
Students with disabilities	8.3	11.3
LEP students[b]	10.1	10.7
Minority students	48.2	41.0

Source: National Center for Education Statistics, *The State of Charter Schools Third-Year Report* (Washington, DC: U.S. Department of Education, National Center for Education Statistics, May 1999). **Notes:** Data comparisons are based on states with charter schools. See tables for lists of states.
a. Public school free and reduced-price lunch eligibility is based on 1994-95 data.
b. Public school LEP designation is based on 1996-97 data.

Furthermore, although charter schools are free of many of the state regulations that govern schools, they are still subject to laws requiring them to provide access to students with disabilities. In fact, some charter schools are specifically designed to serve students with disabilities. For example, during the 1997–98 school year in Florida, 25.1 percent of charter school students had disabilities, compared with 13.4 percent of traditional public school students. According to recent data, students with disabilities made up 8 percent of the population in charter schools overall, compared with 11 percent of public school students. Limited English proficiency (LEP) students are concentrated in a few states in both charter and public schools, but the percentage in both is similar, nearly 10 percent. (See tables 5.2 and 5.3.)[14]

Table 5.2: **Students with Disabilities**
Selected States, 1997–98

State	Charter schools		All public schools	
	Students	Percent of all students	Students	Percent of all students
Alaska	43	5.0%	16,005	12.1%
Arizona	1,730	7.1	75,240	9.2
California	3,576	7.1	547,309	9.6
Colorado	857	7.9	65,734	9.6
Connecticut	84	0.8	69,352	13.0
Florida	720	25.1	307,149	13.4
Georgia	1,122	8.7	133,347	9.7
Illinois	172	10.9	250,193	12.5
Louisiana	30	6.5	84,690	10.9
Massachusetts	546	9.9	148,364	15.6
Michigan	853	5.3	181,678	10.8
Minnesota	491	17.2	92,966	10.0
New Jersey	10	2.1	189,219	15.1
New Mexico	673	17.4	15,319	13.7
North Carolina	523	14.3	142,628	11.5
Pennsylvania	77	13.4	202,655	11.2
Texas	362	7.2	443,341	11.4
Wisconsin	137	8.6	100,027	11.3
Total	**12,243**	**8.3**	**3,552,284**	**11.3**

Source: National Center for Education Statistics, *The State of Charter Schools Third-Year Report* (Washington, DC: U.S. Department of Education, National Center for Education Statistics, May 1999). **Note:** The total number of students with disabilities is based on 554 of the 619 open charter schools that responded to the survey, although the exhibit does not show breakdowns for states with 3 or fewer charter schools. The percentage of students with disabilities in Florida is inflated by 1 school that reported large numbers of charter students with disabilities. Of the 554 charter schools, 10 schools in the District of Columbia and 5 states (Delaware, Hawaii, Kansas, Rhode Island, and South Carolina) are not displayed in the table because each state has 3 or fewer charter schools and percentages are not meaningful. The "Total" row includes data from all 24 charter states, including the 6 states not included in the table.

Table 5.3: **Students with Limited English Proficiency**
Selected States

| State | Charter schools (1997–98) | | All public schools (1996–97) | |
	Students	Percent of all students	Students	Percent of all students
Alaska	6	70.0%	34,942	27.7%
Arizona	1,643	6.7	93,528	11.9
California	9,208	18.3	1,381,393	24.6
Colorado	120	1.1	24,675	7.4
Connecticut	8	80.0	19,813	3.8
Florida	7	20.0	288,603	12.2
Georgia	382	30.0	14,339	1.1
Illinois	54	3.4	118,246	6.0
Louisiana	2	40.0	6,494	0.9
Massachusetts	339	6.1	44,394	4.7
Michigan	407	2.5	25,988	1.6
Minnesota	321	11.2	28,237	3.4
New Jersey	3	60.0	49,300	4.0
New Mexico	954	24.6	78,107	24.0
North Carolina	90	2.5	24,771	2.0
Pennsylvania	20	3.5	na	na
Texas	1,140	22.7	513,634	13.4
Wisconsin	22	1.4	23,270	2.6
Total	**14,856**	**10.1**	**2,814,982**	**10.7**

Source: National Center for Education Statistics, *The State of Charter Schools Third-Year Report* (Washington, DC: U.S. Department of Education, National Center for Education Statistics, May 1999). **Note:** The total number of LEP students is based on 611 of the 619 open charter schools that responded to the survey, although the exhibit does not show breakdowns for states with 3 or fewer charter schools. Of the 611 schools, 9 schools in the District of Columbia and 5 states (Delaware, Hawaii, Kansas, Rhode Island, and South Carolina) are not displayed in the table because each state has 3 or fewer charter schools and percentages are not meaningful. The "Total" row includes data from all 24 charter states, including the 6 states not included in the table.

In examining data for the states that have charter schools, slightly more than 50 percent of charter school students are white, compared with almost 60 percent in public schools. NCES concluded that charter schools are more likely to serve black, Hispanic, and Native American students, compared to traditional public schools. (See table 5.4 and figure 5.2.)[15]

Table 5.4: **Racial Composition of Charter School Students 1997–98**

| | Students | | Racial distribution | |
| | Charter schools | All public schools[a] | Charter schools | All public schools[a] |
Race				
White, not of Hispanic origin	71,943	16,367,055	51.8%	58.7%
Black, not of Hispanic origin	26,393	4,680,563	19.0	16.8
Hispanic	28,554	5,395,949	20.6	19.3
Asian or Pacific Islander	5,157	1,164,334	3.7	4.2
American Indian or Alaska Native	5,310	278,392	3.8	1.0
Other	1,578	na	1.1	na
Total	**138,935**	**27,886,307**		

Source: National Center for Education Statistics, *The State of Charter Schools Third-Year Report* (Washington, DC: U.S. Department of Education, National Center for Education Statistics, May 1999) **Note: a.** All public school students in the 24 states with charter schools.

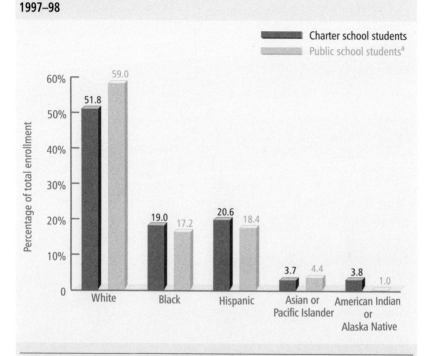

Figure 5.2: **Race and Ethnicity of Charter School and Public School Students**
1997–98

Charter school students
Public school students[a]

Percentage of total enrollment

60% — 59.0
51.8
50%
40%
30%
20% — 19.0 17.2 20.6 18.4
10%
0 — White Black Hispanic 3.7 4.4 3.8 1.0 Asian or Pacific Islander American Indian or Alaska Native

Sources: National Center for Education Statistics, *The State of Charter Schools Third-Year Report* (Washington, DC: U.S. Department of Education, National Center for Education Statistics, May 1999); National Center for Education Statistics, *The State of Charter Schools Fourth-Year Report* (Washington, DC: U.S. Department of Education, National Center for Education Statistics, January 2000).
Note: a. Only public schools in the 24 charter school states.

Large discrepancies are not apparent between charter school and public school demographics. Furthermore, based on evidence from Arizona and Michigan, competition from charter schools may actually improve public school achievement and cost less. For example, in Michigan, during the 1999–2000 school year, the average per-pupil expenditure for public school students was $7,440, compared to $6,600 for charter school students. Moreover, in Arizona, public schools exposed to charter school competition recorded dramatic improvements in test scores, two to six times more improved than those public schools that did not have competition. Michigan public schools exposed to competition from charter schools also experienced a greater improvement in test scores than those schools not exposed to competition. (See figures 5.3 and 5.4.)[16]

Figure 5.3: **Public School Performance in Response to Charter Competition**
Arizona, 2000

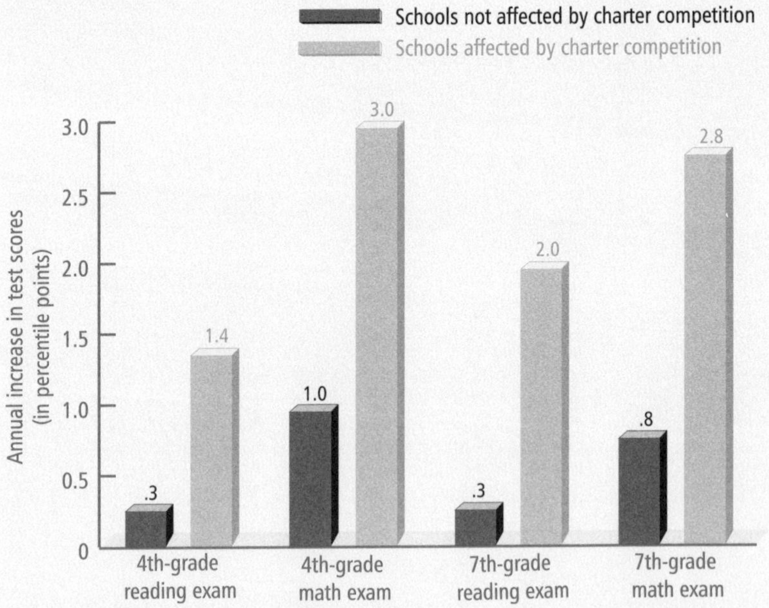

■ Schools not affected by charter competition
▨ Schools affected by charter competition

Annual increase in test scores (in percentile points)

4th-grade reading exam: .3 / 1.4	4th-grade math exam: 1.0 / 3.0	7th-grade reading exam: .3 / 2.0	7th-grade math exam: .8 / 2.8

Source: Caroline M. Hoxby, "Rising Tide," *Education Next* 1, no. 4 (Winter 2001), pp. 69–74.
Note: The difference between "Schools not affected by charter competition" and "Schools affected by charter competition" in every comparison is statistically significant at the .05 level.
Students in districts in Arizona that lost more than 6 percent of enrollment to charter schools began increasing achievement at rates greater than in schools that weren't affected by charters.

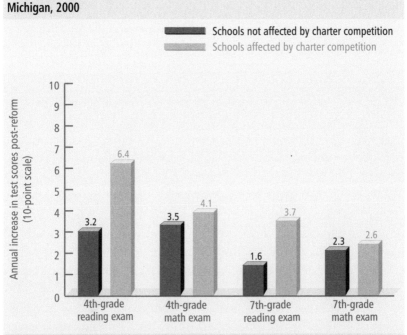

Figure 5.4: **Public School Performance in Response to Charter Competition**
Michigan, 2000

Legend:
- Schools not affected by charter competition
- Schools affected by charter competition

Y-axis: Annual increase in test scores post-reform (10-point scale)

Exam	Schools not affected	Schools affected
4th-grade reading exam	3.2	6.4
4th-grade math exam	3.5	4.1
7th-grade reading exam	1.6	3.7
7th-grade math exam	2.3	2.6

Source: Caroline M. Hoxby, "Rising Tide," *Education Next* 1, no. 4 (Winter 2001), pp. 69–74.
Notes: Charter competition occurs when a school district has lost more than 6 percent of its students to charter schools.
The difference between "Schools not affected by charter competition" and "Schools affected by charter competition" in every comparison is statistically significant at the .05 level.

Vouchers and Achievement

Over the past 10 years in the Milwaukee school system, which operates the country's longest-running publicly provided school voucher program, the performance of students has increased remarkably. In fact, their increases have outstripped those of students in the rest of the state. There may be disputes about the performance of the students who have used vouchers and left the Milwaukee public school system, but the data show that the students left behind are faring quite well. Competition to keep students and concomitant funding may be providing an incentive for the administrators and teachers in Milwaukee to pick up the pace and improve overall performance.[17]

If critics' arguments against school choice had merit, one would expect to see a decline in test scores in school districts with voucher programs because the lower-performing students had been left behind. There are some revealing data from the Milwaukee Public Schools (MPS) and the Milwaukee Parental School Choice Program. That program—in existence since 1990, when 341 students participated (approximately 0.4 percent of MPS enrollment)— expanded to include 9,638 students in the 2000–2001 school year, approximately 9.2 percent of MPS enrollment. Interestingly, as participation increased, the scores of students left behind increased, not decreased as alarmists predicted.[18]

When comparing test scores of MPS students with those from the rest of the state, students in Milwaukee showed remarkable improvement in both absolute and relative terms. In tests measuring the fourth-, eighth-, and tenth-grade levels in reading, math, science, and social studies, Milwaukee students improved in local, state, and national assessments between 1997 and 2000. The national percentile rank of Milwaukee public school fourth-grade students, for example, improved from a 36 percentile ranking to a 50 percentile ranking in math, 29 to 51 in science, and 35 to 52 in social studies. (See table 5.5 and figures 5.5, 5.6, and 5.7.)[19]

Table 5.5: Proficiency Levels of Wisconsin Public School Students

Percentage Change in Number of Students at or above Proficient Level, 1997–2000

Subject area[a]	4th grade		8th grade		10th grade	
	Milwaukee public schools	Wisconsin	Milwaukee public schools	Wisconsin	Milwaukee public schools	Wisconsin
Reading	27%	13%	56%	23%	23%	10%
Math	124	42	38	40	43	11
Science	162	40	59	18	40	21
Social studies	130	37	41	17	38	15

Source: Wisconsin Department of Public Instruction, *Wisconsin School Performance Report* (Madison: Wisconsin Department of Public Instruction), available online at http://208.170.76.100/DPI/query.asp?yr=...=3619&school=&subject.
Note: a. Based on Wisconsin Knowledge and Concepts Examination.

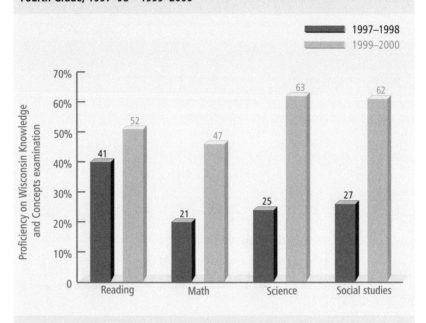

Figure 5.5: **Milwaukee Public School Students' Proficiency in Wisconsin Knowledge and Concepts Examination**
Fourth Grade, 1997–98—1999–2000

Sources: Wisconsin Department of Public Instruction, *Wisconsin School Performance Report* (Madison: Wisconsin Department of Public Instruction), available online at http://208.170.76.100/DPI/query.asp?yr=...=3619&school=&subject; Wisconsin Department of Public Instruction, School Management Services, *Milwaukee Parental Choice Program* (Madison: Wisconsin Department of Public Instruction), available online at wysiwyg://6/http://www.dpi.state.wi.us/dpi/dfm/sms/mpcxgrde.html.

Figure 5.6: **Milwaukee Public School Students' National Percentile Rankings**
Fourth Grade, 1997–98—1999–2000

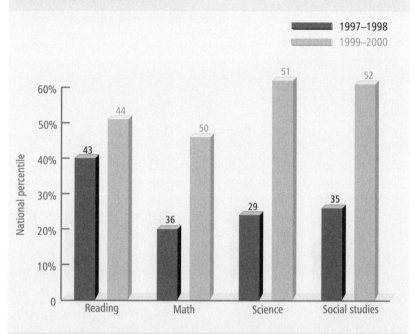

Sources: Wisconsin Department of Public Instruction, *Wisconsin School Performance Report* (Madison: Wisconsin Department of Public Instruction), available online at http://208.170.76.100/DPI/query.asp?yr=...=3619&school=&subject; Wisconsin Department of Public Instruction, School Management Services, *Milwaukee Parental Choice Program* (Madison: Wisconsin Department of Public Instruction), available online at wysiwyg://6/http://www.dpi.state.wi.us/dpi/dfm/sms/mpcxgrde.html.

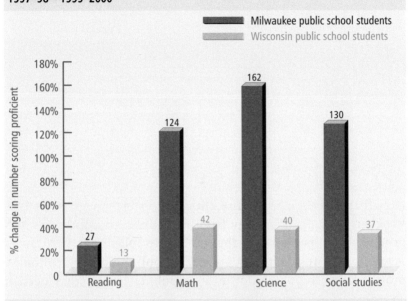

Figure 5.7: **Milwaukee and Wisconsin Public School Fourth-Grade Proficiency Comparisons**
1997–98—1999–2000

Sources: Wisconsin Department of Public Instruction, *Wisconsin School Performance Report* (Madison: Wisconsin Department of Public Instruction), available online at http://208.170.76.100/DPI/query.asp?yr=…=3619&school=&subject; Wisconsin Department of Public Instruction, School Management Services, *Milwaukee Parental Choice Program* (Madison: Wisconsin Department of Public Instruction), available online at wysiwyg://6/http://www.dpi.state.wi.us/dpi/dfm/sms/mpcxgrde.html.
Note: a. Scoring at or above proficiency level.

Milwaukee Public Schools should be applauded. Whether the improvement is due to changing pedagogy, improved academic standards, an increase in resources, or in response to competition remains to be determined.

The success or failure of school choice should be determined by results. If it were successful, all students—those that stay and those that leave the traditional public school system—would be better off, academically and otherwise. A cautious observation is that all students in Milwaukee public schools are doing better.

Proposition: Vouchers are becoming more popular by the day, and they are not a solution solely supported by the rich.

Those in favor of school choice view vouchers as a free-market solution to a failing public school system and as an opportunity to provide choice to those who have no options. In contrast, voucher foes have spent millions of dollars fighting vouchers; for them the very idea of school choice is unconstitutional and anti–public school. Despite the U.S. Supreme Court's recent ruling affirming the constitutionality of vouchers, arguments that vouchers will divert money from the public school system at a crucial time persist. In the words of National Education Association president Bob Chase, school choice is "siphoning money from the communities and public schools that need it the most."[20]

At the heart of the arguments against vouchers is the presumption of inequality, that the rich and more educated will receive even more benefits than the poor. Diminishing resources in the schools that most need them and concerns regarding "leaving children behind" are further examples of antagonists' fears.

The Milwaukee school voucher program, the nation's oldest, portrays the opposite scenario. Resources in Milwaukee public schools have increased, not decreased, and test scores have risen dramatically. In the Milwaukee public school district, from 1990 (when vouchers were introduced) to 2001, enrollment increased from nearly 93,000 to 98,000, and total spending increased from $580 million to more than $990 million. Since vouchers were introduced in Milwaukee, spending increased by nearly 70 percent in the public schools, while enrollment increased by a mere 5 percent. Furthermore, during the same time period, per-pupil expenditures increased from approximately $6,200 to $9,700, and achievement gains in the public schools are apparent. (See table 5.6.)[21]

Table 5.6: **Wisconsin Fourth-Graders Scoring at or above Proficiency on the Knowledge and Concepts Examination 1997–98—1999–2000**

Subject	1997–98	1999–2000
Reading	41%	52%
Math	21	47
Science	25	63
Social studies	27	62

Source: Wisconsin Department of Public Instruction, *Wisconsin School Performance Report* (Madison: Wisconsin Department of Public Instruction), available online at http://208.170.76.100/DPI/query.asp?yr=...=3619&school=&subject.

Moreover, many contend that voucher support is decreasing in the general public and, therefore, undesirable. To the contrary, overall voucher support, whether for public or privately funded vouchers, is on the rise, particularly among poor minorities,[22] who also show strong support for school choice in general.[23] A 1999 survey found that 60 percent of blacks favored vouchers, a higher figure than the general public. Moreover, support swelled to 72 percent among blacks earning less than $15,000 a year.[24] In addition, parents whose children attend private schools or have a choice in regard to the public school their children attend have a higher degree of satisfaction with their children's education than those parents whose children attend assigned public schools. (See figures 5.8 and 5.9.)

School Figures: The Data behind the Debate

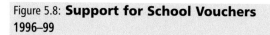

Figure 5.8: **Support for School Vouchers 1996–99**

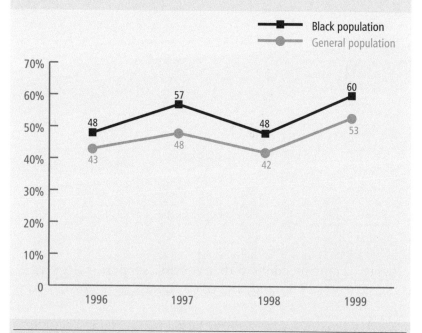

Source: David A. Bositis, *1999 National Opinion Poll—Education* (Washington, DC: Joint Center for Political and Economic Studies, 1999), available online at http://www.jointcenter.org.

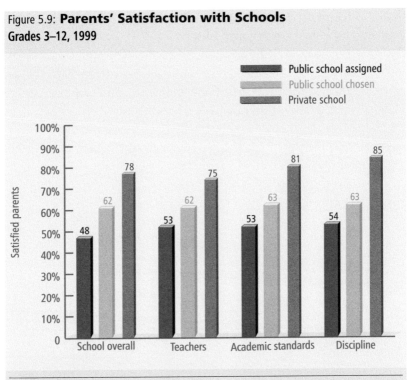

Figure 5.9: **Parents' Satisfaction with Schools**
Grades 3–12, 1999

Source: Howard Fuller, "The Continuing Struggle against Unequal Educational Opportunity," speech delivered at the National Press Club, Washington, DC (24 August 2000).

Over the past 10 years, vouchers have moved from the outer edge of acceptability to the center of education reform discussions. Moreover, the voucher programs in existence serve not the rich but the poor. In the 1999–2000 school year, there were 3 publicly funded voucher programs and 60 privately funded voucher programs. Of those existing voucher programs, every one served needy children.

School choice, specifically voucher programs, actually bridges the divide between the rich and the poor. With philanthropists funding the majority of the 60 private voucher programs, and vouchers providing the opportunity for less-advantaged children to attend private schools or schools of their choice, the advantaged and the disadvantaged can work for the same ends. Parents, regardless of socioeconomic status, want a good education for their children, and school choice may provide that opportunity.

▶ PROPOSITION: CATHOLIC SCHOOLS PROVIDE HIGH MARKS AT LOW COSTS.

Historically, Catholic schools have played a significant role in educating America's children. They continue to be important and effective players in the field, despite substantial changes in the size and makeup of their collective student body over the last 4 decades. Studies show that Catholic schools advance the academic, moral, and religious development of the students in their care and they do it at less than half the cost of public schools.

Catholic schools are characterized by a strong sense of community, high academic standards, and a committed faculty. Students are disciplined and orderly. Academic achievement is notable, particularly among inner-city black families, where parental satisfaction also is high.

The number of children that Catholic schools educate has fallen in recent decades. It peaked in 1960, when about 1 in every 8 children was attending a Catholic school; by 2000, the ratio had fallen to 1 in 20. (See table 5.7.)[25]

Table 5.7: **Catholic School Enrollment**
1919–20—2000–01

| School year | Catholic school enrollment | | | Catholic school enrollment as a percentage of: | |
	Elementary	Secondary	Total	Total national enrollment	Total private school enrollment
1919–20	1,795,673	129,848	1,925,521	8.3%	na
1929–30	2,222,598	241,869	2,464,467	8.7	93.0%
1939–40	2,035,182	361,123	2,396,305	8.5	91.8
1949–50	2,560,815	505,572	3,066,387	10.8	90.7
Fall 1960	4,373,422	880,369	5,253,791	12.9	92.6
1970–71	3,355,478	1,008,088	4,363,566	8.5	81.4
1975–76	2,525,000	890,000	3,415,000	7.6	68.3
1985–86	2,061,000	760,000	2,821,000	6.3	50.8
1990–91	1,883,906	591,533	2,475,439	5.3	47.3
1995–96	1,884,461	606,650	2,491,111	4.9	44.0
1996–97	1,885,037	612,161	2,497,198	4.8	43.1
1997–98	1,879,737	618,157	2,497,894	4.7	42.6
1998–99	1,876,211	620,277	2,496,488	4.7	42.1
1999–2000	1,877,236	623,180	2,500,416	4.9	44.2
2000–01	2,004,037	643,264	2,647,301	4.8	44.1

Source: Thomas D. Snyder, ed., *Digest of Education Statistics, 2001* (Washington, DC: U.S. Department of Education, National Center for Education Statistics, 2002), table 62, p. 73.
Notes: Excludes prekindergarten enrollment.
Data reported by the National Catholic Educational Association and data reported by the National Center for Education Statistics are not directly comparable because survey procedures and definitions differ.

The composition of the student body has undergone a dramatic change, as well. Enrollment changed in terms of race, ethnicity, and religion. For example, in the 1970–71 school year, minority enrollment in Catholic schools was 10.7 percent of total enrollment. In the 1999–2000 school year, minority enrollment had more than doubled to 24 percent. Furthermore, in 1970, only 2.7 percent of Catholic school enrollment was non-Catholic; in 2000, 13.4 percent of enrollment was non-Catholic. (See table 5.8 and figure 5.10.)[26]

Table 5.8: **Catholic School Enrollment**
By Race/Ethnicity, 1970–2000

Ethnicity	1970	1983–84	1993–94	1994–95	1999–2000
Black	6.5%	8.6%	8.4%	8.3%	7.8%
Hispanic	5.2	8.9	10.7	10.6	10.7
Asian American	0.5	2.4	4.0	3.9	3.5
Native American	na	0.3	0.6	0.4	0.3
All others	87.8	79.8	76.3	76.9	77.7

Source: Dale McDonald, *United States Catholic Elementary and Secondary School Statistics 1994–1995* (Washington, DC: National Catholic Educational Association, 1995), available online at http://www.ncea.org.

Figure 5.10: **Catholic School Demographics**
1970–2000

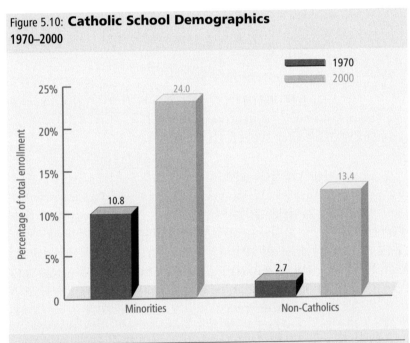

Source: Dale McDonald, *United States Catholic Elementary and Secondary School Statistics 1999–2000* (Washington, DC: National Catholic Educational Association, 2000), available online at http://www.ncea.org.

School Figures: The Data behind the Debate

A 1990 study comparing Catholic schools and public schools in New York City showed very different outcomes for minority and disadvantaged youth.

- Catholic high schools graduated 95 percent of their senior class each year; the public schools graduated slightly more than 50 percent of their seniors.
- More than 66 percent of the Catholic school graduates received the New York State Regents diploma; only about 5 percent of the public school students received this distinction.
- Catholic school students achieved an average combined SAT I score of 803; the average combined score for public school students was 642.
- Sixty percent of black Catholic school students scored above the national average for black students on the SAT I; less than 30 percent of public school black students in New York City scored above the average.[27]

Early studies comparing Catholic and public schools were often discounted. Critics claimed that they failed to account for the possibility of selectivity bias in Catholic schools and that selectivity bias left the worst-performing and -behaving students in public schools. Paying special attention to selectivity bias, by restricting comparisons to like students and using data from the U.S. Department of Education's *High School and Beyond* study and other recent reports, the evidence confirms that Catholic schools still produce outstanding long-run results and lifetime advantage.[28]

- Attending a Catholic high school raises an inner-city student's probability of finishing high school and entering college by 17 percentage points.
- Black and Hispanic students attending urban Catholic schools are more than twice as likely to graduate from

college as their counterparts in public schools: 27 percent of black and Hispanic Catholic school graduates who started college went on to graduate, compared with 11 percent from urban public schools.

- When compared with their public school counterparts, minority students in urban Catholic schools can expect roughly 8 percent higher wages in the future.[29]

A study of New York City schools released in 2001 confirms the stellar results of Catholic schools. When comparing per-student costs and student performances in public and Catholic schools in 88 public and 77 Catholic elementary and middle schools located in three New York boroughs—the Bronx, Brooklyn, and Manhattan—evidence shows that Catholic schools are at least twice as efficient and their students perform better on state tests.[30]

To ensure a fair comparison, all expenditures that did not have a private school counterpart were deducted, including, but not exclusively, all monies spent on transportation, special education, school lunch, and bureaucratic functions. After removing all of these expenditures—which make up nearly 40 percent of the cost of running the New York City public schools—the analysis showed that public schools still spent more than $5,000 per pupil each year, compared to the $2,400 spent by Catholic schools.[31]

Test score comparisons also were revealing. When schools serving populations with similar poverty levels were compared, excluding special education student test scores, Catholic schools outperformed public schools on state-administered math and reading tests for the third- and sixth-grade levels in all comparisons. Additional analysis showed that test scores remained higher in Catholic schools even after adjustments were made for race and ethnicity. Other studies show that black students from low-income schools learn more—or at least as much—at half the cost. (See figure 5.11.)[32]

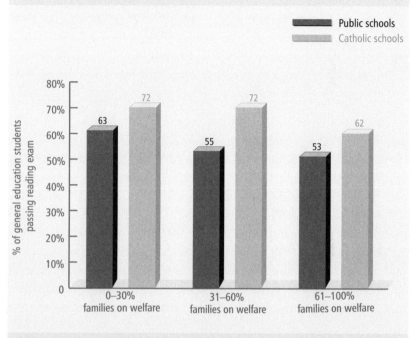

Figure 5.11: **Reading Scores and Welfare Dependency**
New York City[a] Sixth-Graders, 1997–98

Public schools
Catholic schools

% of general education students passing reading exam

0–30%
families on welfare

31–60%
families on welfare

61–100%
families on welfare

Source: New York State Education Department, *1997–98 School Expenditure Report.*
Notes: a. Bronx, Brooklyn, and Manhattan borough elementary and middle schools only, 88 public and 77 Catholic.
Differences are statistically significant at the 5 percent confidence level for each category.

Although their enrollments have declined, the effect of Catholic schools still stands out. Catholic schools continue to contribute to the fabric of American education.

PROPOSITION: HOME EDUCATION IS THE FASTEST-GROWING ALTERNATIVE TO PUBLIC SCHOOLING, AND A GOOD ONE AT THAT.

Many view home education as a fringe alternative and an option for the paranoid or overly protective parent. Within the last decade, however, home schooling has become part of the mainstream in education reform discussions. Moreover, it appears to produce results worth acknowledging. Data from the largest survey and testing program for students in home schools provide a look at the exponential growth of the number of children home-schooled, their academic performance, and motivating factors for those who choose to home-school.[33]

Home education has grown faster than voucher and charter school enrollments combined. With virtually zero "enrollees" in 1978, home-schooled students now comprise more than 3 percent of total elementary and secondary education enrollment in the United States.[34] Their numbers are growing at an estimated 15–25 percent annually; in the year 2000, approximately 1,700,000 elementary and secondary students were home educated. (See table 5.9.)[35]

Table 5.9: **Home School Enrollment**
1978–2000

Year	Enrollment
1978	12,500
1985	183,000
1990	301,000
1996	1,225,000
2000	1,700,000

Source: Home School Legal Defense Association, *Homeschooling Research* (Purcellville, VA: Home School Legal Defense Association, National Center for Home Education), available online at www.hslda.org.
Note: Enrollment data for home education are limited.

What is known about those who are home-schooling? Most parents who choose to home-school their children are motivated by a desire to teach specific philosophical or religious values, control social interaction, develop close families, or encourage high academic achievement. The ability to be flexible and tailor curricula to the specific needs of their children is an additional incentive.[36] The demographics of home school families are not representative of the general U.S. population, and neither are their results.

- In 1998, 94 percent of home-schooled children were white, 0.8 percent black, 0.2 percent Hispanic, and 5 percent unknown. In contrast, total enrollment in public elementary and secondary schools by race was 63 percent white, 17 percent black, 15 percent Hispanic, and 5 percent unknown.[37]

- Some 97 percent of home-schooled children were in married-couple families; nationwide in 1997, only 72 percent of all families with 1 or more children enrolled in school were in married-couple families.[38]

- The majority of home school families (62.1 percent) have 3 or more children, with a mean of about 3.1 children per family. Nationwide nearly 80 percent of all families with school-age children have 1 or 2 children, with a mean of about 1.9 children per family.[39]

- A large percentage of home school mothers are stay-at-home moms not participating in the labor force; in 1998, 76.9 percent of home school mothers did not work for pay. Contrast that to national figures, where only about 30 percent of married women with children under 18 were not labor force participants.[40]

- Nearly 88 percent of home school students have parents who continued their education after high school; less than 50 percent of the general population attended or graduated from college.[41]

- Almost one out of every four home school students has at least one parent who is a certified teacher: 19.7 percent of home school mothers and 7.1 percent of home school fathers are certified. Teachers make up only approximately 3 percent of the national labor force.[42]

- The median family income for home school families in 1997 was about $52,000; nationwide the median income for all families with children was approximately $43,545.[43]

- Only 1.7 percent of fourth-grade home-schooled children watch 4 or more hours of television per day; nationwide 38.5 percent of all fourth-graders watch 4 or more hours of television per day.[44]

Achievement is the best barometer for success or failure in the education arena. When comparing the achievement of home school students with public and private school students, home school students stand out. The median scale scores for home school students on the Iowa Tests of Basic Skills (ITBS) or the Tests of Achievement and Proficiency (TAP) are well above those of their public and private school counterparts in every subject and in every grade. (See table 5.10.)[45]

Table 5.10: **Home and Private School Student Performance**
Iowa Tests of Basic Skills, 1998

Grade	National median	Home school students Median composite score	Percentile	Private and Catholic school national percentile
1	150	170	91%	89%
2	168	192	90	88
3	185	207	81	74
4	200	222	76	72
5	214	243	79	71
6	227	261	81	71
7	239	276	82	72
8	250	288	81	72
9	260	292	77	63
10	268	310	84	71
11	275	310	78	63
12	280	326	86	74

Source: Lawrence M. Rudner, "Scholastic Achievement and Demographic Characteristics of Home School Students in 1998," *Education Policy Analysis Archives* 7, no. 8 (23 March 1999), available online at http://www.epaa.asu.edu.

Instead of comparing specific grades and their corresponding test scores, another way to evaluate test scores is to look at the composite scale score in relationship to relative grade placement, the grade equivalent score. For example, the sixth-grade home school student's median composite score of 261 is the median score for a ninth-grader nationwide. Over time, the achievement gap between home school students and their peers nationwide widens. By the time home school students reach eighth grade, their median scores are four grade equivalents above their public school peers. (See figure 5.12.)[46]

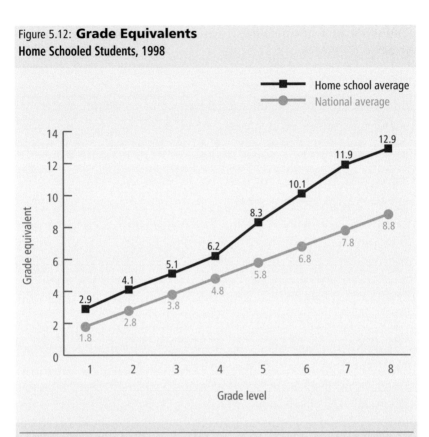

Figure 5.12: **Grade Equivalents**
Home Schooled Students, 1998

Home school average
National average

Grade equivalent

2.9
4.1
5.1
6.2
8.3
10.1
11.9
12.9

1.8
2.8
3.8
4.8
5.8
6.8
7.8
8.8

Grade level

Source: Lawrence M. Rudner, "Scholastic Achievement and Demographic Characteristics of Home School Students in 1998," *Education Policy Analysis Archives* 7, no. 8 (23 March 1999), available online at http://www.epaa.asu.edu.

An interesting sidebar is the performance of home-schoolers in national geography bees. In the 2002 national geography bee, for example, 4 of the 10 finalists were home-schooled. The winner—who was the youngest finalist, at age 10, and the third-place finisher were both home-schooled.

Home school students and their families are not a representative cross-section of the United States population; there are distinct demographic differences. Furthermore, it is evident by the degree of parental involvement that there is a very strong

School Figures: The Data behind the Debate

commitment to education and children among home school parents.

There are a few things, however, we can learn from this small, select group. What they're doing appears to be working, and working quite well. According to a recent study by Caroline Hoxby, various family aspects have a greater impact on school achievement than school inputs; the growth and achievement of home school students, by definition in homes where parents have made a serious commitment to education, appears to validate this point.[47]

PROPOSITION: THE PUSH FOR INCREASED ACCOUNTABILITY IS APPARENT, BUT BETTER SCHOOLS ARE STILL TO COME

Dissatisfaction regarding public schools has grown, and with it mounting pressure to hold schools responsible for their results. Until the 1966 Coleman report, *Equality of Educational Opportunity,* accountability efforts focused on the measuring and tallying of resources (inputs). The Coleman report, followed by *A Nation at Risk* (1983), shifted attention to the measurement of outcomes and achievement. In the early 1990s, states, districts, and schools began to establish measurable standards to gauge progress and improvement. Establishing an effective accountability program takes careful planning, strategic implementation, and patience. However, because of poor design, accountability programs have often been ineffective, and poor evaluation techniques and bad programs lead to unintended consequences.

Although there are critics, the majority of the general public, parents and teachers included, greatly favor holding students accountable to standards. An August 1999 survey by Peter D. Hart reported that 73 percent of teachers and 92 percent of principals endorse standards-based reform.[48] Furthermore, according to an August 2000 Business Roundtable survey, 65 percent of parents and 70 percent of the general public answered "Yes" when asked whether students should be required to pass state tests before graduating from high school, "even if they have passing grades in their classes." Support was notably higher, 76 and 81 percent, respectively, as long as students were allowed to take the state exams several times, which is common in most states.[49]

A good accountability program does not consist of requirements and tests alone. Currently, there are many requirements and tests at all different grade levels, none of which necessarily ensures competence or effectiveness. For example, nearly all states administer some form of norm-referenced exam, a test where results are reported on a comparative basis—kids are measured relative to one another, not against established academic standards. Most states, however, also use a standardized test that is developed, administered, and scored under controlled conditions, and a minimum score must be achieved to pass.[50] Neither norm-referenced nor standardized tests can stand alone in their guarantee of effective accountability. An effective accountability program consists of four primary components:

- Standards
- Testing
- Incentives
- Flexibility

Providing an objective viewpoint on the effectiveness of state accountability programs can be difficult. As of August 2000, the Education Commission of the States (a clearinghouse for educational issues across the states), *Education Week's* "Quality Counts 2000," and the Thomas B. Fordham Foundation's *State of the State* Standards provided the most comprehensive comparison. (See table 5.11 and figure 5.13.)

Table 5.11: **Standards and Accountability By State**

State	Students must master 10th-grade standards to graduate[a]	Rewards	Criterion-referenced assessments aligned to state standards				Strong accountability, assessments, and high standards
			English	Math	History	Science	
Alabama	yes		yes	yes		yes	yes
Alaska	yes		yes	yes			
Arizona	yes		yes	yes			
Arkansas			yes	yes			
California	future	yes	yes	yes			yes
Colorado	future		yes	yes		yes	
Connecticut			yes	yes	yes	yes	
Delaware	yes		yes	yes	yes	yes	
Florida		yes	yes	yes			
Georgia	yes	yes	yes	yes	yes	yes	
Hawaii							
Idaho	future						
Illinois			yes	yes	yes	yes	
Indiana		yes	yes	yes			
Iowa							
Kansas			yes	yes			
Kentucky		yes	yes	yes	yes	yes	
Louisiana	future		yes	yes	yes	yes	
Maine			yes	yes	yes	yes	
Maryland	future	yes	yes	yes	yes	yes	
Massachusetts	future		yes	yes	yes	yes	
Michigan			yes	yes	yes	yes	
Minnesota			yes	yes			
Mississippi			yes	yes	yes	yes	
Missouri			yes	yes	yes	yes	
Montana							
Nebraska							
Nevada	yes		yes	yes			
New Hampshire			yes	yes	yes	yes	
New Jersey	future	yes	yes	yes		yes	
New Mexico	yes	yes	yes	yes	yes	yes	
New York	yes		yes	yes	yes	yes	
North Carolina		yes	yes	yes	yes	yes	yes
North Dakota							
Ohio	future		yes	yes	yes	yes	
Oklahoma			yes	yes	yes	yes	
Oregon			yes	yes	yes	yes	
Pennsylvania		yes	yes	yes			
Rhode Island			yes	yes			
South Carolina	future		yes	yes			yes
South Dakota							
Tennessee		yes	yes	yes			
Texas	yes	yes	yes	yes	yes	yes	yes
Utah	yes						
Vermont			yes	yes		yes	
Virginia	future		yes	yes	yes	yes	
Washington	future		yes	yes			
West Virginia							
Wisconsin	future						
Wyoming			yes	yes			
U.S. total	8	13	40	40	21	25	5

Sources: Chester E. Finn Jr. and Michael J. Petrilli, eds., *The State of the State Standards, 2000* (Washington D.C.: The Thomas B. Fordham Foundation; January 2000); Lori Meyer, Greg F. Orlofsky, Ronald A. Skinner, and Scott Spicer, *Quality Counts 2002* (Bethesda, MD: Education Week on the Web, 2002), available online at http://www.edweek.org.
Note: a. 1999–2000.

Figure 5.13: **Education Accountability**
By State

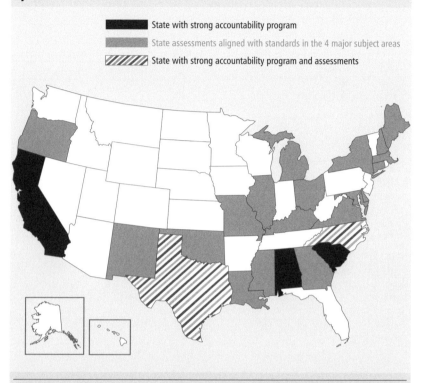

■ State with strong accountability program

▨ State assessments aligned with standards in the 4 major subject areas

▨ State with strong accountability program and assessments

Sources: Lori Meyer, Greg F. Orlofsky, Ronald A. Skinner, and Scott Spicer, *Quality Counts 2002* (Bethesda, MD: Education Week on the Web, 2002), available online at http://www.edweek.org; Chester E. Finn, Jr., and Michael J. Petrilli, eds., *The State of the State Standards, 2000* (Washington DC: The Thomas B. Fordham Foundation, January 2000).
Note: According to Finn and Petrilli's report, states with strong academic accountability systems have both clear and high academic standards and assessments designed to measure progress toward those standards.

Education Week data disclose the trend toward increasing accountability.

- In the 1997–98 school year, 45 states had adopted standards in at least one subject; by the 1999–2000 school year, 49 states had.

- In the 1997–98 school year, 38 states had adopted standards in English, math, social studies, and science; 44 had by 1999–2000.

- In the 1997–98 school year, 35 states had tests or some form of assessment that measured achievement according to set standards in at least one subject; 41 had by 1999–2000.

- In the 1997–98 school year, 17 states had tests or assessments that measured achievement according to set standards in English, math, social studies, and science; 21 had by 1999–2000.[51]

Furthermore, recent reports regarding the 2000–2001 and 2001–2002 school years show states continuing in their efforts toward increased accountability.[52]

Despite these efforts, the Fordham study found that only five states (Alabama, California, North Carolina, South Carolina, and Texas) had strong accountability programs, that is, high standards coupled with tests to measure progress and effectiveness.

Evidence that testing is on the rise can be seen by looking at test-scoring companies. National Computer Systems (NCS) works with states to develop customized, criterion-referenced exams and also scores them. In the spring of 1998, the number of test sheets that the company scored leapt to 177.7 million, up from 88.3 million in the spring of 1997.[53] Although elementary and secondary enrollment increased less than 2 percent between the 1997 and 1998 school years, the number of test sheets scored by NCS increased by more than 100 percent.[54] Some of this increase is a result of more open-ended questions, which require longer answers and more test sheets than multiple-choice questions. Regardless of these changes, there has been a decided overall increase in the number of tests taken.

Changes in test sales, compared to enrollment in grades K–12, for the period from 1960 to 1990 are notable, as well.

Revenues from sales of commercially published standardized tests increased from approximately $35 million to about $95 million (in 1982 dollars), while enrollment grew by only 15 percent.[55] The increase in the number of tests taken by students and ballooning revenues is revealing; however, test-taking does not necessarily equate to effective accountability or improved achievement.

Time is still needed to show large-scale improvements, but the state of Florida provides a snapshot of the possibilities when high-stakes standards, regular and tailored assessment, and flexibility are integrated simultaneously. In 1999, Governor Jeb Bush's A+ Plan for Education became the first program to offer state-paid tuition scholarships for children in failing public schools to attend public, private, or parochial schools of choice. In Florida, schools are given a grade of A, B, C, D, or F, based on student performance. Schools that improve their scores are rewarded with up to $100 per pupil. Students in schools that get a failing grade for 2 consecutive years are entitled to choose another school by using their "opportunity scholarship," worth up to $4,000 a year, regardless of their income or their grades. In the first year (1999–2000), 134 families from two elementary schools were offered scholarships; children from 78 of these families attended public schools. It was projected that as many as 78 schools would qualify in the 2000 school year. However, no new schools received a grade of F in 2000, and all 78 schools that were given grades of F in 1999 made substantial progress on the writing part of their state's standardized tests.[56]

Many believe that the higher scores prove that the A+ Plan works and that raising expectations in the classroom gets results. A recent survey of more than 750 public school teachers in Florida found a large number who concede that the possibility or threat of vouchers this year helped cause a dramatic improvement in test scores at some of Florida's worst public schools. Of the respondents expressing an opinion, 65 percent said that Florida's A+ Plan for Education played a role in education changes. Only 17 percent said it did not.[57]

Early results indicate that accountability, combining high-stakes standards, integrated testing and assessment, and flexibility, produces better schools. If, however, accountability becomes merely another form of increased regulation—failing to give parents, teachers, and administrators the opportunity to participate and tailor solutions to their children, their school, and their community—it will not be successful.

Proposition: Summer school gives clear evidence that accountability is changing the way we educate.

As student achievement has waned, social promotion—where students are allowed to pass from grade to grade with their peers without satisfying academic requirements or meeting performance indicators—has become increasingly common. Thus, the desire to improve achievement has led to a renewed focus on decreasing social promotion. This leaves teachers begging for solutions for children who have fallen behind.

A majority of teachers surveyed in 1996 indicated that they had promoted unprepared students in the past year, and 60 percent of teachers surveyed felt under pressure to promote students out of fear that high failure rates reflected poorly on schools and administrators.[58] Not surprisingly, research shows that passing students on to the next grade when they are unprepared neither increases student achievement nor properly prepares students for college or future employment. Thus, the new emphasis on summer school is a by-product of the national movement to raise academic performance, improve scores on standardized tests, and end automatic promotion based on age rather than achievement.

More students than ever before were enrolled in summer school in the year 2000; approximately one in five students in the nation's 53 largest urban districts attended summer school. Districts in Chicago, Miami, and St. Louis led the increased attendance, with more than 40 percent of students enrolled during the summer months, some required to attend and others accepting the option to attend. In recent years, other districts have also experienced dramatic increases in both summer-time remediation and enrichment programs.[59]

- Cleveland's summer school enrollment jumped to 18,000 students in the summer of 2000; enrollment was only 1,000 in 1998.
- New Orleans's summer school enrollment increased from 500 in 1995 to 11,000 in 2000.
- Boston's anticipated summer school enrollment in the 2000 school year was 12,000, up from 2,800 five years earlier.
- New York, in an effort to end social promotion, projected 2000 summer school enrollment to be roughly 264,000.
- By June 2000, 14 states had enacted legislation expanding summer school requirements, and 24 of the nation's 53 largest urban districts had mandatory attendance for some students.[60]

A recent survey of the nation's 100 largest school districts found that 59 percent of the districts offer summer school as an alternative to social promotion and 55 percent are using the extra weeks to help students meet more challenging state and local standards. More than 80 percent of the districts offering remedial summer programs held back students who did not successfully complete summer school. Every one of the 100 largest school districts in the nation reported some type of summer program in operation during the summer of 1999. Twenty-five years earlier, a similar survey indicated that only half of U.S. school systems offered summer school.[61]

Past studies on the effectiveness of summer school programs have been mixed; however, recent comprehensive studies report that the vast majority of programs have had positive effects on student achievement. In Harris Cooper's study *Making the Most of Summer School*, a recent compilation of 93 summer school research reports, 85 percent of students who attended summer school outperformed their nonattending peers.[62]

Chicago's 2000 summer school program, for example, reported its best promotion rates since they began requiring their failing third-, sixth-, and eighth-grade students to attend summer school. According to their 2000 district report, 83 percent of the 9,722 Chicago third-graders required to attend summer school met promotion criteria at summer's end, nearly double the rate for each of the 3 years prior. Of the summer school students in the third-, sixth-, and eighth-grade, less than 10 percent were held back.[63]

New Orleans results, however, were not as encouraging. Hundreds of eighth-graders failed to pass a retest of the newly required ninth-grade advancement exam. Of the 1,416 students who took the language arts retest after 4 weeks of study, 80 percent still failed. In math, 86 percent of the 2,819 who took the retest failed. Reports did show, however, that 75 percent of the students who attended summer school did improve their test scores, perhaps just not enough to pass the advancement exam.[64]

Data from New York City provides the most recent and accurate assessment of a large school district's summer school program. In the summer of 2000, the New York City Board of Education instituted a large-scale summer school program for students in grades 3–12 who had failed to meet standards for promotion to the next grade, as well as for students who met promotion criteria but who were believed to be still at risk of failing to achieve high academic standards. This program represented the largest summer program ever offered anywhere in the United States. In 2001, the program enrolled nearly 375,000 students in more than 800 locations in the five boroughs of New York City. The results appear to confirm that summer school makes a difference when it comes to achievement. (See table 5.12.)[65]

Table 5.12: **Recent New York City Summer School 2000 & 2001**

	Summer school students	
	2000 (%)	2001 (%)
Enrollment		
Total, grades K–12	279,927	374,411
Total, grades 3–12	237,509	314,674
Enrichment students, grades K–12	185,423	184,047
Mandated students, grades 3–12[a]	94,504	190,364
Achievement in reading and math, grades 3–8[b]		
Mandated students scoring at Level 2 or above in reading	10,710 (41.2%)	16,301 (48.0%)
Mandated students scoring at Level 2 or above in math	12,587 (37.5%)	16,601 (39.6%)
Promotion and retention, grades 3–9		
Mandated students who were promoted, grades 3–8	38,960 (64.0%)	46,539 (64.7%)
Mandated students who were retained, grades 3–8	21,105 (35.0%)	23,942 (33.3%)
Passing of Regents Examinations, grades 9–12		
Mandated students who took one Regents examination and passed at 55% or higher	2,268 (37.3%)	8,981 (50.5%)
Mandated students who took one Regents examination and passed at 65% or higher	1,185 (19.5%)	5,091 (28.6%)

Source: New York City Board of Education, *Summer School 2001 Evaluation Report* (New York: Metis Associates, March 2002), available online at http://www.nycenet.edu.
Notes: a. There are no mandated students in grades K–2.
b. Does not include ESL students.

The accountability push has encouraged many districts to work toward ending social promotion. The increasing availability of summer schools and their burgeoning enrollments are signs of this endeavor.

▶ Proposition: California's class size reduction appears to be an education reform initiative gone bad.

Identifying effective school reform policies sounds easy enough; however, a seemingly good idea implemented in haste can bring more harm than good. California's class size reduction (CSR) initiative is a perfect example. At face value, everyone would agree that achievement should be enhanced by more teachers teaching fewer students. With smaller class size, however, more teachers, more classroom space, and more money are needed. Class size reduction may be politically savvy—60 percent of parents surveyed in a *U.S. News* poll said they would be more likely to vote for a political candidate who wants to raise taxes if the money went to pay for smaller class sizes in kindergarten through third grade—but across-the-board cuts in class size do not appear to be the most cost-effective or achievement-effective way to spend education money.[66]

Nearly one-eighth of the nation's public elementary and secondary students are enrolled in California.[67] Prior to 1996, California had the highest student-teacher ratio in the nation;[68] in 1996, California's state legislature passed SB 1777, a reform measure aimed at cutting class size in the early school grades from what had been an average of 28 students to a maximum of 20 students. According to many, the CSR initiative was and still is the largest state educational reform in history. The program incurs costs of approximately $1.5 billion annually and affects more than 1.8 million students.[69]

The policy was inspired by Tennessee's Project Student/ Teacher Achievement Ratio (STAR), which suggested that reducing class size to 15 students positively affects student achievement. For example, 69 percent of STAR project first-graders in smaller classes passed the state's reading test, compared to 58 percent of students in larger classes.[70]

California, however, differs from Tennessee in many respects. California's policy targets all students; Tennessee's included only 10,000 carefully controlled students. California's program reduced its maximum class size of 33 students down to 20; Tennessee took its class size of 22–26 students down to 13–17. This translated to approximately 250 additional teachers needed in Tennessee and more than 25,000 new teachers needed in California.

Moreover, because of the comprehensive nature of California's program, it lacked two important ingredients that Tennessee schools had—adequate space and enough qualified teachers for program implementation. The greatest concern, however, is that a study of Tennessee's Project STAR did not provide convincing evidence of long-term achievement gains.[71] The study shows that students in substantially smaller classes in their first year of schooling (whether kindergarten or first grade) perform better than those remaining in classes of larger size. No similar benefits, however, were observed for older grades.[72]

Despite this shaky evidence, California proceeded with the CSR policy. At the time of implementation, the nation's education system was short on teachers who were skilled and willing to teach. With California's CSR initiative, the lack of available, experienced, effective teachers was exacerbated. In 1997, for example, school districts had 18,000 new slots to fill, and as a result, nearly two-thirds of the new hires had little or no teaching experience.[73] Decades of research confirm that the quality of teacher affects the level of student achievement, and many consider it the single most important factor in ensuring that students learn. When there are not enough good teachers, students suffer.[74]

CSR costs, both economic and otherwise, were further exacerbated by space shortages. For example, throughout the state, schools began parking portable classrooms on their playgrounds as fast as they could purchase them. By 1997, 7,000 portable classrooms were already back-ordered, and several thousand of the "temporary" structures were only permitted to be used for 2 years, according to state law. When total costs for new construction are considered, the true costs of the CSR initiative are actually much higher.[75]

Numerous studies show that teacher quality has a greater proven impact on student performance than class size.[76] Two important observations can be made when evaluating California's CSR initiative: (1) The teacher quality in California's schools has dramatically decreased, particularly in already low-performing schools; and (2) economic costs are very high. Recent evaluations comparing the whole 1997–98 fourth-grade class, which had little or no exposure to reduced size classes, with the complete 1998–99 fourth-grade class, which had over a year of exposure to CSR, found, on average, no difference in achievement. Furthermore, the program has not reduced the gap in achievement between low-income, minority, or English language students and other students.[77] Did CSR work? Preliminary evaluations say marginally, at best.

Education reform policies should be well researched and have identifiable outcomes before implementation. Despite the lack of solid evidence, though, numerous states have already followed California's trend.[78] To be successful, the benefits or results must outweigh the costs. In 1997, the cost of implementation included a 7.5 percent increase in state-level education spending, with no noticeable impact on achievement.

► Chapter Notes

1. Thomas D. Snyder, ed., *Digest of Education Statistics, 2001* (Washington, DC: U.S. Department of Education, National Center for Education Statistics, 2002), table 3, p. 12; Dale McDonald, *United States Catholic Elementary and Secondary School Statistics 1994–1995* (Washington, DC: National Catholic Educational Association, 1995), available online at http://www.ncea.org; Dale McDonald, *United States Catholic Elementary and Secondary School Statistics 1999–2000* (Washington, DC: National Catholic Educational Association, 2000), available online at http://www.ncea.org; Center for Education Reform, *Charter School Highlights and Statistics* (Washington, DC: Center for Education Reform, 2000), available online at http://www.edreform.com; Marquette University, Institute for the Transformation of Learning, Office of Research, *School Choice Enrollment Growth* (Milwaukee, WI: Marquette University, 2000), available online at http://www.schoolchoiceinfo.org; Children First America, *The Road to Success: Private Vouchers Helping American Children* (Bentonville, AR: Children First America, 1999); Home School Legal Defense Association, *Homeschooling Research* (Purcellville, VA: Home School Legal Defense Association, National Center for Home Education), available online at www.hslda.org.

2. Center for Education Reform, *Charter School Highlights and Statistics.*

3. National Center for Education Statistics, *The State of Charter Schools Third-Year Report* (Washington, DC: U.S. Department of Education, National Center for Education Statistics, May 1999).

4. Snyder, *Digest of Education Statistics, 2001,* table 3, p.12; Marquette University, *School Choice Enrollment Growth;* Children First America, *The Road to Success: Private Vouchers Helping American Children.*

5. David A. Bositis, *1999 National Opinion Poll—Education* (Washington, DC: Joint Center for Political and Economic Studies, 1999), available online at http://www.jointcenter.org.

6. Nina H. Shokraii, "Why Catholic Schools Spell Success for America's Inner-City Children," *Backgrounder,* no. 1128 (30 June, 1997), available online at http://www.heritage.org.

7. Ibid.

8. Home School Legal Defense Association, *Homeschooling Research.* Note: A study by the Department of Education entitled "Homeschooling in the United States: 1999" was recently released;

however, the sample size for the study was quite small (275 home-school students). The results from this study were quite similar to the results of Lawrence Rudner's study "Scholastic Achievement and Demographic Characteristics of Home School Students in 1998"; however, Rudner's sample size was much larger (20,760 students). One distinct difference between the studies was the projected number of students home-educated within the United States. The Department of Education based 2000 "enrollment" projections at roughly 1,000,000. In this proposition, the larger study results (Rudner, 1999) were used as the primary data source.

9. Education Commission of the States, *ECS State Notes* (Denver, CO: Education Commission of the States, August 2000), available online at www.ecs.org.

10. Jodi Wilgoren, "Summer Classes Expanding in Push to Improve Skills," *New York Times* (5 July 2000).

11. Ibid.

12. National Center for Education Statistics, *The State of Charter Schools Third-Year Report;* National Center for Education Statistics, *The State of Charter Schools Fourth-Year Report* (Washington, DC: U.S. Department of Education, National Center for Education Statistics, January 2000).

13. National Center for Education Statistics, *The State of Charter Schools Fourth-Year Report.*

14. Ibid.

15. National Center for Education Statistics, *The State of Charter Schools Third-Year Report.*

16. Caroline M. Hoxby, "Rising Tide," *Education Next* 1, no. 4 (Winter 2001), pp. 69–74.

17. Wisconsin Department of Public Instruction, *Wisconsin School Performance Report* (Madison: Wisconsin Department of Public Instruction), available online at http://208.170.76.100/DPI/query.asp?yr=...=3619&school=&subject; Wisconsin Department of Public Instruction, School Management Services, *Milwaukee Parental Choice Program* (Madison: Wisconsin Department of Public Instruction), available online at wysiwyg://6/http://www.dpi.state.wi.us/dpi/dfm/sms/mpcxgrde.html.

18. Wisconsin Department of Public Instruction, *Wisconsin School Performance Report;* Wisconsin Department of Public Instruction, *Milwaukee Parental Choice Program.*

19. Wisconsin Department of Public Instruction, *Wisconsin School Performance Report.*

20. Frederick M. Hess, "The Work Ahead," *Education Next* 1, no. 4 (Winter 2001), pp. 8–13.

21. Ibid.

22. Bositis, *1999 National Opinion Poll—Education.*

23. Bositis, *1999 National Opinion Poll—Education.*

24. Howard Fuller, "The Continuing Struggle against Unequal Educational Opportunity," speech delivered at The National Press Club, Washington, DC (24 August 2000).

25. Snyder, *Digest of Education Statistics, 2001*, tables 3 and 63, pp. 12 and 73.

26. McDonald, *United States Catholic Elementary and Secondary School Statistics 1994–1995*; McDonald, *United States Catholic Elementary and Secondary School Statistics 1999–2000.*

27. Shokraii, "Why Catholic Schools Spell Success for America's Inner-City Children."

28. Ibid.

29. Ibid.

30. Paul E. Peterson and Herbert Walberg, "In New York City, Catholic Schools Do a Better Job—at Half the Cost," *Columbus Dispatch* (2 March 2001).

31. Ibid.

32. Ibid.

33. See note within endnote 8 starting, "A study by the Department of Education entitled 'Homeschooling in the United States: 1999' was recently released."

34. Snyder, *Digest of Education Statistics, 2001*, table 3, p. 12; Home School Legal Defense Association, *Homeschooling Research.*

35. Home School Legal Defense Association, *Homeschooling Research.*

36. Lawrence M. Rudner, "Scholastic Achievement and Demographic Characteristics of Home School Students in 1998," *Education Policy Analysis Archives* 7, no. 8 (23 March 1999), available online at http://www.epaa.asu.edu. Note: This study is comprised of the largest sample size ever used to evaluate home school students and their families; however, it should be noted that it was not possible within the parameters of the study to evaluate whether the sample is truly representative of the entire population of home school students.

37. Rudner, "Scholastic Achievement and Demographic Characteristics"; Jeanne Nathanson, *The Condition of Education 2000 in Brief* (Washington, DC: U.S. Department of Education, National Center for Education Statistics, 2001), available online at http://nces.ed.gov.

38. Rudner, "Scholastic Achievement and Demographic Characteristics."

39. Ibid.

40. Ibid.

41. Ibid.

42. Rudner, "Scholastic Achievement and Demographic Characteristics"; Bureau of Labor Statistics, available online at ftp://ftp.bls.gov.

43. Rudner, "Scholastic Achievement and Demographic Characteristics"; Bureau of Labor Statistics; Bureau of the Census, available online at http://ferret.bls.census.gov.

44. Rudner, "Scholastic Achievement and Demographic Characteristics."

45. Ibid.

46. Rudner, "Scholastic Achievement and Demographic Characteristics." Note: Approximately 20 percent of eighth-grade students in public schools score similarly.

47. Hoxby, "If Families Matter Most, Where Do Schools Come In?"

48. Standards-based reform requires that achievement be measured against a set standard.

49. Diane Ravitch, "The Backlash against the Backlash," *The Weekly Standard* 6, no. 23 (26 February 2001).

50. Merrill Lynch, *The Book of Knowledge* (San Francisco: Merrill Lynch, Global Securities Research & Economics Group, 1999).

51. Lori Meyer, Greg F. Orlofsky, Ronald A. Skinner, and Scott Spicer, *Quality Counts 2002* (Bethesda, MD: *Education Week on the Web,* 2002), available online at http://www.edweek.org.

52. Ibid.

53. Merrill Lynch, *The Book of Knowledge.*

54. Snyder, *Digest of Education Statistics, 2001,* table 3, p. 12.

55. Gregory J. Cizek, "Filling in the Blanks: Putting Standardized Tests to the Test," *Fordham Report* 2, no. II (October 1998).

56. Nina Shrokraii Rees, "Florida State Profile," *School Choice 2000* (Washington, DC: Heritage Foundation, October 2000), available online at http://www.heritage.org.

57. Ibid.

58. National Center for Education Statistics, *Taking Responsibility for Ending Social Promotion: A Guide for Educators and State and Local*

Leaders (Washington, DC: U.S. Department of Education, National Center for Education Statistics, May 1999), available online at http://www.ed.gov.

59. Jodi Wilgoren, "Summer Classes Expanding in Push to Improve Skills."

60. Ibid.

61. G.D. Borman, "Summers Are for Learning," *Principal* 80, no. 3 (January 2001).

62. Ibid.

63. Robert C. Johnston, *Bumper Summer School Crop Yields Mixed Test Results* (Bethesda, MD: *Education Week on the Web*, 2000), available online at http://www.edweek.org.

64. Ibid.

65. New York City Board of Education, *Summer School 2001 Evaluation Report* (New York: Metis Associates, March 2002), available online at http://www.nycenet.edu.

66. Thomas Toch, Betsy Streisand, and Steven Butler, *Does Class Size Matter?* (Washington, DC: *U.S. News Online*, 13 October 1997), available online at http://www.usnews.com.

67. Ibid.

68. Policy Analysis for California Education, *California Class Size Reduction Evaluation Project*, available online at http://www.gse.berkeley.edu/research/PACE/pace_cal_class_size.html.

69. CSR Research Consortium, *Class Size Reduction in California: The 1998–99 Evaluation Findings*, available online at http://www.classize.org.

70. Toch, Streisand, and Butler, *Does Class Size Matter?*

71. Ibid.

72. Eric A. Hanushek, "Deconstructing RAND," *Education Matters* 1, no. 1 (Spring 2001), pp. 65–67.

73. Toch, Streisand, and Butler, *Does Class Size Matter?*

74. Lynn Olson, "Finding and Keeping Competent Teachers," *Education Week* XIX, no. 18 (13 January 2000); Education Trust, "New Frontiers for a New Century," *The Education Gadfly* 1, no. 9 (12 July 2001).

75. Toch, Streisand, and Butler, *Does Class Size Matter?*

76. Hanushek, "Deconstructing RAND"; Olson, "Finding and Keeping Competent Teachers."

77. CSR Research Consortium, *Class Size Reduction in California: The 1998–99 Evaluation Findings*.

78. Toch, Streisand, and Butler, *Does Class Size Matter?*

Chapter 6:
Students and
Their Families

Propositions

▶ WHEN IT COMES TO A GOOD EDUCATION, FAMILY MAY
MATTER MOST.

▶ A POSITIVE HOME ENVIRONMENT IS RELATED TO
HIGH ACADEMIC PERFORMANCE.

▶ PARENTS ARE WELL ABLE TO DETERMINE THE
DIFFERENCE BETWEEN HIGH-PERFORMING SCHOOLS
AND LOW-PERFORMING SCHOOLS.

▶ DESPITE LEGISLATIVE LIMITATIONS, PARENTS STILL
EXERCISE CHOICE WHEN IT COMES TO THEIR CHILD'S
EDUCATION.

Highlights

- In 2000, there were approximately 53 million students enrolled in public and private schools at the elementary and secondary school levels in the United States.[1]

- In 2000, of the students enrolled in public elementary and secondary schools, approximately 38 percent were minorities, nearly 17 percent black and 16 percent Hispanic.[2]

- Of America's school-age children, nearly one-fifth speak a language other than English at home; 7 in 10 of these speak Spanish.[3]

- More than 13 percent of students in public elementary and secondary schools have been diagnosed as having a disability. Six percent have been diagnosed with a learning disability, the largest designated category by far.[4]

- In 1960, 88 percent of children under 18 were living with 2 parents; in 1998, only 68 percent of children were living with 2 parents.[5]

- The median family income for 2-parent families is more than double that of families headed by a divorced single mother and more than 4 times as much as that of families in which the single mother never married.[6]

- In 1990, 21 percent of children under 18 were living in poverty; in 1999, 17 percent of children were living in poverty.[7]

- In 1998, 9 percent of children in married-couple families were living in poverty, compared to 46 percent in single-parent families.[8]

According to the public, the number one "major problem" facing public schools is lack of parental involvement. It is ranked ahead of drugs, undisciplined students, overcrowded classrooms, violence and lack of school safety, inequality in school funding, and inadequate academic standards.[9]

School Figures: The Data behind the Debate

Overview

hildren are a valuable resource, and educating children—seeking to ensure the development of an informed citizenry, the transfer of a common culture, and the creation of a trained workforce—is one of society's most important functions. In the 2000 school year, there were nearly 53 million children enrolled in elementary and secondary grades in the United States. Educating them costs more than $420 billion—4.3 percent of the nation's GDP. Education is an important and an expensive endeavor and it plays a significant role in the shaping of America's future.

Throughout the 20th century, the size of the 5- to 18-year-old age group relative to the rest of the population has fluctuated. The postwar Baby Boom put enormous pressure on the education infrastructure, but it was followed by a massive decline in birth rates. This decline rebounded with the Baby Boom bounce, as the boomers started their own families. Not only were the sheer numbers changing, but as the 20th century came to a close, the effects of immigration and divergent birth rates among ethnic groups led to a changing face of the composite classroom. In 1977, for example, nearly 24 percent of K–12 students were nonwhite compared to 38 percent just 25 years later. Bilingual education and multiculturalism, footnotes to the educational process a mere 25 years ago, are now important elements of the everyday classroom.

Through all this change, education researchers agree that some things have remained constant: The family and the home environment have as much to do with children's education as what is taught in the classroom. The formative years before children start formal education remain vital to preparing children for school. Furthermore, research shows that parents and the home environment are instrumental throughout their children's formal education. This chapter explores the relationships between families, students, and the classroom.

PROPOSITION: WHEN IT COMES TO A GOOD EDUCATION, FAMILY MAY MATTER MOST.

For too long, suggestions for educational improvement have focused on prescribing and implementing remedies for falling educational achievement. Remedies have included increased spending, smaller class size, more testing, and new methodology and curricula; most exclude the parent. Research shows, however, that the family and student achievement are directly related—and that family matters most, not least.

Since the 1960s, popular assumptions and recommendations regarding achievement disparity have centered on total resources and their distribution. It was presumed, for example, that the achievement gap between whites and blacks stemmed more from resource allocation than from differences in abilities, black students attending schools with smaller budgets, fewer teachers, and fewer textbooks. In 1966, however, an Equality of Educational Opportunity Commission (EEOC) report disclosed evidence that even after controlling for differences in family backgrounds, differences in school resources accounted for next to none of the achievement disparities. In short, families mattered more and schools mattered less when it came to measuring the impact on student achievement.[10]

Furthermore, recent research indicates that the EEOC report, commonly known as the Coleman Report, underestimated the effect that family has on achievement. Report results confirmed the importance of schools' and parents' working together—schools and parents instead of schools versus parents—to enhance achievement. These results and further study led Caroline Hoxby to the following conclusion:

> Indeed, the combined explanatory power of school input variables and neighborhood variables (such

as the education, income, and racial composition of the local population) do not come close to matching that of family background variables.[11]

Hoxby studied the 1996 National Educational Longitudinal Survey (NELS), which tracked nearly 25,000 eighth-graders through their high school careers. She used regression analysis, a sophisticated statistical technique that ascribes differences in results, outcomes, or performance to a set of underlying factors—the explanatory variables. In her study, Hoxby used family, neighborhood, and school characteristics to describe differences in student performance in four subject areas: reading, mathematics, history, and science.[12]

Her statistical analysis revealed that family characteristics were 35 to 105 times more powerful in explaining student performance differences than school input variables were, and they were 12 to 24 times more important than neighborhood variables were in explaining variation in students' scores. (See figure 6.1.)[13]

The family characteristic variables in the analysis included individual family measures for parental education, family income, race and ethnicity, family size, and parents' involvement in their children's educational experience. The school input variables included class size, per pupil expenditures, teachers' average education and experience, various measures of teachers' salaries, and the number of books and computers per student. The neighborhood variables included income measures for the neighborhood, education level, and race and ethnicity (where the neighborhood is defined by school district and metropolitan area).[14]

School Figures: The Data behind the Debate

Figure 6.1: **Contribution of Explanatory Variables for Math Score Variation**
Twelfth-Graders, 1996

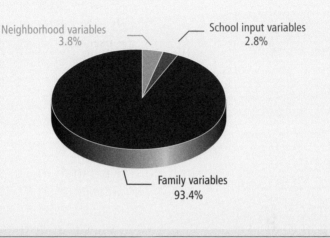

Neighborhood variables
3.8%

School input variables
2.8%

Family variables
93.4%

Source: Caroline M. Hoxby, "If Families Matter Most, Where Do Schools Come In?" in *A Primer on America's Schools,* ed. Terry M. Moe (Stanford, CA: Hoover Institution Press, 2001), pp. 89–123.

Technically, test scores are a predictive but not perfect measure of success; however, they often provide a glimpse of long-term outcomes, such as ultimate educational attainment, occupation, and income. The 1999 National Longitudinal Survey of Youth (NLSY), another survey that followed nearly 13,000 young Americans from their teens into their middle 30s, provides a picture of results beyond the classroom.[15]

- Various family components exerted 14 times greater impact on future income levels than school variables and 23 times greater impact than neighborhood variables.

- Comparing educational attainment, various family components exerted 19 times greater impact than school input variables and 24 times greater impact than neighborhood variables.

- In total, family variables accounted for 9 to 11 times as much variation in later outcomes as school inputs and neighborhood variables combined.[16]

In educational reform, families should not be removed from the equation. Clearly, they play a pivotal role in educational achievement and long-term success. The statistical analyses confirm what many grassroots organizations advocate: Families make the most significant difference in academic outcomes, achievement and otherwise. To ignore them would be negligent.

PROPOSITION: A POSITIVE HOME ENVIRONMENT IS RELATED TO HIGH ACADEMIC PERFORMANCE.

Recent data from Caroline Hoxby suggest that students whose parents take a more active role in their education have higher academic achievement. Parents, for example, who have made a personal investment in their child's education—whether it be through choosing their place of residence based upon the quality of schools, moving their child from public to private school, or exercising some other form of choice—are more likely to supplement their child's schooling at home. Parents may create a designated study area for their child and provide important resources and opportunities—books, calculators, computers, trips to libraries or museums. According to the 1996 NELS, when comparing children who score in the bottom quartile on reading and math tests to those who score in the top quartile, these complementary actions appear to make a difference. (See table 6.1.)[17]

Table 6.1: **Parental Involvement, Home Environment, and Student Achievement**

Activity	High achievers[a]	Low achievers[b]
Use libraries with their parents	79%	48%
Visit science museums with their parents	63	27
Come from homes with more than fifty books	96	76
Come from homes with an atlas	81	55
Come from homes with a calculator	98	89
Come from homes with a computer	60	27

Source: Caroline M. Hoxby, "If Families Matter Most, Where Do Schools Come In?" in *A Primer on America's Schools,* ed. Terry M. Moe (Stanford, CA: Hoover Institution Press, 2001), p. 116.
Notes: a. Students scoring in the top quartile when tested.
b. Students scoring in the bottom quartile when tested.

While the NELS was conducted, some families switched their children from public to private schools. These families, although a small number relative to the entire survey, provided laboratories for further study because many of the underlying characteristics remained constant. After switching to private schools, there were statistically significant changes in family behavior; for example, the families were more likely to own an atlas and more likely to have a specific place for their children to study. These data further solidify the connection between parental involvement and the home environment. After making conscious choices regarding their children's education, parents participated to an even greater degree.[18]

Moreover, in metropolitan areas where there is a choice between public school districts (where parents have made a large financial investment to live in a high-achieving school district, bearing higher housing costs, property taxes, or both), parents are more likely to make their home environment complement their child's school. In metropolitan areas with choice between districts, several learning enhancements stand out.

- 18 percent more families have a computer.
- 4 percent more have an atlas.
- 4 percent more have a calculator.
- 14 percent more parents use libraries with their children.
- 5 percent more visit science museums with their children.[19]

Data suggest that the home environment is more complementary to the educational process than parents perceive and that real involvement in their child's education increases performance. Both private schools and an expanded choice of schools provide the opportunity for parents to be more a part of their child's education. If higher test scores are an indication of better schooling, parents should be encouraged to explore as many venues for involvement as possible.

PROPOSITION: PARENTS ARE WELL ABLE TO DETERMINE THE DIFFERENCE BETWEEN HIGH-PERFORMING SCHOOLS AND LOW-PERFORMING SCHOOLS.

Some question whether parents are informed enough to determine the best for their children when it comes to their education. Do parents know the difference between schools that provide a good education and those that do not? The answer appears to be yes. Results from the 1996 NELS demonstrate that parents can accurately estimate the value added to their children's education each year. (A longitudinal survey, the NELS surveyed the same approximately 20,000 families beginning in 1988.) Furthermore, there is a correlation between the value added and the effectiveness ratings parents give schools.[20]

The NELS asked parents to rate the school their child attends based on three factors:

1. whether the school placed a high priority on learning

2. whether the parents were satisfied with their child's education

3. whether the teaching was good[21]

Parents' answers to the questions were consistent with the value added to achievement scores in the respective schools. Value-added comparisons gauge the relative progress students make over a given time period, versus solely comparing raw test scores. In other words, parents were able to differentiate between high-performing and low-performing schools. (See table 6.2.)[22]

Table 6.2: **Parents' Ratings of Schools**

Question	Parents' response	School rank for value-added achievement	
		Highest quartile	Lowest quartile
School placed a high priority on learning	"Strongly agree(d)"	32%	19%
School placed a high priority on learning	"Disagree(d)" or "strongly disagree(d)"	10	25
"Very satisfied" with education	"Yes"	44	15

From the 1988 to 1996 period of the NELS, the achievement records from the schools changed, and some dramatic shifts in parents' attitudes and opinions occurred in metropolitan areas where there was extensive choice. In cases where schools' achievement performance improved from the lowest value-added quartile to the highest, parents' opinion ratings of the schools reflected the improvement. For example, in responding to a question of whether the "teaching is good," parents with students in low-performing schools generally "disagreed" or "strongly disagreed." At a later date, the same survey was taken; these same parents, with children in the same school (but now better performing), "agreed" or "strongly agreed" that "teaching is good" when their schools' achievement scores had moved to the top quartile.[23]

A similar pattern was exhibited by parents when queried as to whether they were "satisfied with education." When their children's schools moved ahead in achievement rankings, the parents were "very satisfied" with the education their children were receiving, as opposed to "very dissatisfied" when their children were in low-performing schools.[24]

The last few decades of education ideology have presumed that the education experts know what is best for children and that parents are not capable of determining what makes for a good education. Recent data, however, tell a different story. Parents are capable of determining the difference between high-performing schools and low-performing schools, and they do. Perhaps education experts need to look back to the 1960s, when it was agreed that "Father knows best."

PROPOSITION: DESPITE LEGISLATIVE LIMITATIONS, PARENTS STILL EXERCISE CHOICE WHEN IT COMES TO THEIR CHILDREN'S EDUCATION.

Many question the value and effectiveness of allowing families to choose the school their children will attend. For onething, they argue that some parents are not interested in being involved in their children's education at this level. Moreover, some say that parents are not informed enough to make good decisions. Parents might be tempted to choose a school for "the wrong reasons." Evidence, however, shows that parents are interested in participating in choosing the school their children attend. In fact, the majority, 69 percent, of parents make intentional decisions regarding the school their child attends. (See table 6.3.)[25]

Table 6.3: **School Choice** 1996	
Parents' decision	Percentage
Sent children to private school	15%
Sent children to magnet school or other public school of choice	17
Sent children to assigned public school but chose residence partially based on neighborhood	37
Sent children to assigned public school	31

Source: Caroline M. Hoxby, "If Families Matter Most, Where Do Schools Come In?" in *A Primer on America's Schools,* ed. Terry M. Moe (Stanford, CA: Hoover Institution Press, 2001), pp. 103–104. **Note:** National Household Education Survey.

Housing purchases, for example, provide evidence that parents do make conscious choices when it comes to the school their child attends. Residential location is a primary means by which families pay more for better educational opportunities. If only a few were willing to pay to locate near a school with higher achievement, then a systematic increase in housing prices in relationship to school quality would not exist; however, recent data provide strong evidence of the relationship between parental choice, housing prices, and educational outcomes. For example, a 1999 study in Massachusetts compared similar houses in the same neighborhood and school district, with the same property tax rates, and the same fire, police, and recreation services, but different schools. The study reported that housing prices were 2.5 percent higher when school test scores were 5 percent higher.[26]

School finance equalization programs, programs that "equalize" expenditures between districts by establishing what districts spend despite what local taxpayers are willing to pay, support the relationship between housing prices and school quality, as well. According to recent survey results, when equalization programs were implemented, housing prices fell, revealing that families do value the ability to choose and pay for school resources. Moreover, data show that when school finance equalization programs were implemented, local foundations were often created to pay for school inputs no longer available but desired by local families.[27]

While families play an important role in education, it is clear that they are sometimes limited in their ability to exert the desired effect on their children's education when faced with income constraints or other impediments, such as houses that are too expensive or few choices in given areas. Parents[28] surveyed in the 1996 NHES, for example, participated in school choice at varying levels, based upon race, income, and education levels.[29] For example, black and Hispanic families, after controlling for income, are more likely than white families to exercise choice by selecting a public or private school but less likely to exercise choice via their residence. Furthermore, when comparing white parents with income levels between $35,000 and $40,000, 63 percent of parents with a baccalaureate degree make intentional choices regarding the school their child attends, while only 55 percent of parents who have only a high school degree do so. (See table 6.4.)[30]

Table 6.4: **School Choice by Family Income Level 1996**

	Family income	
Parents' decision	$10,000–15,000	$75,000 or more
Private school	5.3%	28.8%
School choice within public school system	21.4	10.4
Chose residence partially based on neighborhood school quality	26.6	42.2

Source: Caroline M. Hoxby, "If Families Matter Most, Where Do Schools Come In?" in *A Primer on America's Schools,* ed. Terry M. Moe (Stanford, CA: Hoover Institution Press, 2001), p. 107.

Studying the enrollment of teachers' children provides interesting insight. Public and private school teachers nationwide are slightly more likely than the general public to choose private schools (17.1 percent to 13.1 percent). However, in select cities of America, the difference is quite remarkable: Public school teachers are two to three times more likely than the general public to use private schools.[31]

- In Washington, D.C., 25.7 percent of the children of the city's public school teachers who make less than $35,000 attend private school.
- In Boston, 24.4 percent of the children of the city's public school teachers attend private school.
- In New York, 21.4 percent of the children of the city's public school teachers attend private school.
- In Miami, 35.4 percent of the children of the city's public school teachers attend private school, whereas only 15.6 percent of K–12 students in Miami-Dade county are not enrolled in public schools.

- In Los Angeles, 18.9 percent of the children of the city's public school teachers attend private school, whereas approximately 12 percent of all K–12 students in Los Angeles are enrolled in private schools.[32]

Parents do care where their child attends school and make choices that reflect the desire for their child to attend a school with high achievement records, and in many cases, they are willing to pay the price.

▶ Chapter Notes

1. Thomas D. Snyder, ed., *Digest of Education Statistics, 2001* (Washington, DC: U.S. Department of Education, National Center for Education Statistics , 2002), table 2, p. 11.

2. Ibid., table 42, p. 58.

3. U.S. Census Bureau, *Census 2000,* available online at http://www.census.gov/main/www/cen2000.html.

4. Snyder, *Digest of Education Statistics, 2001,* table 52, p. 66.

5. William J. Bennett, *The Index of Leading Cultural Indicators 2001* (Washington, DC: Empower.org, 2001), p. 51, available online at http://www.empower.org.

6. Ibid., p. 54.

7. Ibid., p. 66.

8. Ibid., p. 67.

9. Public Agenda Online, *Education: People's Chief Concerns* (New York: Public Agenda Online), available online at http://www.publicagenda.org.

10. Caroline M. Hoxby, "If Families Matter Most, Where Do Schools Come In?" in *A Primer on America's Schools*, ed. Terry M. Moe (Stanford, CA: Hoover Institution Press, 2001), pp. 89–123.

11. Ibid.

12. Ibid.

13. Ibid.

14. Ibid.

15. Ibid.

16. Ibid.

17. Ibid.

18. Ibid.

19. Ibid. Note: All estimates control for family background characteristics, control for metropolitan areas' demographic characteristics, and use instruments for public school choice based on natural boundaries.

20. Hoxby, "If Families Matter Most."

21. Ibid.

22. Ibid.

23. Ibid.

24. Ibid.

25. Ibid.

26. Ibid.

27. Ibid.

28. Rural parents were excluded from the analysis of NHES data because in many a rural area, there is only one school that is reasonably nearby.

29. Hoxby, "If Families Matter Most."

30. Ibid.

31. Denis Doyle and James Hirni, *Business/Education Insider*, no. 42 (October-November 1995), available online at http://www.heritage.org.

32. Doyle and Hirni, *Business/Education Insider;* California Department of Education, available online at www.cde.ca.gov; Florida Department of Education, available online at www.firn.edu/doe.

Appendix: Basic Data

Table A.1: **Population by Race**
1970–2000

	Thousands					
Year	All races	White	Black	Hispanic origin	American Indian, Eskimo, and Aleut	Asian and Pacific Islander
1970	152,689	125,708	17,649	na	na	na
1980	226,546	188,372	26,495	14,609	1,420	3,500
1990	248,710	199,686	29,986	22,354	2,065	7,462
1995	262,803	218,023	33,116	27,107	2,256	9,408
1996	265,229	219,636	33,537	28,099	2,290	9,765
1997	267,784	221,333	33,989	29,182	2,326	10,135
1998	270,248	222,980	34,427	30,252	2,361	10,479
1999	272,691	224,611	34,862	31,337	2,397	10,820
2000	281,422	216,931	36,419	35,306	4,119	12,773

	Percent of total population					
1970	100%	82.3%	12.0%	na	na	na
1980	100	83.1	12.0	6.4%	0.6%	1.5%
1990	100	80.3	12.0	9.0	0.8	3.0
1995	100	83.0	13.0	10.3	0.9	3.6
1996	100	82.8	13.0	10.6	0.9	3.7
1997	100	82.7	13.0	10.9	0.9	3.7
1998	100	82.5	13.0	11.2	0.9	3.9
1999	100	82.4	13.0	11.5	0.9	4.0
2000	100	77.1	13.0	12.5	1.5	4.5

Source: U.S. Census Bureau, *CensusCD 1970, CensusCD1980, Census 2000.*
Note: Totals may add up to more than 100% due to individuals' listing of two or more races.

Table A.2: **Family Structure**
1970–2000

Thousands of families								
Family status	1970	1980	1990	1995	1996	1997	1998	2000
All families	**51,456**	**59,550**	**66,090**	**69,305**	**69,594**	**70,241**	**70,880**	**75,579**
Married couple family	**44,728**	**49,112**	**52,317**	**53,858**	**53,567**	**53,604**	**54,317**	**56,497**
No own children	19,196	24,151	27,780	28,617	28,647	28,521	29,048	30,726
With own children	25,532	24,961	24,537	25,241	24,920	25,083	25,269	25,771
Other family, male householder, no spouse present	**1,228**	**1,733**	**2,884**	**3,226**	**3,513**	**3,847**	**3,911**	**4,286**
No own children	887	1,117	1,731	1,786	1,885	2,138	2,113	2,242
With own children	341	616	1,153	1,440	1,628	1,709	1,798	2,044
Other family, female householder, no spouse present	**5,500**	**8,705**	**10,890**	**12,220**	**12,514**	**12,790**	**12,652**	**14,797**
No own children	2,642	3,261	4,290	4,606	4,859	4,916	4,960	5,116
With own children	2,858	5,445	6,599	7,615	7,656	7,874	7,693	9,681

Percent of families								
Family status	1970	1980	1990	1995	1996	1997	1998	2000
Married couple family	**86.9%**	**82.5%**	**79.2%**	**77.7%**	**77.0%**	**76.3%**	**76.6%**	**74.8%**
No own children	37.3	40.6	42.0	41.3	41.2	40.6	41.0	40.7
One own child	15.9	16.3	14.5	13.8	13.4	13.5	13.5	12.8
Two own children	15.6	15.9	14.8	14.9	14.8	14.5	14.4	13.8
Three or more own children	18.1	9.7	7.8	7.7	7.6	7.7	7.8	7.4
Other family, male householder, no spouse present	**2.4%**	**2.9%**	**4.4%**	**4.7%**	**5.0%**	**5.5%**	**5.5%**	**5.7%**
No own children	1.7	1.9	2.6	2.6	2.7	3.0	3.0	3.0
One own children	0.3	0.6	1.1	1.3	1.4	1.4	1.6	1.7
Two own children	0.2	0.3	0.5	0.6	0.7	0.7	0.6	0.7
Three or more own children	0.1	0.1	0.2	0.2	0.2	0.3	0.3	0.3
Other family, female householder, no spouse present	**10.7%**	**14.6%**	**16.5%**	**17.6%**	**18.0%**	**18.2%**	**17.8%**	**19.6%**
No own children	5.1	5.5	6.5	6.6	7.0	7.0	7.0	6.8
One own child	2.0	4.0	4.9	5.2	5.3	5.4	5.3	6.9
Two own children	1.6	3.1	3.3	3.5	3.5	3.7	3.4	3.9
Three or more own children	2.0	2.1	1.8	2.2	2.2	2.0	2.2	2.0

Source: Thomas D. Snyder, ed., *Digest of Education Statistics, 2001* (Washington, DC: U.S. Department of Education, National Center for Education Statistics, 2002), table 18, p. 25.
Notes: Detail may not sum to totals due to rounding.
"Children" always refers to children under 18.

Table A.3: **Poverty Status of Individuals and Families**
All Races, 1980–2000

| | Below poverty level (thousands) | | | Percent below poverty level | | |
| | | In families | | | | In families | |
Year	Individuals	Total	Related children under 18	All persons	Total	Related children under 18
1980	29,272	22,601	11,114	13.0%	11.5%	17.9%
1990	33,585	25,232	12,715	13.5	12.0	19.9
1995	36,425	27,501	13,999	13.8	12.3	20.2
1996	36,529	27,376	13,764	13.7	12.2	19.8
1997	35,574	26,217	13,422	13.3	11.6	19.2
1998	34,476	25,370	12,845	12.7	11.0	18.3
1999	32,258	23,396	11,510	11.8	10.2	16.3
2000	31,138	22,015	11,018	11.1	9.6	15.6

Source: Thomas D. Snyder, ed., *Digest of Education Statistics, 2001* (Washington, DC: U.S. Department of Education, National Center for Education Statistics, 2002), table 21, p. 28.

Table A.4: **Poverty Status of Individuals and Families** By Race, 1980–2000

| | Below poverty level (thousands) | | | | Percent below poverty level | | |
| | | In families | | | | In families | |
Year	Individuals	Total	Related children under 18	All persons		Total	Related children under 18
			White[a]				
1980	19,699	14,587	6,817	10.2%		8.6%	13.4%
1990	22,326	15,916	7,696	10.7		9.0	15.1
1995	24,423	17,593	8,474	11.2		9.6	15.5
1996	24,650	17,621	8,488	11.2		9.6	15.5
1997	24,396	17,258	8,441	11.0		9.3	15.4
1998	23,454	16,549	7,935	10.5		8.9	14.4
1999	21,922	15,141	7,123	9.8		8.1	12.9
2000	21,292	14,392	6,838	9.8		7.7	12.3
			Black[a]				
1980	8,579	7,190	3,906	32.5%		31.1%	42.1%
1990	9,837	8,160	4,412	31.9		31.0	44.2
1995	9,872	8,189	4,644	29.3		28.5	41.5
1996	9,694	7,993	4,411	28.4		27.6	39.5
1997	9,116	7,386	4,116	26.5		25.5	36.8
1998	9,091	7,259	4,073	26.1		24.7	36.4
1999	8,361	6,688	3,644	23.9		22.7	32.7
2000	7,901	6,108	3,417	21.7		20.7	30.4
			Hispanic origin[b]				
1980	3,491	3,143	1,718	25.7%		25.1%	33.0%
1990	6,006	5,091	2,750	28.1		26.9	37.7
1995	8,574	7,341	3,938	29.2		27.0	52.8
1996	8,697	7,515	4,090	29.4		28.5	39.9
1997	8,308	7,198	3,865	27.0		26.2	36.4
1998	8,070	6,814	3,670	25.6		24.3	33.6
1999	7,438	6,349	3,382	23.7		21.7	29.9
2000	7,156	6,025	3,173	20.3		20.1	27.3
			Asian, Pacific Islander				
1980	na	na	na	na		na	na
1990	858	712	356	12.2%		11.3%	17.0%
1995	1,411	1,112	532	26.6		na	13.0
1996	1,454	1,172	553	14.5		13.2	19.1
1997	1,468	na	na	14.0		na	na
1998	1,360	na	na	12.5		na	na
1999	1,162	na	na	10.7		na	na
2000	1,226	na	na	9.6		na	na

Source: Thomas D. Snyder, ed., *Digest of Education Statistics, 2001* (Washington, DC: U.S. Department of Education, National Center for Education Statistics, 2002), table 21, p. 28
Notes: a. Includes persons of Hispanic origin.
b. Persons of Hispanic origin may be of any race. As a result, numbers may not total as expected.

School Figures: The Data behind the Debate

Table A.5: **Population Enrolled in School**
3- to 34-Year-Olds, 1950–2000

	Thousands of people									
Year	Total, 3–34 years	3–4 years	5–6 years	7–13 years	14–17 years	18–19 years	20–21 years	22–24 years	25–29 years	30–34 years
1970	56,999	1,461	7,000	28,943	14,796	3,322	1,949	1,410	1,011	466
1980	52,902	2,280	5,853	23,751	14,411	3,788	2,515	1,931	1,714	1,105
1990	55,506	3,292	7,207	25,016	12,653	4,044	2,852	2,231	2,013	1,281
1995	61,368	4,042	7,901	27,003	14,648	4,274	3,025	2,545	2,216	1,284
1996	61,696	3,959	7,893	26,936	14,818	4,539	3,017	2,605	2,265	1,286
1997	63,056	4,194	7,964	27,616	15,282	4,618	3,231	2,754	2,223	1,159
1998	63,473	4,164	7,902	27,846	15,109	4,914	3,197	2,607	2,216	1,322
1999	63,681	4,273	7,774	28,209	15,352	4,840	3,256	2,664	2,018	1,215
2000	63,515	4,097	7,648	28,296	15,226	4,926	3,314	2,731	2,030	1,292

	Percent of the population									
Year	Total, 3–34 years	3–4 years	5–6 years	7–13 years	14–17 years	18–19 years	20–21 years	22–24 years	25–29 years	30–34 years
1950	na	na	74.4%	98.7%	83.7%	29.4%	na	na	3.0%	0.9%
1960	na	na	80.7	99.5	90.3	38.4	na	na	4.9	2.4
1970	56.4%	20.5%	89.5	99.2	94.1	47.7	31.9%	14.9%	7.5	4.2
1980	49.7	36.7	95.7	99.3	93.4	46.4	31.0	16.3	9.3	6.4
1990	50.2	44.4	96.5	99.6	95.8	57.2	39.7	21.0	9.7	5.8
1995	53.7	48.7[a]	96.0	98.9	96.3	59.4	44.9	23.2	11.6	5.9
1996	54.1	48.3[a]	94.0	97.7	95.4	61.5	44.4	24.8	11.9	6.1
1997	55.6	52.6[a]	96.5	99.1	96.6	61.5	45.9	26.4	11.8	5.7
1998	55.8	52.1[a]	95.6	98.9	96.2	62.2	44.8	24.9	11.9	6.6
1999	56.0	54.2[a]	96.0	98.7	95.8	60.6	45.3	24.5	11.1	6.2
2000	56.2	52.1[a]	95.6	98.3	95.7	61.2	44.1	24.6	11.4	6.7

Source: Thomas D. Snyder, ed., *Digest of Education Statistics, 2001* (Washington, DC: U.S. Department of Education, National Center for Education Statistics, 2002), table 6, p. 15.
Notes: Data are based upon sample surveys of the civilian noninstitutional population. Includes enrollment in any type of graded public, parochial, or other private school. Includes nursery schools, kindergartens, elementary schools, high schools, colleges, universities, and professional schools. Attendance may be on either a full-time or part-time basis and during the day or night. Enrollments in "special" schools, such as trade schools, business colleges, or correspondence schools, are not included.
a. Preprimary enrollment collected using new procedures. May not be comparable to figures for earlier years.

Table A.6: **High School Graduates as Percentage of 17-Year-Olds**
1951–52—1999–2000

School year	17-year-old population (thousands)[a]	High school graduates (thousands)			Graduates as a percentage of the17-year-old population
		Public school[b]	Private school[c]	Total	
1951–52	2,086	1,056	141	1,197	57.4%
1960–61	2,892	1,725	239	1,964	67.9
1970–71	3,872	2,638	300	2,938	75.9
1980–81	4,212	2,725	295	3,020	71.7
1990–91	3,421	2,235	268	2,503	73.2
1995–96	3,641	2,273	267	2,540	69.8
1996–97	3,773	2,341	267	2,608	69.1
1997–98	3,930	2,431	277	2,708	68.9
1998–99	3,948	2,500	286	2,786	70.6
1999–2000	4,019	2,545	294	2,839	70.6

Source: Thomas D. Snyder, ed., *Digest of Education Statistics, 2001* (Washington, DC: U.S. Department of Education, National Center for Education Statistics, 2002), table 103, p. 126.
Notes: Includes graduates of regular day school programs. Excludes graduates of other programs, when separately reported, and recipients of high school equivalency certificates.
Some data have been revised from previously published figures.
Details may not sum to totals due to rounding.
a. Derived from *Current Population Reports,* Series P-25. 17-year-old population adjusted to reflect October 17-year-old population.
b. Based on state estimates.
c. For most years, private school data have been estimated based on periodic private school surveys.

Table A.7: **High School Dropouts**
By Race, 1960–2000

Year	% of all races	White, non-Hispanic	Black, non-Hispanic	Hispanic origin
1960[a]	27.2%	na	na	na
1970	15.0	13.2%[b]	27.9%[b]	na
1980	14.1	11.4	19.1	35.2%
1990	12.1	9.0	13.2	32.4
1995[c]	12.0	8.6	12.1	30.0
1996[c]	11.1	7.3	13.0	29.4
1997[c]	11.0	7.6	13.4	25.3
1998[c]	11.8	7.7	13.8	29.5
1999	11.2	7.3	12.6	28.6
2000	10.9	6.9	13.1	28.6

Source: Thomas D. Snyder, ed., *Digest of Education Statistics, 2001* (Washington, DC: U.S. Department of Education, National Center for Education Statistics, 2002), table 108, p. 130.
Notes: These are "status" dropouts who are 16- to 24-year-olds who are not enrolled in school and who have not completed a high school program, regardless of when they left school. People who have received GED credentials are counted as high school completers.
All data except for 1960 are based on October counts. Data are based upon sample surveys of the civilian noninstitutionalized population.
a. Based on the April 1960 decennial census.
b. White and black include persons of Hispanic origin.
c. Because of changes in data collection procedures, data may not be comparable with figures from previous years.

Table A.8: **Per-Pupil Expenditures**
1919–20—2000–01

School year[a]	Total expenditures per pupil (2000–01 dollars[b])	Current expenditures per pupil (2000–01 dollars[b])
1919–20	$440	$367
1929–30	919	734
1935–36	948	801
1939–40	1,148	957
1945–46	1,193	1,115
1949–50	1,708	1,380
1955–56	2,304	1,752
1959–60	2,622	2,088
1965–66	3,331	2,739
1969–70	4,075	3,482
1974–75	4,811	4,250
1975–76	4,934	4,371
1979–80	5,164	4,710
1984–85	5,721[c]	5,334
1985–86	5,992[c]	5,599
1989–90	7,135	6,402
1994–95	7,227	6,436
1995–96	7,302	6,447
1996–97	7,453	6,527
1997–98	7,731	6,700
1998–99	8,016	6,925
1999–2000[c]	8,155	7,045
2000–01[c]	8,194	7,079

Source: Thomas D. Snyder, ed., *Digest of Education Statistics, 2001* (Washington, DC: U.S. Department of Education, National Center for Education Statistics, 2002), table 167, p. 191.
Notes: a. Data for 1919–20 to 1953–54 are based on school-year enrollment. Later data based on fall enrollment.
b. Based on the consumer price index, prepared by the Bureau of Labor Statistics, U.S. Department of Labor, adjusted to a school-year basis.
c. Estimated.

Table A.9: **Public School Instructional Staff**
By Functional Area, 1949–50—1999

Year	Teachers[a]	Instructional aides	Pupils per instructional staff[a]
1949–50	913,671	b	26.1
1959–60	1,353,372	b	24.1
1969–70	2,016,244	57,418	19.9
1980	2,184,216	325,755	14.3
1985	2,205,987	306,860	14.3
1990	2,398,169	395,959	13.5
1995	2,598,220	494,289	13.4
1996	2,667,419	516,356	13.2
1997	2,746,157	557,453	12.9
1998	2,830,286	588,108	12.6
1999	2,906,554	621,385	12.3

Source: Thomas D. Snyder, ed., *Digest of Education Statistics, 2001* (Washington, DC: U.S. Department of Education, National Center for Education Statistics, 2002), table 82, p. 91.
Notes: Employed in elementary and secondary school systems.
a. Data after 1985 not comparable to figures for years prior to 1985.
b. Data included in "Teachers" column.

Table A.10: **Performance on National Assessment of Educational Progress (NAEP)**

By Average Score and Proficiency by Age and Subject, 1971–99

Reading

| | Average reading scores | | | Percent of students proficient at each reading level | | | | | | | | |
| | 9-year-olds | 13-year-olds | 17-year-olds | 9-year-olds | | | 13-year-olds | | | 17-year-olds | | |
Year	9-year-olds	13-year-olds	17-year-olds	Level 150[a]	Level 200[b]	Level 250[c]	Level 200	Level 250	Level 300[d]	Level 200	Level 250	Level 300
1971	207.6	255.2	285.2	90.6%	58.7%	15.6%	93.0%	57.8%	9.8%	96.0%	78.6%	39.0%
1975	210.0	255.9	285.6	93.1	62.1	14.6	93.2	58.6	10.2	96.4	80.1	38.7
1980	215.0	258.5	285.5	94.6	67.7	17.7	94.8	60.7	11.3	97.2	80.7	37.8
1984	210.9	257.1	288.8	92.3	61.5	17.2	93.9	59.0	11.0	98.3	83.1	40.3
1988	211.8	257.5	290.1	92.7	62.6	17.5	94.9	58.7	10.9	98.9	85.7	40.9
1990	209.2	256.8	290.2	90.1	58.9	18.4	93.8	58.7	11.0	98.1	84.1	41.4
1992	210.5	259.8	289.7	92.3	62.0	16.2	92.7	61.6	15.3	97.1	82.5	43.2
1994	211.0	257.9	288.1	92.1	63.3	16.5	91.7	60.4	14.1	96.8	80.8	41.0
1996	212.5	257.9	287.6	93.5	64.2	16.7	92.1	59.9	13.5	97.5	81.8	39.4
1999	211.7	259.4	287.8	93.0	63.7	15.9	93.2	60.9	14.5	97.6	82.0	39.6

Notes: a. Able to follow brief written directions and carry out simple, discrete reading tasks.
b. Able to understand, combine ideas, and make inferences based on short, uncomplicated passages about specific or sequentially related information.
c. Able to search for specific information, interrelate ideas, and make generalizations about literature, science, and social studies material.
d. Able to find, understand, summarize, and explain relatively complicated literacy and informational material.

Mathematics

| | Average mathematics scores | | | Percent of students proficient at each mathematics level | | | | | | | | |
| | 9-year-olds | 13-year-olds | 17-year-olds | 9-year-olds | | | 13-year-olds | | | 17-year-olds | | |
Year	9-year-olds	13-year-olds	17-year-olds	Level 150[a]	Level 200[b]	Level 250[c]	Level 200	Level 250	Level 300[d]	Level 200	Level 250	Level 300
1973	219.0	266.0	304.0	na	na	na	na	na	na	na	na	na
1978	218.6	264.1	300.4	96.7%	70.4%	19.6%	94.6%	64.9%	51.5%	99.8%	92.0%	51.5%
1982	219.0	268.6	298.5	97.1	71.4	18.8	97.7	71.4	48.5	99.9	93.0	48.5
1986	221.7	269.0	302.0	97.9	74.1	20.7	98.6	73.3	51.7	99.9	95.6	51.7
1990	229.6	270.4	304.6	99.1	81.5	27.7	98.5	74.7	56.1	100.0	96.0	56.1
1992	229.6	273.1	306.7	99.0	81.4	27.8	98.7	77.9	59.1	100.0	96.6	59.1
1994	231.1	274.3	306.2	99.0	82.0	29.9	98.5	78.1	58.6	100.0	96.5	58.6
1996	231.0	274.3	307.2	99.1	81.5	29.7	98.8	78.6	60.1	100.0	96.8	60.1
1999	232.0	275.8	308.2	98.9	82.5	30.9	98.7	78.8	60.7	100.0	96.8	60.7

Notes: a. Simple arithmetic facts.
b. Beginning skills and understanding.
c. Numerical operations and beginning problem solving.
d. Moderately complex procedures and reasoning.

School Figures: The Data behind the Debate

Table A.10: **Continued**

<table>
<tr><th></th><th colspan="3">Average
science scores</th><th colspan="9">Percent of students
proficient at each science level</th></tr>
<tr><th></th><th>9-
year-
olds</th><th>13-
year-
olds</th><th>17-
year-
olds</th><th colspan="3">9-year-olds</th><th colspan="3">13-year-olds</th><th colspan="3">17-year-olds</th></tr>
<tr><th>Year</th><th></th><th></th><th></th><th>Level
150[a]</th><th>Level
200[b]</th><th>Level
250[c]</th><th>Level
200</th><th>Level
250</th><th>Level
300[d]</th><th>Level
200</th><th>Level
250</th><th>Level
300</th></tr>
<tr><td>1973</td><td>220.0</td><td>250.0</td><td>296.0</td><td>na</td><td>na</td><td>na</td><td>na</td><td>na</td><td>na</td><td>na</td><td>na</td><td>na</td></tr>
<tr><td>1977</td><td>219.9</td><td>247.4</td><td>289.5</td><td>93.5%</td><td>68.0%</td><td>25.7%</td><td>86.0%</td><td>48.8%</td><td>11.1%</td><td>97.1%</td><td>81.6%</td><td>41.7%</td></tr>
<tr><td>1982</td><td>220.8</td><td>250.1</td><td>283.3</td><td>95.2</td><td>70.7</td><td>24.3</td><td>89.8</td><td>50.9</td><td>9.6</td><td>95.7</td><td>76.6</td><td>37.3</td></tr>
<tr><td>1986</td><td>224.3</td><td>251.4</td><td>288.5</td><td>96.2</td><td>72.0</td><td>27.5</td><td>91.6</td><td>52.5</td><td>9.1</td><td>97.1</td><td>80.7</td><td>41.3</td></tr>
<tr><td>1990</td><td>228.7</td><td>255.2</td><td>290.4</td><td>97.0</td><td>76.4</td><td>31.1</td><td>92.3</td><td>56.5</td><td>11.2</td><td>96.7</td><td>81.2</td><td>43.3</td></tr>
<tr><td>1992</td><td>230.6</td><td>258.0</td><td>294.1</td><td>97.4</td><td>78.0</td><td>32.8</td><td>93.1</td><td>61.3</td><td>12.0</td><td>97.8</td><td>83.3</td><td>46.6</td></tr>
<tr><td>1994</td><td>231.0</td><td>256.8</td><td>294.0</td><td>97.2</td><td>77.4</td><td>33.7</td><td>92.4</td><td>59.5</td><td>11.8</td><td>97.1</td><td>83.1</td><td>47.5</td></tr>
<tr><td>1996</td><td>229.7</td><td>256.0</td><td>295.7</td><td>96.8</td><td>76.1</td><td>32.2</td><td>92.0</td><td>57.6</td><td>12.3</td><td>97.8</td><td>83.8</td><td>48.4</td></tr>
<tr><td>1999</td><td>229.4</td><td>255.8</td><td>295.3</td><td>97.0</td><td>77.4</td><td>31.4</td><td>92.7</td><td>57.9</td><td>10.9</td><td>98.0</td><td>85.0</td><td>47.4</td></tr>
</table>

Notes: a. Know everyday science facts.
b. Understand simple scientific principles.
c. Apply general scientific information.
d. Analyze scientific procedures and data.

Sources: U.S. Department of Education, National Assessment of Educational Progress, *NAEP Trends in Academic Progress* (Educational Testing Service); Thomas D. Snyder, ed., *Digest of Education Statistics, 2001* (Washington, DC: U.S. Department of Education, National Center for Education Statistics, 2002), tables 112, 124, 130, pp. 133, 143, 149.

Table A.11: **SAT Scores**
By Race, 1970–71—2000–01

SAT Combined

Year	All students	White	Black	Hispanic
1970–71	1,035	na	na	na
1980–81	1,018	na	na	na
1986–87	1,008	1,038	839	926
1990–91	999	1,031	846	920
1995–96	1,013	1,049	856	931
1996–97	1,016	1,052	857	934
1997–98	1,017	1,054	860	927
1998–99	1,016	1,055	856	927
1999–2000	1,019	1,058	860	928
2000–01	1,020	1,060	859	925

Source: Thomas D. Snyder, ed., *Digest of Education Statistics, 2001* (Washington, DC: U.S. Department of Education, National Center for Education Statistics, 2002), tables 134, 138, pp. 152, 156.
Note: Data for 1967 to 1986 were converted to the recentered scale by using a formula applied to the original mean and standard deviation.
For 1987 to 1995, individual student scores were converted to the recentered scale and recomputed. For 1996 to 2001, most students received scores on the recentered scale score. Any score on the original scale was converted to the recentered scale prior to recomputing the mean.

Table A.12: **ACT Scores**
1970–2001

American College Testing (ACT) score averages

Year	Composite score
1970	18.6
1975	18.5
1980	18.5
1985	18.6
1990	20.6
1995	20.8
1996	20.9
1997	21.0
1998	21.0
1999	21.0
2000	21.0
2001	21.0

Source: Thomas D. Snyder, ed., *Digest of Education Statistics, 2001* (Washington, DC: U.S. Department of Education, National Center for Education Statistics, 2002), tables 134, 138, pp. 152, 156.
Note: Test scores for 1990 and later data are not comparable with previous years because a new version of the ACT was introduced.

Index

academic achievement
  apportionment of resources and, 208
  class size and, 283–84
  education funds and, 192
  explanatory variables for, 299–300, 299f
  family and, 297
  homework and, 149–50
  parental involvement, home environment and, 301, 301t, 302
  parents' ratings of schools and, 303, 304
  per pupil expenditures and, 197–203, 202t, 229n20
  social promotion and, 279
  summer school and, 280–81
  teacher quality and, 285
  television viewing and, 155–6, 158, 160–1, 163
  Title I participants and, 222–24, 223f
  U.S. *vs.* international education expenditures and, 208
accountability programs
  primary components of, 273
  standards and, 274t
Advisory Panel on the Scholastic Aptitude Test (SAT) Score Decline, 155
African Americans
  vouchers and, 235
AFT. *See* American Federation of Teachers (AFT)
alcohol
  students' use of, 46–47, 47t
alternative education, 10
  opponents to, 12
American College Testing (ACT)
  scores by race on, 324t
American Federation of Teachers (AFT), 70, 82, 104, 108

education *(continued)*
American *vs.* international student achievement and, 125–6, 127–8
apportionment of resources and, 208
changing demographics of, 295
class size and, 283
community service and, 177–8
cost of, 295
country rankings, physics, mathematics and, 134–5, 135t
expenditures, student performance and, 192, 197, 200–1, 201f, 202t
expenditures for, 78f, 189, 191, 198, 205t, 210f
expenditures of public, private institutions for, 209t
expenditures per student on, 205–6, 206t
expenditures *vs.* outcomes and, 208
family and, 295–300
family characteristic variables and, 297–98
federal government's role in, 192, 219
home environment and, 295–96, 302
homework and, 149–50, 151t
hours of instruction time and, 33, 34t, 35f
importance of, 295
instruction time, subject and, 36t, 37t, 38f, 39f, 40f
international comparisons of math achievement and, 123
international comparisons of science achievement and, 123
international performance differences in, 34–35
international value-added comparisons, literacy and, 136t
international value-added comparisons, mathematics and, 132, 133t
international value-added comparisons, science and, 132, 134t
lack of progress in, 237
national goals of, 127
national student performance, eighth graders and, 130–1t
national student performance, fourth graders and, 129t
national student performance, twelfth graders and, 132t
parental choice, housing prices and, 307
parents and, 304–5